Labour Relations and Health Reform

Labour Relations and Health Reform

A Comparative Study of Five Jurisdictions

By Kurt Wetzel
With contributions from Stephen Bach, Mark Bray and Nadine White

palgrave
macmillan

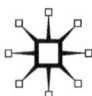

First published 2005 by
PALGRAVE MACMILLAN
Houndmills, Basingstoke, Hampshire RG21 6XS and
175 Fifth Avenue, New York, N. Y. 10010
Companies and representatives throughout the world

PALGRAVE MACMILLAN is the global academic imprint of the Palgrave Macmillan division of St. Martin's Press, LLC and of Palgrave Macmillan Ltd. Macmillan® is a registered trademark in the United States, United Kingdom and other countries. Palgrave is a registered trademark in the European Union and other countries.

ISBN-13: 978–1–4039–9865–1   hardback
ISBN-10: 1–4039–9865–5   hardback

This book is printed on paper suitable for recycling and made from fully managed and sustained forest sources.

A catalogue record for this book is available from the British Library.

Library of Congress Cataloging-in-Publication Data
Wetzel, Kurt.
   Labour relations and health reform : a comparative study of five jurisdictions / by Kurt Wetzel ; with contributions from Stephen Bach, Mark Bray, and Nadine White.
      p. cm.
   Includes bibliographical references and index.
   ISBN 1–4039–9865–5 (cloth)
   1. Health care reform–Cross-cultural studies. 2. Labour laws and legislation–Cross-cultural studies. I. Title.

RA394.9.W48 2005
362.1′0425–dc22   2005049327

10   9   8   7   6   5   4   3   2   1
14   13 12 11 10 09 08 07 06 05

Printed and bound in Great Britain by
Antony Rowe Ltd, Chippenham and Eastbourne

I am indebted to my wife, Eva, for her consistent, if occasionally ungracious support.

Contents

List of Tables and Figures

Tables

Figures

Foreword

Health reform is an ongoing, organizationally and politically complex undertaking that involves establishing new organizational structures through which to deliver services. It is a highly political process and is subject to intense media and public scrutiny. And for the labour-intensive, unionized health sector, it has extensive industrial relations implications.

This book examines the industrial relations of health care reform in five jurisdictions: Great Britain, New Zealand, the Australian state of New South Wales, and the provinces of Alberta and Saskatchewan in Canada. Each chapter deals with the period of health reform during which labour relations restructuring was particularly intense, as established industrial relations structures and practices changed to what was intended to become the new order. While the authors provide a look at current industrial relations developments in each jurisdiction's health sector, their primary focus is on the restructuring periods.

These five jurisdictions share important features that make them suitable for comparative study. First, each is a parliamentary democracy in the British tradition and has a comprehensive publicly funded health care delivery system. These national or sub-national governments have meaningful powers in the area of health policy and primary responsibility for funding health services. This means that they are politically accountable for the provision and quality of health services. Moreover, in each jurisdiction the health sector has been the object of a major reform initiative. Each has an extensively unionized health care sector as well as legislative authority over health sector labour policy. Finally, the ideologies of the political parties forming the respective governments are spread across the political spectrum, from neoconservative to social democratic, enabling one to examine the impact of different ideologies.

The chapters that comprise this book explore the genesis of health reform policies in the respective jurisdictions and the industrial relations that develop over the medium term. Accordingly, the chapters discuss governments' labour policies and the methods that governments and management use to address the industrial relations issues generated by health reform. They also examine health unions' roles in and responses to the reform process. The concluding section compares the five jurisdictions' approaches to health industrial relations restructuring and examines the respective outcomes.

This book reflects an institutionalist industrial relations systems perspective of the type pioneered by the Webbs and John R. Commons and more recently associated with John Dunlop and Thomas Kochan.[1] That framework provides a checklist for examining the impact of reform on health industrial relations systems. In addition to the actors, it identifies contexts, rule making and ideologies as elements of any system. It recognizes that industrial relations systems operate at multiple levels.

The authors of these chapters have a deep and abiding interest in health care industrial relations.[2] They have drawn upon the literature as well as government and other public documents, and have interviewed industrial relations practitioners and policy makers employed by government, management and labour. The authors thank those individuals for their time and hope that this product is in some way useful to them.

I would like to thank the College of Commerce, University of Saskatchewan, for its support and to acknowledge the thorough, competent editorial assistance of Loretta Fritz.

Kurt Wetzel
University of Saskatchewan

Notes

1. John T. Dunlop, *Industrial Relations Systems* (Boston: Harvard Business School Press), 1993.
2. Stephen Bach, *Employment Relations and the Health Service* (London: Continuum), 2003; K. Wetzel and D. G. Gallagher, "Management Structures to Accommodate Multi-Employer Hospital Bargaining in Western Canada," in *Conflict or Compromise: The Future of Public Sector Industrial Relations*, G. Swimmer and M. Thompson, eds. (Ottawa: Institute for Research on Public Policy), 1984, pp. 285–313.

1
Introduction

Kurt Wetzel

Comprehensive publicly funded health care delivery systems were centrepieces of postwar welfare state programs. In the closing decades of the twentieth century, these systems were plagued by escalating costs and stretched by a burgeoning demand for services. The pressures reflected such factors as rising labour costs, aging populations, increased service intensity across all age groups, soaring drug costs, and expensive technological breakthroughs in diagnostic and treatment procedures. The four countries that are the focus of this book – Britain, Australia, New Zealand and Canada – saw total expenditures on health care rise between 1980 and 2000. According to the Organization for Economic Cooperation and Development (OECD), the four-country average climbed from 6.4 percent of GDP to 8.2 percent. See Table 1.1.[1]

Table 1.1   Total Expenditure on Health – % GDP

	1980	1985	1990	1995	2000
Australia	7	7.4	7.8	8.2	8.3
Canada	7.1	8.2	9	9.1	9.1
New Zealand	5.9	5.2	6.9	7.2	8
United Kingdom	5.6	5.9	6	7	7.3
Mean	6.4	6.7	7.4	7.9	8.2

Rising costs threatened the sustainability of these countries' health systems and diverted resources from other important public program areas. Under fiscal pressure that was aggravated by falling tax revenues and reluctance to raise taxes, governments undertook health reform initiatives designed to improve cost effectiveness, constrain service expenditures and maintain service quality. This involved rationalizing, reorganizing and refocusing health care delivery systems. The four countries (five jurisdictions) have a number of circumstances, institutional characteristics and reform policies in common. First, despite the anti-statist proclivities of some, the governments have remained the primary funders of health services. OECD data (Table 1.2) reveal that the four-country average of public expenditures on health as a total of health spending from 1980 to 2000 dipped only slightly, from 79 percent to 76 percent.[2]

Table 1.2 Public Expenditure on Health – % Total Expenditure on Health

	1980	1985	1990	1995	2000
Australia	63	71.4	67.1	67.1	72.4
Canada	75.6	75.6	74.6	71.4	72
New Zealand	88	87	82.4	77.2	78
United Kingdom	89.4	85.8	83.6	83.9	81
Mean	79	80	76.9	74.9	75.8

Second, in order to achieve the savings and efficiencies they sought, governments restructured their health care delivery systems. With the notable exception of the United Kingdom, pre-reform service delivery systems were typically fragmented. Services were usually provided by freestanding and sometimes rival institutions variously associated with government, municipalities, universities, independent boards and religious groups. While Britain decentralized health service delivery, health reform elsewhere led to the creation of larger and more organizationally complex regional health organizations, variously called health authorities, districts or regions. Authorities encompassing major urban centres dwarf teaching hospitals, previously the largest health organizations. The range of services the new organizations were called upon to oversee could include home, acute and long-term care, as well as mental and public/community health. They also assumed responsibility for rationalizing, reconfiguring and delivering services in ways designed to meet local needs. Health reform presented management with enormous organizational restructuring and operational challenges.

Third, to varying degrees different conceptions of "health" and how and what services might be most appropriately delivered are evident in the health reform orthodoxy. It has been increasingly acknowledged that health systems focused primarily on providing medical care and treatment within institutional settings are neither cost effective nor optimal for meeting overall population health needs. Reform attempts to shift the focus to the delivery of primary care by community-based frontline service providers.

Broadly construed, the "wellness" concept captures this policy agenda. It emphasizes maintaining and achieving good health by preventing illness and injury. It promotes public education about practices that contribute to better health and encourages individuals to assume responsibility for improving their own health status. Wellness programs focus on de-institutionalizing service delivery. Thus, home care is preferred to protracted hospital stays or institutionalization in long-term care facilities. Wellness emphasizes working in and through the community to identify and address factors affecting health at the local level. And it generally involves providers working in multidisciplinary teams rather than in the hierarchical roles delineated by their respective professional designations.[3]

Fourth, the health industrial relations systems of the five jurisdictions share some defining characteristics. Prior to reform, the health sector in each jurisdiction was relatively stable, with the number of employees, institutions and services growing steadily. Because some 80 percent of operating costs in this 24-hour/day, year-round labour-intensive industry are labour related, the bulk of any savings or efficiencies to be achieved by reform involved reducing the size of the workforce, cutting its compensation, altering its composition and/or deploying it more effectively. Health workers in these jurisdictions are unionized. At the outset of reform, they were covered by long-standing collective agreements with provisions that addressed myriad aspects of the employment relationship. Moreover, their unions' structures as well as the structures under which bargaining occurred reflected the pre-reform era.

Health reform profoundly affects each of the actors in the sector's industrial relations system – government, management, and workers/workers' representatives – and their relationships with each other. The process of reconfiguring industrial relations to accommodate a new health regime is complex and disruptive. At the same time, it is politically sensitive, carries a high profile and involves high stakes. This book examines the industrial relations of health reform in five selected jurisdictions, focusing on the roles and relationships of the actors.

Government

In the health sector, government is the industrial relations system's preponderant actor. It can use state fiat to accomplish its ends. It has a complex array of interrelated roles – legislative, policy, fiscal, administrative, legal, political, managerial – which enable it to initiate action and pursue reforms. As the strategic decision maker, government initiates, provides the vision, specifies objectives, funds and oversees health reform. It determines the structures that will be put into place to deliver services and implement reform measures. It specifies the pace at which reform will proceed. As the public health care system's funder, government prescribes how reformed health organizations will be managed and how outcomes will be measured.

Since governments are accountable for public health care systems and health care is a high-profile political issue, reforming the system can become a priority on which they are prepared to act boldly. All governments are driven by fiscal concerns as they restructure health organizations and reorder service delivery. Political beliefs and values determine how the process unfolds. Governments' beliefs address such issues as whether public sector organizations can effectively provide health services or if market(-like) forces must be brought to bear to ensure system efficiencies. Their values are reflected in their policies and programs and in the sector's operating modes and implementation mechanisms. In addition to governments' beliefs specified as industrial relations/human resource management, this amalgam of beliefs and values is reflected in the industry's health labour relations restructuring regimes.

By the 1980s, two distinct sets of political beliefs, or ideologies, were evident: social democracy and neoconservativism, although there are no pure types in practice and not all governments subscribe to a body of beliefs. Some governments function in ways that do not manifest a broader set of ideals or values; rather, they are opportunistic, driven by temporal factors and particular circumstances.

These beliefs can be associated with likely scenarios. A neoliberal government, for example, may seek market mechanisms by creating smaller, decentralized and competing units in which the roles of health services purchasers and providers are split. It may also create opportunities for private (for-profit and not-for-profit) providers to compete with public sector providers for public funding and even allow a private for-profit health care system to operate. A social democratic government, on the other hand, may call for the creation of larger, more highly integrated health organizations and more circumscribed roles for the private sector.

Government controls and defines the role of the health bureaucracy. It can also determine the structure and role of health boards and management. Even where responsibility for providing services, determining operating policy, hiring and evaluating senior management has been devolved to health authorities, government may limit those organizations' capacity to exercise independent initiative through its power to fund them and appoint some or all of their board members. Government decides what management's role in health reform will be. Will it be to administer perhaps far-reaching structural and operational change intended to make the publicly funded and provided health care delivery system more sustainable and viable over the long run? Or, will it be to oversee a radical transformation designed to make the health system strive for market efficiency using market-like mechanisms? Government also determines the extent to which industrial and employee relations will be treated as strategic considerations, with elements that should be addressed centrally as well as locally, or whether these are *ad hoc* or *post hoc* concerns that under ideal circumstances can be devolved.

Government has powers that no private sector employer has. It can set industrial relations policy and enact legislation that enumerates workers' collective rights. It specifies workers' rights to take collective action. It appoints statutory administrative and judicial tribunals. It also sets policy in related social program areas, e.g., publicly funded educational and training institutions, which are predominant sources of professional and technical health workers. Government chooses how to balance the use of state fiat to implement health reform *vis-à-vis* providing opportunities for stakeholders (e.g. unions) to have input into decision making that affects them. In large measure, this choice reflects the government's political predisposition. Similarly, government determines its own and management's predominant operating mode, i.e. whether changes are imposed unilaterally, negotiated or introduced in some other way.

Health reform raises structural and procedural questions about the level at which collective bargaining and pay determination should occur. Should negotiations take place locally or at a more centralized level? If bargaining is not local, who should represent government and management? If conditions of employment are not negotiated, what should there be in lieu – legislation or a third party tribunal? Government can decide these matters. Government can also decide if management will participate in bargaining, if there will be an employers' association, and, if there is an employers' association, whether it is broadly mandated to represent and coordinate the industry's interests or has a limited role.

Governments' industrial relations restructuring policies can differ substantially. Restructuring may be done to unions or with them.

Government and management may implement change in ways that destabilize unions, or they may attempt to accommodate unions' and workers' needs and concerns in the restructuring process. The industrial relations consequences of governments' choices in these matters are immense.

Management

Implementing health sector reform is a huge managerial task. Management may be charged with creating and managing larger, more complex organizations that are expected to be more efficient, effective and responsive to local needs, or overseeing smaller, more market-driven organizations toward similar ends. New regimes may be required to introduce different concepts of health and new approaches to service delivery. With transitional funding typically limited or non-existent, the requisite resources must generally be found within existing or reduced operating budgets. The managerial undertaking is complicated by two realities: first, the high profile of the industry makes the implementation of reform the object of intense public, government, workforce and media scrutiny; second, reform must be implemented without interrupting the ongoing delivery of health services.

Management is typically not well positioned to shape the health sector's strategic industrial relations, and its operating modes are largely prescribed by government policies. Management is a weathervane rather than a rudder. Its role is to implement reform and oversee the health care delivery system at the workplace, organization and, in some cases, industry levels in ways consistent with government policies. Regional boards and senior managers have a certain amount of autonomy to develop policy, reconfigure services, and restructure their organizations. They are, however, accountable to the government or its health bureaucracy, which have the capacity to set standards, monitor performance and intervene in their affairs. Government may expect management to operate with decisive unilateralism, or it may direct management to administer change using a consultative or negotiating model. One of senior management's abiding concerns is that government will intervene in health authorities' affairs, thereby reducing local discretion. Politicians and bureaucrats are often reluctant to abandon control and may be inclined to reclaim it on an *ad hoc* basis. Regardless, by appointing some or all regional board trustees and influencing the choice of key managers hired by those boards, government can ensure that its reform vision is pursued locally.

Employee and industrial relations practices follow the government's lead. Where a government is hostile to unionism, maintaining cordial working relationships with trade unions and staff is less important than acting with dispatch to contain costs and enact a reform agenda. Where a government wants to cultivate cordial relationships with unions, managerial prerogative is more circumscribed. For example, a social democratic government may insist that organizational restructuring be postponed until accords are reached with the unions whose members will be affected. Thus, the implementation of reform may be less precipitous and more likely to reflect consensus born of delays that frustrate management.

In this labour-intensive industry dedicated to providing caring services, one might expect management to embrace human resource strategies that treat employees as assets, invest in skills and empower employees to satisfy patient needs autonomously. However, the government's vision, inadequate resources and the enormity of the health reform undertaking may slow the emergence of these practices. The pressure to get the job done can be overwhelming. Instead of evolving into progressive organizations characterized by healthy workplaces, health organizations may become stretched, stressed and unhealthy. Strategic human resource management programs that involve broadening participation and communication are not concerns that initially draw the attention of those in charge of reforming a health system.

Management also takes direction on another important front. Governments determine whether health authorities view each other as cohorts and potential sources of colleagues or as competitors. As well, governments specify the level at which bargaining occurs and the arrangements through which the interests of the funder and operational management are represented at the bargaining table.

Governments that advocate market-like mechanisms may encourage health authorities to regard themselves as distinct and autonomous and to treat other health organizations as competitors. Where uniqueness is emphasized, organizations are not encouraged or inclined to establish active multi-purpose industry associations. Rather, they may be attracted to limited purpose associations, or have none, and be drawn to the idea, if not the practice, of local bargaining. In these cases, management's ambit is more likely to be confined to the organization and workplace levels, and government-health authority relationships are more apt to be managed using personal political contacts.

Where the health sector is encouraged to see itself as a group of interdependent organizations with common interests and concerns, governments are likely to facilitate the establishment of industry associations to help address the collective issues. This may allow health organizations and their managers to develop a formal industry-level presence. Where health sector bargaining is centralized, industry associations typically represent the combined interests of government and employers. They may serve as a front for government in bargaining, thereby distancing policy makers from the bargaining tables. They may also become the vehicles through which the industry lobbies and communicates with government.

Unions and their members

The hierarchically structured, predominantly female health sector labour force is drawn from a variety of labour markets. Its main occupational groups include: medical; registered and auxiliary nursing; myriad specialized paramedical technical (e.g. lab/imaging technologists) and professional (e.g. physiotherapists, pharmacists); and support personnel including maintenance, housekeeping, clerical and dietary workers. There is little organic solidarity among these occupational groups. The increasingly numerous and important (sub)professional occupations cultivate distinct identities and try to defend their job territory. Many belong to professional associations that have statutory licensing and standard setting authority and to occupationally based unions.

To appreciate the impacts of heath reform on workers and their unions, it is important to understand that pre-reform representational and collective bargaining structures were the result of unions bargaining for occupational family groups. Some form or degree of centralized bargaining was the norm. Health sector industrial relations were routinized, and they were characterized by mature, traditional relationships. In some jurisdictions, unions representing certain occupational groups had histories of militancy. Collective agreements addressed a wide array of issues but did not anticipate the restructuring that accompanied reform. It is also important to remember that health services are widely treated as "essential," and unions' freedom to take industrial action is generally restricted.

Unions experience health reform as a process that destroys the stability they had come to regard as normal. They want to be consulted about and have input into those aspects of reform that affect them and their members. Regardless of the political leanings of the government, the unions are apprehensive. If reform coincides with budgetary and/or political circumstances that have the effect of reducing union power, governments are better positioned to implement change unilaterally. Health reform raises three sets of concerns for unions. The first involves union members' issues, some of which flow from organizational/workplace restructuring to rationalize service delivery (e.g. site closings, service unit amalgamations). These issues, along with "contracting out," generate anxiety about employment status and security, seniority, transfer and bidding rights, compensation rates and workload. If collective agreements lack provisions to address these issues, union leaders are unable to respond to their members' concerns. Government may then be called upon to implement and fund labour adjustment programs to provide laid-off workers with early retirement or severance packages and arrangements that allow them to bid for jobs elsewhere in the system.

Second, health reform can raise high-stakes institutional issues for unions and occasion extensive collateral union restructuring. This may involve reconfiguring union representation to reflect the new regionalized or decentralized organizational structures. Resolution of these matters may affect a union's prospects for survival, provide it opportunities for growth and determine its capacity to operate effectively. Representational restructuring may prompt union mergers and the creation of larger, stronger unions; it may also spell the demise of small, weak unions which management can safely ignore. Representational restructuring can aggravate inter-union rivalries. Where competing unions are unable to reach accommodations, reform may occasion the establishment of mechanisms to determine which union will represent employees in the restructured health organization. Indeed, until representational restructuring arrangements are completed and it is clear as to which unions and which collective agreements will prevail, full organizational restructuring may be blocked.

Reform can also precipitate internal union change. For instance, where health organizations are decentralized, unions that had previously accommodated the centralized system focus are forced to reconfigure themselves to accommodate the change. This can involve profound operational and organizational restructuring. As management shifts its operational and employment patterns to favour categories of workers who are cheaper and can be deployed more flexibly (e.g. auxiliary nurses, health care assistants), unions that had previously denied these workers membership may broaden their organizing scope to capture members in the expanding group. Health restructuring can raise issues for occupational groups that belong to professional bodies that certify and can discipline their members.

The third set of industrial relations issues relates to the structure of bargaining and negotiating under a new regime. Health industrial relations restructuring may lead to new bargaining structures. The structure of bargaining is a major determinant of a union's capacity to bargain effectively. While unions generally prefer centralized bargaining, which occurs closer to government, government and management may prefer decentralized bargaining. Organization-specific agreements are particularly attractive to larger, newly empowered health organizations and to those entities faced with operating under competitive regimes.

The bargaining rounds immediately following health sector restructuring can be complex. If a variety of service sectors and unions have been merged into integrated health organizations, the parties must negotiate consolidated agreements to replace the pre-existing service sector-specific agreements. A similar situation occurs where bargaining moves from a decentralized to a centralized structure. Agreeing on common language for amalgamated agreements can be enormously difficult. Government/management efforts to contain compensation costs and craft agreements that offer greater flexibility for labour deployment can be particularly contentious.

At the outset of health reform, unions negotiating collective agreements may find themselves reacting to a barrage of concessionary demands from fiscally and operationally constrained employers. Governments, however, can change. Poor economic conditions and labour markets can rebound. And bargaining power can shift. Where bargaining units are amalgamated and union representation is rationalized, the bargaining power of unions initially staggered by health reform may increase. Union members may become less hesitant to take job actions, and those job actions, in the aftermath of health reform, are likely to have a greater impact than they did before reform was undertaken.

It is clear that health reform has manifold cascading consequences for employees and their unions as well as for management. It raises an array of generic institutional, organizational and *ad hominem* issues that draw the actors' attention: tendering work to the non-public sector providers, closing/merging sites and redundancies; changing the employment status of workers as less than regular full-time work becomes more common; intensifying work processes; changing the composition of the labour force; and restructuring union representation.

The chapters that follow look at these and related issues, examining how the actors in each jurisdiction approached reform, how they managed and/or responded to its implementation, and how they have addressed its various outcomes. The case studies are exploratory. They document the institutional complexities of health labour relations restructuring. They are not driven by *a priori* assumptions or hypotheses. The conclusion identifies themes that cross the five jurisdictions and makes observations about what might be learned from the experiences reported in the case studies.

Notes

1. Organization for Economic and Cooperative Development, 2002, http://www.oecd.org/dataoecd/1/31/2957323.xls.
2. Organization for Economic and Cooperative Development, 2002, http://www.oecd.org/dataoecd/1/30/2957329.xls.
3. R. Dobson and R. Lepnurm, "Wellness Activities Address Inequities," *Social Science and Medicine* 50 (2000): 108.

2
Health Service Reform and the Modernization of Employment Relations: The Case of the United Kingdom

Stephen Bach

There can be few organizations whose restructuring has been as controversial and as subject to so much media scrutiny as the reforms of the National Health Service (NHS) over the last twenty years. Health service reform is not confined to the UK; across all continents governments are struggling to reconcile increased patient expectations with the reluctance of employers and employees to contribute more resources to maintain the growth of health services. The distinctiveness of the UK experience, however, is the degree to which health sector reform has formed a central component of the domestic political agenda for more than two decades. This reform process has altered employment relations but there is uncertainty about the consequences for employees, employers and trade unions. In the health service the degree to which the market-style reforms of Conservative governments and the modernization agenda of the Labour government has transformed employment relations has been a source of controversy. During the 1990s, Conservative government ministers suggested that their reforms were leading to staff working to higher performance standards; managers had acquired the autonomy and influence to establish their own organizational employment practices, without hindrance from trade unions or interventionist governments. Since 1997, Labour government ministers have emphasized the centrality of human resource (HR) management issues to their modernization agenda; developing an HR strategy for the health service, incorporating specific HR targets into the NHS performance management framework, and embarking on a fundamental reform of the system of pay determination. The scope and significance of these changes have been disputed. What is clear, is that the restructuring of the health service has prompted unprecedented interest in health service employment relations.

This chapter assesses this programme of reform and the tensions exposed by the modernization project of the Labour government. It outlines the changing pattern of health service employment and the far-reaching reforms of management and organization over the last two decades. It explores attempts to modernize the pay system to encourage reforms of working practices and to eradicate unequal pay and conditions between women and men employed in different occupations in the health service. This chapter starts with an overview of the main developments in the structure of the NHS before considering the role of employers in shaping employment relations practice and the degree to which this has led to the reform of pay determination systems and working practices. The implications for trade unions of this reform agenda are then examined. The final section concludes that a continuous process of health care reform has uprooted traditional patterns of industrial relations and these trends are intensifying as the Labour government implements far-reaching reforms of pay determination and work organization.

Organization and financing of health care

In Britain, debate about the health sector is synonymous with the centralized, tax funded system of public services provided by the NHS, comprising hospital and community services and general practitioner (GP) based primary health care. The NHS is financed almost entirely through general taxation. At the apex of the system is the Secretary of State for Health who is responsible to Parliament for the provision of health services. This has had an important bearing on how the health service has been administered. In contrast to other countries in which responsibilities are devolved to lower tiers of government, British politicians have been acutely aware that problems in the NHS invariably translate into political difficulties. In 1990, for example, the Conservative government almost delayed their planned market-style reforms because of their fear that its unpopularity would jeopardize their re-election (Ham, 2000).

This degree of integration and political centralization has also facilitated the growth of what has been termed the Audit Society (Power, 1997). As the NHS became more fragmented under the market type reforms of the 1990s, with the establishment of separate NHS trusts, more auditing and inspection of outcomes was instigated. This ensured that formal devolution of managerial authority to trusts did not weaken political control and accountability. Consequently the establishment of performance indicators, and processes such as medical audit (comparisons of surgical outcomes), proliferated under successive Conservative governments. This process was developed further under the Labour government because of the centrality of performance management to their reforms of the NHS. The proliferation of service targets, however, was identified as a key source of dissatisfaction amongst public service employees (Audit Commission, 2002). This led the government to reduce the number of national targets from 62 to 20 during 2004 with greater scope for local target setting (Department of Health, 2004a).

Historically, the percentage of national expenditure allocated to health services has been relatively low in comparison to other OECD countries. In 1997 the UK spent 6.8 per cent of Gross Domestic Product (GDP) on health care, well below other countries in this study (i.e. Australia 8.5 per cent, Canada 8.9 per cent, New Zealand 7.4 per cent) (OECD, 2004a). Funding was allocated largely on historically derived fixed budgets rather than being activity based. Budgetary monitoring rested with central government, facilitating tight central control of expenditure but providing limited incentives to use existing capacity more effectively (OECD, 2004b). Clinicians were not rewarded on a fee for service basis and their access to medical technology was regulated, ensuring that incentives to over supply medical services were largely absent in the UK. General practitioners act as gate keepers to secondary care, moderating the demands on the hospital services.

The NHS in England comprised a small number of regional health authorities sub-divided into more numerous district health authorities. Both tiers aided the government to implement national policy, undertake service planning and monitor performance. There have been numerous changes to health authority roles, culminating in the abolition of the regional tier in 2003. A year earlier, 28 strategic health authorities (SHAs) were established with a strategic planning and performance management role; holding to account NHS trusts and primary care trusts (PCTs) through performance agreements. Important changes have also arisen from the process of political devolution instigated by the Labour government that has led to differences in health policy and HR strategy emerging between England, Scotland, Wales and Northern Ireland. These differences are largely beyond the scope of this chapter that focuses on England.

The Conservative government aspired to make the NHS 'primary-care led' by creating GP fundholders in which some family doctors held budgets to purchase health care. It proved controversial because patients of GP fundholders were able to access hospital services more rapidly than non-fundholders, undermining equity. GP commissioning of services remained in place under Labour but it was made universal with GP practices grouped into primary care trusts. PCTs control in excess of 75 per cent of the NHS budget, providing primary and community services directly and commissioning secondary care services from acute NHS trusts and the independent sector. PCTs have a pivotal role in the Labour government's vision for the NHS because through their control of resources they are responsible for accelerating the shift of activity from hospitals to the community, facilitating the utilization of a variety of providers, and from 2006 are responsible for promoting patient choice by offering patients a choice of four or five local NHS providers together with other nationally accredited providers (Department of Health, 2005a: 21).

Employment trends

One of the clichés beloved of government ministers is that the NHS is the largest single employer in Europe. The workforce has grown rapidly in the last five years, mirroring the sharp rise in NHS expenditure; a contrast with the fluctuations in staff numbers during the 1990s (Department of Health, 2004b). Its size is reflected in the NHS paybill. In 2003–04 the NHS cost £63.7 billion and the largest component, 59 per cent, comprised staff and pay costs (cited in King's Fund, 2005: 15). In England, the NHS employed approximately 1.3 million people (1,071,203 fte) with almost 1.2 million (968,435 fte) employed in the NHS hospital and community health services (HCHS) in September 2004, excluding staff that are contracted out (Table 2.1).

A distinctive feature of the health service workforce is the centrality of professional staff to the delivery of health care and this has given NHS employment relations a particular form. This is reflected in the high levels of education amongst NHS workers; 20 per cent are graduates compared to 12 per cent of the UK workforce overall (Wanless, 2001: 184). It is also evident from the composition of the workforce. Medical and dental staff constitute almost 9 per cent of the workforce, 30 per cent comprise qualified nurses, midwives and health visitors which are the numerically dominant group. The only staff category in which professional staff do not constitute a majority is within the NHS

Table 2.1   NHS Staff by Occupation Code Staff Groups 1997–2004 (full-time equivalent) England as at 30 September each year

	1997	1999	2001	2003	2004
Total employed staff (inc. GP & Practice staff)	846,298	873,226	930,633	1,026,976	1,071,203
Total employed staff (HCHS only)	758,059	782,106	837,196	928,059	968,435
Total non-medical staff (inc. GP Practice staff)	761,540	784,855	838,138	924,939	961,979
Total non-medical staff (HCHS only)	700,961	721,767	773,141	855,799	889,973
Professionally qualified clinical staff	436,646	450,678	477,169	525,196	549,839
All doctors (excl. retainers[1])	84,758	88,371	92,495	102,037	109,224
Total qualified nursing staff	256,093	261,340	277,334	304,892	315,440
Total qualified scientific, therapeutic & technical staff	81,601	86,837	93,085	102,912	108,585
Qualified ambulance staff	14,193	14,129	14,255	15,355	16,587
Support to clinical staff	215,129	226,585	249,198	277,178	284,394
NHS Infrastructure support:	141,637	142,071	149,598	167,916	178,098
Central functions	60,643	63,190	69,277	78,784	85,498
Hotel, property & estates	59,560	55,503	54,036	55,323	56,593
Manager & senior manager	21,434	23,378	26,285	33,810	36,007
Other non-medical staff or those with unknown classification	2390	1494	834	512	432
Other GP practice staff	50,497	52,398	53,835	56,173	58,443

Source: Abbreviated from Department of Health, 2005b

[1] All doctors (excluding GP Retainers) also excludes hospital practitioners and clinical assistants, most of whom are GPs working part-time in hospitals

infrastructure support staff category which comprise a variety of managerial, estates and support services functions. The NHS has always employed a high proportion of women and in 2004, 82 per cent of the non-medical workforce were female and 12 per cent were from ethnic minority groups. The latter figure is substantially higher than in the past (6–7 per cent) because new ethnic categories were introduced from 2001 (see Department of Health, 2005b).

Doctors comprise three main categories: consultant medical and dental staff, medical and dental staff in training, and GPs, totaling 109,224 (ftes) (Table 2.1). In September 2004 of the 28,141 (fte) consultant medical staff 25 per cent were female, an increase from 18 per cent in 1994 and the proportion of women amongst doctors in training was 43 per cent. Approximately 35 per cent of the hospital medical workforce are consultants, an increase on average, of 5.5 per cent growth per year since 1994.

GPs comprise 30,762 (fte) staff and in contrast to hospital medical staff are self-employed (Department of Health, 2005c,d).

There have been very significant changes in the composition of the workforce. In the NHS infrastructure support staff category, the work-force in hotel services (cleaning, catering, portering) has been particu-larly hard hit by the impact of outsourcing. Since 1997 the number of hotel, property and estates staff has decreased by an average of 553 per year to 73,932 in 2004, which is over and above the rapid decline in the previous decade (Department of Health, 2005b). Employment levels have increased amongst all other staff categories in the last decade with a surge in employment growth from 2000. There have been large increases amongst hospital medical staff and occupational groups that support doctors and nurses. There has also been significant growth amongst registered nurses. In recent years, a substantial contri-bution to this increase has arisen from international recruitment. In the year to March 2004, there were more than 14,000 newly registered overseas-trained nurses placed on the Nursing and Midwifery Council Register in comparison to 19,000 UK trained registrations (Nursing and Midwifery Council, 2004).

The Labour government has also sponsored a rapid growth of non-registered nursing staff and other forms of support staff to compensate for shortages amongst qualified staff. To replace the leakage from the workforce arising from the shift to student status for trainee nurses there has been a substantial growth in the numbers of health care assis-tants (HCAs). Although there are data limitations because of the variety of titles used to describe non-registered nursing staff, the number of HCAs more than doubled in numbers from 13,000 to 27,000 between 1995 and 2001 in England (Buchan and Seccombe, 2002: 29). The sharp increase in HCAs suggests that in response to continuing short-ages of registered nursing staff, trust managers have tilted the balance of the workforce towards the use of more non-registered nursing care – a less 'rich' skill-mix in the NHS jargon. The Labour government has enthusiastically embraced such an approach and has committed itself to doubling the number of HCAs by 2005 (from a 2002 baseline) and a key objective for the workforce is to:

> Increase workforce capacity and productivity through skill mix and continuing professional development; moving work from doctors to other healthcare professionals and from healthcare professionals to the support workforce, supported by pay modernisation, and service redesign (Department of Health, 2002a: 23).

The growth of the medical workforce reflects the UK's historically low levels of medical staff and government policy to shift towards a consultant-provided service. Another catalyst for change has been the phased reduction in long working hours for doctors in training, with the European Union Working Time Directive providing the impetus for change. From August 2004 doctors in training were subject to a maximum average of 58 hours per week which will reduce to 48 hours by August 2009. This has required the establishment of more training posts in conjunction with new roles for medical staff and altered working patterns to ensure compliance (Department of Health, 2004c: 15). It has been possible to increase the medical workforce rapidly, despite lengthy periods of training, because the UK has actively recruited internationally. The number of HCHS medical staff qualified outside the European Economic Area increased from 16,241 (25 per cent of the total) in 1999 to 25,676 (31 per cent of the total) in 2004 (Department of Health, 2005c: 4). This growth is reflected in OECD (2004a) data which indicates that in 2002 the UK had 2.1 practising physicians per 1,000 population, the same figure as Canada, although the UK figure remains low in comparison to many other OECD countries.

A contentious issue has been the increase in the numbers of managerial staff with an increase of 5 per cent per year over the last decade. This increase remains a sensitive issue for the Labour government which has emphasized that staff increases are targeted on 'front-line staff' i.e. nurses and doctors. The Labour government implicitly distinguishes between the positive impact of increases in 'front-line staff' in contrast to the detrimental consequences of the growth of 'back-office' managerial staff. The contradictions of this policy position in a highly interdependent organization such as the NHS are evident, not least because the Labour government's support for more effective financial management, information technology and human resources capabilities have contributed to the growth of the managerial workforce.

Health sector reform: the conservative legacy and new labour

Since its establishment, governments of all political persuasions have proclaimed their support for the NHS and attempts to reform its structure have been viewed with intense suspicion by staff and public alike. The distinctiveness of the eighteen years of Conservative government was that it allowed a more sustained and ideologically motivated reform agenda to be pursued. The most important Conservative legacy was the establishment of a cadre of managers drawn from non-clinical backgrounds that were able to convert government aspirations for a more 'business like' NHS into concrete managerial initiatives. The increased focus on the individual employer unit – the trust – rather than the NHS as a whole legitimated managerial attempts to accelerate the shift from administered organizations, centred on a diverse set of frequently conflicting professional priorities, to managed organizations whose primary obligation was to ensure its future financial viability and that evaluated professional service aspirations according to whether they coalesced with the 'business' priorities of the trust.

Successive Conservative governments diffused market-type mechanisms across the public services to put pressure on managers and employees to alter employment practices. Compulsory competitive tendering (CCT) for support services (i.e. hospital cleaning, catering and laundry services) was introduced in the health sector in the early 1980s. Regardless of whether a service was retained in-house or outsourced, this policy led to substantial reductions in the workforce, and accompanying pay-roll savings (Colling, 1999). The imposition of mandatory competitive tendering provided managers with an incentive to alter working practices, erode national terms and conditions of employment and shifted industrial relations activity from national to local level.

In the early 1990s market relationships were further embedded in the health service. An internal market was established that separated purchasing by district health authorities (DHAs) from providing roles. The service providers, NHS trusts, typically comprised a single large hospital or hospitals that competed against each other for government revenue. Trusts were established as corporate bodies with their own board of directors; had scope to employ their own staff directly on trust terms and conditions of employment; were required to meet target rates of return on assets; could borrow subject to annual financing limits and had discretion to dispose of surplus assets. Trust status allowed managers to opt out of nationally determined pay and conditions of employment and the chance to manage budgets more flexibly (Department of Health, 1989).

Devolved management in trusts covered pay and terms and conditions of service, as well as the operational aspects of recruitment, appraisal and training. Managers experimented with changes in work organization, skill-mix, and working time arrangements and made greater use of temporary employment – altering the composition of the workforce and the roles undertaken (Arrowsmith and Mossé, 2000; Grimshaw, 1999). There was also a harder edge to many of the reforms, with more assertive policies on the control of sickness absence and increases in workload throughout the health service (Bach, 2004).

The central assumption of the internal market was that workload would be linked more closely to resources, with competiton between providers stimulating increased efficiency and responsiveness. The problem was that this form of 'dictated competition' (Light, 2001) embodied contradictory tendencies. Increased managerial autonomy came up against increased centralized control as the Conservative government became anxious about the political costs of the internal market (e.g. job losses). The Conservative government wanted the benefits of competition without the pain of market adjustment. In a planned health system, the market was inevitably highly regulated and incentive structures were relatively weak. Nonetheless Tony Blair's health policy advisor concluded that 'some things did change for the better during the internal market period and that whatever efficiency gains were made in the mid-1990s are now in danger of being lost' (Le Grand, 2002: 141). These comments foreshadowed the re-introduction of market-type incentives in the health service from the end of the second term of Labour government.

New labour: modernizing the NHS

The Labour government's mantra has been the modernization of public services which signalled an attempt to broaden out the reform agenda and a rejection of the more ideological elements of the Conservative government's market-based reforms. In practice the Labour government left much of the architecture of the internal market in place, but shifted the dynamics of health policy away from a focus on cost minimization towards a concern with increasing the volume and quality of health service provision. Its approach has combined unprecedented investment in infrastructure and staff with a requirement that increases in resources are accompanied by reforms of public services and alterations in working practices.

The Labour government, elected in 1997, used a sustained period of economic growth to address long-standing under-investment in public services. It was initially cautious, however, adopting restrictive conservative plans for public expenditure for its first two years in office to signal that it had shed its image as a 'tax and spend' party. This approach proved successful in these terms, but the government was increasingly besieged by tales of NHS financial crisis. This led to a government commitment that the UK would increase its share of GDP that it spends on health care to the average of the European Union (EU) by 2006. This policy was reaffirmed when the Chancellor, Gordon Brown, commissioned Derek Wanless a retired banker, to undertake a review of the long-term trends affecting the NHS. His reports (Wanless 2001; 2002) concluded that the UK would have to devote a far higher proportion of national income to health care expenditure. The government unveiled unprecedented increases in health service expenditure in the 2002 budget. Planned health service expenditure was to increase in real terms by 7.4 per cent per year on average until 2008 which corresponded to an increase in NHS spending in the UK from £65.4 billion in 2002–03 to £105.6 billion in 2007–08. These increases in health service expenditure have contributed to shorter waiting times for treatment, improved hospital infrastructure and increased staffing levels, although NHS productivity has declined (Department of Health, 2004d; King's Fund, 2005: 18–19).

Alongside investment, the Labour government's NHS reform programme combines an emphasis on national standards, a shift in governance to focus on partnership working between public, private and voluntary sector providers, the development of a devolved patient-led NHS and a comprehensive approach to HR issues. First, there has been an emphasis on national standards underpinned by systems of performance management and new inspectorates to direct and monitor performance against centrally defined standards. The government has been more explicit than its predecessors in establishing national targets which are set out in each government department's Public Service Agreement (PSA) with the Treasury. In the NHS these goals include targets for maximum waiting times, reductions in death rates and improvements in efficiency alongside broader National Service Frameworks (NSFs) for mental health, care of older people, coronary heart disease and other services. These NSFs guide the development of local services and enable NHS organizations to measure their clinical performance against national standards.

To enforce national standards the government established the Commission for Health Improvement (subsequently termed the Health Care Commission) with a remit to examine and maintain standards by regular inspections of NHS trusts, health authorities and PCTs. The Health Care Commission and other forms of performance management have increased the pressure on staff as they attempt to achieve government targets. A crucial dimension of this performance framework are the annual star ratings that are allocated to each NHS trust linked to managerial, clinical effectiveness and the survey responses of staff and patients. The ratings are graded from 3 stars, the highest level of performance, to zero stars, the poorest level of performance. Depending on the level of performance, trusts receive different levels of autonomy and the option for the top performing trusts to apply for foundation status.

The star ratings system and target culture has proved contentious because doubts have been expressed about the yardsticks used, the lack of staff involvement in setting targets and evidence of cheating to meet targets because of the financial and managerial consequences that arise from failure. For example, staff redesignated corridors as 'pre-admission units' to circumvent waiting time targets for accident and emergency care treatment (Public Administration Select Committee, 2003). Staff resent the imposition of targets that they have not devised and the workload involved in documenting outcomes, which militates against the government's emphasis on staff involvement and empowerment of front-line staff (Bach, 2004). The Audit Commission (2002: 22) has pin-pointed targets and the paperwork associated with them as the most important reason why public sector workers leave their jobs, cited by half of former public sector workers. The Labour government, however, suggests that the establishment of targets has raised NHS performance by focusing on delivery and increased accountability.

A second component of the modernization agenda has been a shift in governance structures from a focus on market-type incentives towards networks. This shift in governance signals that services are to be provided by a variety of public, private or voluntary organizations, necessitating partnership working across organizational boundaries in conjunction with resource allocation linked to incentive structures. The Labour government is therefore combining forms of collaboration and competition (King's Fund, 2005: 11). Services are being re-designed around the needs of the 'patient journey' requiring closer working relations between a variety of health service, social care and voluntary agencies. An increasingly important element of this agenda has been the role of the private sector as the Labour government has signalled that it favours a more pluralistic 'mixed economy of welfare' in which services are publicly funded but not necessarily publicly provided.

A core element has been the establishment of treatment centres, provided by the NHS or the independent sector, which undertake standard elective treatments (e.g. cataract operations) contributing to reduced waiting times. It is anticipated that the independent sector will undertake up to 15 per cent of operations for NHS patients by 2008. By commissioning services from overseas independent sector providers the government argues that it has enhanced NHS capacity, an essential pre-cursor to its patient choice initiatives:

> We are clearly beginning to see a fundamental shift in the pricing structure of private providers as we use the corporate buying power of the NHS more effectively. The Independent Sector Treatment Centre (IS-TC) programme will bring additional benefits as they spread new ways of working, spur NHS providers to increase their responsiveness to patients and, as a result of increased contestability, drive down the level of inefficient spot purchasing (Department of Health, 2004d: 52).

The potential to alter working practices is evident from experience at the first (NHS) treatment centre, based at the Central Middlesex hospital, in which surgeons are paid a fee for each patient they treat rather than an annual salary; if an operation is cancelled the surgeon is not paid (*Financial Times*, August 19th 2003). There have also been concerns that IS-TCs will poach staff from the NHS, leading to an agreed HR framework for staffing arrangements. If IS-TCs undertake additional work for the NHS, staff will be recruited from overseas or from staff that have not worked in the NHS for the previous 6 months. If IS-TCs undertake work transferred from an NHS trust, staff will be seconded to the independent sector (NHS Employers, 2005).

A third element concerns a focus on users and a shift towards a devolved patient-led NHS. These reforms have been underpinned by the phasing in of activity-based funding for hospitals, termed 'payment by results' which is designed to improve efficiency and foster competition between providers. The government has established a central system of national tariffs (prices) for operations and procedures and hospitals that attract more patients will receive more income and *vice versa*. Foundation trusts, which already operate under this financial model, are an important element of the attempt to establish market-based incentives and to promote a more decentralized model of health service management. They are intended to have more local community control over their activities (*via* an elected Board of Governors) and have been granted some independence to borrow for investment and to depart from standard NHS employment conditions and pay levels. The first 24 NHS trusts gained foundation status in 2004 and it is intended that all trusts bid for foundation status by 2008. There remains uncertainty about the willingness of the Treasury to loosen central control and allow greater financial independence of foundation trusts. There has also been strong resistance from trade unions concerned about the additional pay freedoms of foundation trusts and hostile to the broader market-based changes of the government (Transport and General Workers Union, 2002; UNISON, 2003).

Finally the Labour government has viewed human resource management as integral to their management reforms in a manner that contrasts with the Conservative government's narrow pre-occupation with decentralized pay determination. The publication, in July 2002, of 'HR in the National Plan' (Department of Health, 2002b) signified an attempt to link the approach to HR to the overall NHS modernization agenda rather than being an adjunct to reform initiatives. It emphasized that making the NHS a model employer was a primary objective and this was to be achieved by measures to improve staff morale, enhanced career development linked to progression on the basis of skill acquisition, and improved recruitment and retention of staff. Central to these efforts has been the Improving Working Lives (IWL) initiative that audits NHS trusts on their HR practice and encompasses a variety of measures: to combat violence against staff, improve the management of diversity, enhance employer provided child care, and boost staff involvement (Department of Health, 2004c).

Employer policy: from crisis management to strategic choice?

The increased attention to employer policy reflects the high priority that all governments have placed on transforming management practice. Over the last two decades the role and status of health service managers has altered markedly. A visible sign of many of these changes have been alterations in the form and level of compensation for managers which from the mid-1980s shifted to incorporate an individual performance-related pay (PRP) element. By the mid-1990s, however, trust boards' enthusiasm for using performance related pay for its top managers had cooled. Tight budgetary constraints often made it difficult to release sufficient resources to reward good performance adequately, so small merit pay increases were distributed across a sizeable number of staff and accounted for only a small proportion of an individual's pay. Forced distributions were frequently used which frustrated managers who believed they were unfairly denied a higher rating. Many trusts discontinued their system of individual merit pay, reflecting more general doubts about the effectiveness of performance related pay in the public services (Marsden and French, 1998).

Devolution of responsibility for employment practices also had consequences for the HR function. In the past, uneven investment in the HR function, an administrative legacy reflecting highly centralized and standardized personnel practice, alongside political constraints, ensured that NHS personnel specialists focused on policy implementation and the provision of administrative services (Lupton and Shaw, 2001). The trend to devolve operational personnel activities to line managers has created some resentment amongst overworked middle managers, whilst the strategic concerns of senior HR specialists, for example, the development of local pay systems have not been shared by other managers (Procter and Currie, 1999). The Department of Health (2002b: 32) has emphasized the importance of building HR skills amongst all managers and ensuring the credibility of the HR function are important elements of the HR strategy. It acknowledges, however, that there is a long way to go because 'human resource management in the NHS is still too often tarnished by its former role as the pejorative 'personnel' function' (*ibid.* 2002b: 32).

During the 1990s, government emphasis on decentralized collective bargaining and trust autonomy, led managers to focus attention on pay and working conditions, not least because staff costs comprised approximately two thirds of trust expenditure. In practice, however, the scope that trust managers had to refashion their employment practices was circumscribed by unpredictable political interventions from above, financial constraints, the scarcity of management resources and skills, and an awareness that devolved bargaining was distrusted by employees and opposed by their union representatives. By the end of the decade it was clear that progress towards devolved bargaining had been very limited (Corby *et al.*, 2001). This is confirmed by analysis of the 1998 Workplace Employee Relations Survey which indicates there was very limited decentralization of authority to managers in the NHS, in comparison to other parts of the public services (Kirkpatrick and Hoque, 2005: 114).

Nonetheless employers used the requirement to establish local pay bargaining machinery as an opportunity to alter relations with trade unions and the workforce. Conservative government hostility towards unions during the 1980s and 1990s created fears that the establishment of NHS trusts would lead to selective union derecognition. This union concern failed to materialize, with the exception of a few ambulance trusts that did not recognize all unions, usually because they favoured a single union deal (Bryson *et al.*, 1995: 123). As Bacon and Storey (2000) demonstrate, in their analysis of three NHS trusts, managers aspired to shift towards more individual relations but held back from wholesale derecognition because it would have engendered employee distrust. They point out that such a step was unnecessary because workplace changes had been imposed without the sanction of derecognition (Bacon and Storey, 2000: 414).

A longitudinal study of three acute hospital trusts between 1995–2001 noted that senior managers greatly increased the amount of direct communication with the workforce. In newsletters and team-briefings, financial information and trust performance against targets invariably gained a high profile in order to shape employee expectations. Employees were much less likely to look towards trade union representatives for information and traditional institutions of joint management-union relations became less important. Trust managers were prepared to tolerate trade unions as institutions but they became more marginal to management-workforce relations. Amongst HR specialists trade unions were viewed more as an adjunct to the management process rather than as an important source of independent employee voice. This view was related to their misgivings about how representative union members that participated in union-management forums were of wider staff opinion. In contrast to this downgrading of forms of indirect participation, alternative approaches to staff involvement were championed, especially by senior nurses. These initiatives were grounded in the particular occupational concerns and aspirations of nurses and were of greater direct relevance to these staff than other more traditional forms of joint consultation (Bach, 2004).

Flexible working practices

In contrast to the very limited developments in pay determination some of the most significant changes in employment practices since the mid-1990s relate to alterations in labour utilization. Analysis of employer practice has frequently differentiated between two labour utilization strategies: numerical flexibility, concerned with adjusting the number of workers to meet fluctuations in demand, and functional flexibility that signifies the range of tasks undertaken by employees. Part-time employment has often been associated with forms of numerical flexibility and within the NHS approximately one third of registered nurses are employed on a part-time basis. Although senior managers have endorsed part-time working as part of a recruitment and retention strategy, line managers that are responsible for the effective implementation of flexible working have been less enthusiastic about its benefits and have highlighted drawbacks. Part-time nurses undertake roles designed on a full-time basis and therefore it is difficult to accommodate them into existing work systems, complicating staff planning for ward managers. There are also drawbacks for full-time staff that work alongside them (Edwards and Robinson, 2004).

McBride (2003) echoes these findings in explaining the limited use of annualized hours, despite the pressures on trust managers to improve recruitment and retention and take account of the work-life balance needs of employees. The limited use of annualized hours is accounted for by the difficulties of making such schemes work in under-staffed services and due to the resistance of some occupational groups to annualized hours because of the effect on overtime earnings. Managers sought to reconcile the tension between their need for cost-effective flexible labour and employees' concerns about work-life balance by the use of additional temporary labour, especially *via* forms of bank working. Bank working involves individuals, especially nurses, registering on the internal staff 'bank' and the trust provides staff with additional shifts as the need arises.

Although public service managers have tried to reduce the incidence of temporary employment because of its potentially detrimental impact on recruitment and retention and on service quality, in the context of chronic staff shortages this has not been achieved. In the case of nursing, an Audit Commission (2001) study found that NHS expenditure on agency staff increased by a third, and expenditure on bank staff by 14 per cent, in 1999/2000. On a typical day about 20,000 bank and agency nurses provided temporary cover for staffing shortfalls on 10 per cent of all shifts. The majority of temporary staff cover the gaps arising from unfilled vacancies and sickness absence; others are employed to meet peaks in workload or to cover for staff on holiday or maternity leave. The Audit Commission also found that the majority of bank and agency nursing staff already had full-time or part-time substantive contracts in the NHS. Almost half of the staff who combined full-time posts with agency or bank employment worked more than 48 hours a week. Moreover, the methods by which temporary staff working less regularly were recruited, trained and appraised sometimes reduced the consistency and quality of patient care. Similar findings were reported in a case study of an NHS trust which noted that although some nurses found it stressful working in an unfamiliar environment, others argued that agency nursing could be relatively stress free in comparison to the responsibilities associated with regular NHS employment (Purcell *et al.*, 2004: 718).

A separate long-standing concern of policy makers has been to alter work organization to encourage 'new ways of working' and break down demarcations between occupational groups by combining jobs such as cleaning and portering into generic worker roles with trust-specific terms and conditions. This process was encouraged by the creation of a new grade of health care assistant (HCA) from 1990 with their pay and conditions excluded from national pay arrangements. Trust managers established starting salaries below the equivalent national rates and defined unilaterally the tasks undertaken by HCAs with knock-on effects for the jobs of registered nursing staff and existing ancillary workers (Grimshaw, 1999).

During the 1990s, Conservative governments persistently blurred the goals of improving patient care and lowering staff costs especially in its approach to the reform of working practices, leading to criticism that the primary concern of reforming working practices was to reduce costs through dilution and work intensification (Kendall and Lissauer, 2003: 9). The Labour government's workforce reform agenda is more ambitious, linked to its belief that organizational reform is insufficient without employment practice change, because 'a modernized workforce is essential to providing modern public services' (Blair, 2002: 26). The emphasis has been placed on making changes in working practices that support a more patient-centred NHS. This has involved the *extension* of existing roles, to improve patient care, alleviate workload pressures and address existing shortages of key professions. For example, more than half NHS trusts have redesigned roles in radiology and radiotherapy services, establishing advanced practitioners that can interpret the results of diagnostic tests (Department of Health, 2004d: 59). The Labour government has encouraged experienced staff to remain in front-line roles by enhancing their salary and status *via* the creation of nurse consultant roles, designed to ensure continued career progression without having to move into solely managerial roles.

There are four distinctive features of the Labour government's approach to changing working practices. First, it has provided resources and an infrastructure through its 'Changing Workforce Programme' to promote new roles with a number of pilot projects used to test job redesign and overcome implementation difficulties (Department of Health, 2002b: 12). Second, flexible working practices are being underpinned by reforms of pay determination and changes in regulatory frameworks. Pay progression is being linked to movement along the skills escalator to encourage life-long learning and career development. Similarly regulatory frameworks have been altered to accomodate enhanced roles, for example nurse prescribing. Third, the government views flexible roles as an integral element of its attempts to increase workforce capacity. It is not only professionally qualified staff that are having their roles extended; the increased use of non-registered nurses and other support staff reflect attempts by the NHS to grow its own professional workforce. This view is predicated on experience indicating a large pool of applicants, with few formal qualifications, are applying for HCA and similar assistant roles. Improved workplace based training along structured pathways would enable many HCAs to become registered nurses (see Thornley, 2003). Finally, the government has started to locate these workforce reforms into an overarching narrative that it has termed 'a new professionalism' which signifies that professional staff should be consumer orientated and responsive to the personalized needs of each service user (Blair, 2002: 25). This not only implies that existing 'old' professionalism places unnecessary barriers between professionals and patients but it also reduces the scope for professional staff to oppose the new professionalism with its aspiration of improved patient care. Indeed the Department of Health (2004d: 59) has suggested that 'there is a significant appetite for developing new roles in the service ... with the Royal Colleges and other professional bodies now actively leading these changes'.

Pay determination: origins and development

Collective bargaining has been the most important method of determining the public services' pay and conditions of employment and regulating the relationship between employers and trade unions for the last fifty years. The essentially 'voluntary' system, with very little direct legal regulation, covered both the private sector and most of the public services. In contrast to the position in most other countries there has been no general obligation on employers to engage in collective bargaining, and collective agreements are not legally binding between the parties; they are recommendations to central government or public employers.

From the establishment of the NHS in 1948 until the early 1990s a system of centralized pay determination existed which exerted a strong influence over trade union and employer organization and practice. This system referred to as 'Whitleyism' derives from the Whitley sub-committees that examined the deterioration in public sector employment relations during the First World War and proposed a system of employment relations based on a number of principles. National pay and terms and conditions of employment were advocated, determined at national level by employers negotiating with trade unions in joint industrial councils. These arrangements incorporated explicit support for trade union membership and a belief in national collective bargaining (Burchill and Casey, 1996: 43–45). The most important decisions on terms and conditions of employment were negotiated in ten functional Whitley Councils, and the two sides resolved any differences within an agreed procedure that included arrangements for arbitration.

Whereas the ten functional councils were set up to determine pay and conditions of particular occupational groups, a general Whitley council established conditions of service common to all NHS staff such as holiday entitlements, travel expenses, redundancy and sick pay provisions. Once national agreements were accepted by the Secretary of State, they were implemented by regulation in a prescriptive and uniform manner which allowed almost no scope for local flexibility. In a similar manner, nationally agreed grading definitions have been very restrictive defining precisely the qualifications and responsibilities attached to specific grades. Managers complained that occupational grading structures had failed to keep pace with changes in working practices and technological developments (Seifert, 1992).

The diversity of occupational groups was reflected in the multiplicity of staff organizations, about forty of which had national recognition but not all of whom were affiliated to the Trade Union Congress (TUC) – the single national union confederation. Staff-side representation was divided therefore between TUC affiliated unions often competing for NHS membership as well as members outside the service, and non-TUC affiliated professional associations which recruited mainly health care staff. Intense organizational rivalry and conflict over bargaining objectives in defence of narrow occupational or professional interests has complicated both national negotiations and local consultation.

Employer side representation has also proved problematic. The management side of the national bargaining arrangements has been dominated by Department of Health officials and health authority appointees of the Secretary of State for Health, to the virtual exclusion of health service managers. With the increased emphasis on strengthening management practice from the 1970s onwards, these tensions became greater as managers argued for more control in shaping the pay determination process, with only modest results. This management predicament reflected the dominance of central government, especially The Treasury, in maintaining tight control over the NHS paybill and the direct control exercised by the Secretary of State for

Health, who was answerable to Parliament for pay matters (Bach, 1999).

During the 1990s many grading structures were reformed and employers had greater scope to respond to local labour market and supply side conditions. Nonetheless a series of parallel but separate grading structures for each occupation remained in place militating against cross-functional working. In addition grading structures were not underpinned by a comprehensive system of job evaluation. This left health service employers vulnerable to legal claims that national grading structures were potentially discriminatory because they failed to provide equal pay for work of equal value. These issues came to a head in the late 1990s with health service trade unions supporting a series of equal pay for work of equal value claims from their membership. These cases had substantial financial implications for NHS trusts, hastening the search for a more durable and equal value proof system of pay determination (Bach and Winchester, 2003).

Pay review bodies

Pay determination in the NHS is complicated by the existence of independent pay review bodies for nurses and doctors. They were created to remove a range of highly sensitive pay settlements from the political arena. The establishment of an independent pay review body for nurses, midwives and other health professionals in 1983 followed a lengthy nurses' pay dispute. Prior to its establishment, only doctors and dentists in the NHS had been outside of collective bargaining arrangements and covered by an independent review body. The removal of more than half a million nurses from the traditional system of pay bargaining was prompted by government expectations that they would never again join with other health service staff in industrial action. The substitution of traditional bargaining arrangements with a more distant form of arms length bargaining for a large and politically sensitive occupational group had obvious attractions for the government, although these have only been partially realized in practice.

The nurses' pay review body receives detailed evidence from government, employers and trade unions prior to making its recommendations to the government. It is presumed that these recommendations will be accepted unless there are 'clear and compelling reasons for not doing so'. In practice, no government has ever rejected a pay review body's report totally, but frequently the implementation of the recommended pay increases has been staged in order to reduce the annual paybill. The NHS review bodies are concerned only with recommendations on pay levels and other monetary allowances, although they do take a broad view of these issues and consider recruitment and retention, morale, career structures and workload.

The system of pay review bodies has increased the visibility and complexity of the NHS pay determination process with considerable political and economic consequences for the government. First, each year the recommendations for all review body groups and the evidence on which these decisions are based – concerning pay trends, workload and morale – are subject to critical scrutiny by the national media. For this reason all governments have been acutely conscious of the phase of the electoral cycle when deciding whether to accept, reject or phase review body recommendations (see White, 2000).

Second, the division between nurses and doctors with their own review bodies whilst other groups remained subject to collective bargaining, encouraged differential pay outcomes for review body and non-review body groups. These differences in annual settlements derived from the labour market position of doctors and nurses rather than the institutional arrangements for pay setting (Elliot and Duffus, 1996). The position of review body groups has, nonetheless, been widely resented. Doctors and nursing organizations have attached the highest importance to the retention of the review bodies and this has reinforced the strong rivalries between occupational groups and their representative organizations in the health sector. The ability of the Labour government to convince trade unions representing non-review body staff that their members' pay would improve, while reassuring nurses and doctors that their privileged status would be maintained, was an important factor influencing the acceptability of the government's proposals for modernizing the NHS pay system.

For most of the period between 1979 and 1997 the earnings of public sector workers declined in relative terms in comparison to the private sector. This general picture disguises important variations between occupational groups. As Elliott and Duffus (1996) have shown between 1981 and 1992 doctors and qualified nurses saw their real earnings grow by more than 30 per cent. This was in marked contrast to the experience of male and female manual workers effected by competitive tendering where real earnings grew by less than 20 per cent. More generally, the growth of earnings of women working full-time was greater than those of men, and non-manual employees' earnings grew more rapidly than those of manual workers.

Comparisons of public and private sector wage movements are complicated by the different composition of the workforce with the public sector increasingly dominated by salaried and professional workers. Analysis by Incomes Data Services (2001a and b) indicates that with a couple of exceptions (nurses and doctors) public sector occupations experienced a fall in their comparative pay from the mid-1990s. The election of the Labour government in 1997 did not precipitate an immediate change in pay policy because of its commitment to maintain the public spending totals of its predecessors for its first two years in office. Since the late 1990s, however, the government has accepted in full the recommendations of the review bodies that granted above-inflation pay rises for doctors and nurses. Movements in average earnings indicate that review body groups have continued to fare much better than their non-review body counterparts (White and Hatchett, 2003). Taking account of the priority attached to boosting health service capacity and against a backdrop of severe recruitment and retention difficulties, it is not surprising that there has been substantial growth in real wages in the NHS for key occupations and more generally public sector wages have been in a 'catch-up' phase. These trends have been reinforced by pay modernization that has fostered strong earnings growth in return for changes in work practices.

Since 1998, New Earnings data indicates that medical practitioners have experienced cumulative increases in real wages per hour that are 13 percentage points greater than the economy-wide average. Complex negotiations with the medical profession resulted in the acceptance of a new consultant contract in England. Hospital consultants were granted a substantial pay increase of between 10–20 per cent depending on age and experience, but in return, consultants are required to offer additional hours over their basic working week to the NHS rather than allocating it to private practice. Other staff have accepted a general 10 per cent pay increase over three years and many will be upgraded to higher pay bands as part of pay modernization. The fiscal position, however, is tightening so it is likely that wage growth in the NHS will moderate substantially in the medium term (OECD 2004b).

The role of the review bodies has altered under the Labour government and there is considerable uncertainty about their future role (Horsman, 2003; White and Hatchett, 2003). First, the Labour government has promoted social partnership as a core element in bringing about changes in pay determination and work organization. As discussed below this led to four years of negotiation between employers, unions and UK health departments to agree to a new pay system. The agreement included a shift from multiple bargaining units to single-table bargaining with the establishment of a joint employer-union NHS Staff Council that has been central to the development and implementation of the pay reforms. It is not only that pay modernization has occurred outside of the pay review body process, but their key role in assessing trends in pay, workload and morale is being usurped by a range of other actors. For example, the NHS Staff Council produced an evaluation of the benefits and problems of the new pay system that could be expected to carry more weight than the nurses' review body's evaluation, considering the Staff Council's pivotal role in implementation.

Second, the Labour government has supported the development of less prescriptive national pay frameworks that allows more local flexibility in grading and job design to encourage the development of new roles and to respond to local labour market conditions. Increased managerial discretion will erode further the regulatory impact of pay review body awards on the actual earnings and pay progression of NHS staff. These trends are being reinforced by the establishment of long-term pay deals, in a climate of low inflation, which will mean that the nurses' pay review body will not make a pay recommendation until 2006. Moreover, the development of foundation hospitals with additional pay freedoms represents a further source of uncertainty about the future role of the pay review bodies. An important counter-veiling trend, however, is the extension of the coverage of the nurses' pay review body to include NHS scientists, ambulance paramedics, pharmacists and health care assistants, reflected in its new name the Review Body for Nursing and Other Health Professionals (RBNOHP).

Pay modernization: *Agenda for Change*

The Labour government's plans to improve recruitment and retention, instil a much stronger performance culture in the NHS and break down job demarcations has been linked to shared public service modernization principles which White and Hatchett (2003: 239–240) argue comprise a number of elements:

- less prescriptive, national pay determination systems that allow more local flexibility in grading and pay design;
- pay increases that are sufficient to recruit and retain, but which include adequate flexibility to allow local occupational and geographical variations;

- the ending of automatic pay progression based on service and the more explicit linkage of performance and pay;
- longer-term pay agreements, which are seen as advantageous for longer-term planning of public spending;
- urgent implementation of pay reviews to end gender pay discrimination and prevent expensive litigation.

The initial *Agenda for Change* proposals to reform the fragmented and disparate terms and conditions for NHS staff and provide better career progression were outlined in 1999 (Department of Health, 1999). Converting *Agenda for Change* from a generalized set of propositions into a workable blueprint that satisfied the aspirations of the government, not least the Treasury, employers and diverse trade union interests proved to be a complex and time-consuming task that was not completed until the end of 2002. The new pay structure comprises two parallel pay spines one for staff covered by the existing nurses' pay review body with extended coverage to incorporate other professional groups and one pay spine for non-pay review body staff to be covered by a new national negotiating council. Each pay spine comprises eight bands each with 4–9 incremental points. A key feature of the agreement was the establishment by the social partners of an NHS specific job evaluation scheme to remove the anomalies and discriminatory pay practice of the previous pay structures and ensure equal pay for work of equal value. Jobs are therefore allocated to one of the bands according to job size and national job profiles have been prepared to facilitate this process. For example, band 1 includes job profiles for catering and domestic assistants, band 5 includes dieticians and physiotherapists, and band 8 nurse consultants. Grading therefore remains largely national and only jobs that do not match national profiles are intended to be graded locally, using the national job evaluation system.

Pay progression is no longer based exclusively on automatic service-based increments, because within each band there are 'gateway' thresholds at which point length of service progression is augmented by a competency-based assessment of knowledge and skills before the individual can progress further. The trade unions have been anxious to ensure a number of safeguards were built into the system to prevent competency assessment becoming a form of *de facto* performance-related progression. The NHS Knowledge and Skills Framework is the national competency framework that underpins pay progression but equally importantly it is intended to establish a new culture of career development for all staff. It also provides an opportunity for employers to establish new roles, using the skills framework to ensure that staff are rewarded fairly for the knowledge utilized in their jobs. Other aspects of the reforms that are designed to simplify pay structures and encourage flexibility include the development of harmonized core national terms and conditions, the introduction of a system of high-cost area allowances and alterations in unsocial hours payments. Although local pay flexibility has been scaled back in comparison to the original proposals, employers can award recruitment and retention supplements in addition to nationally determine basic rates, but strict criteria and regulation of these premia have been put in place (Department of Health, 2002c; Incomes Data Service, 2003).

All seventeen health service trade unions involved consulted their membership and balloted them on the proposals with differing results. These variations arise from the differing membership composition and historical identities of individual trade unions (see Bach and Givan, 2004). Trade unions with a relatively homogenous membership and strong professional identities were attracted by the strong emphasis on professional development. This led to strong affirmation of the agreements by the Royal College of Nursing, the Royal College of Midwives and the Chartered Society of Physiotherapists with between 80–90 per cent of votes cast supportive of the agreement. The only exception was the narrow vote (51%) against the agreement by the Society of Radiographers attributed to frustration with endemic recruitment and retention difficulties and hostility to the proposal to increase their standard working week by 2.5 hours (Labour Research, 2003).

Amongst the large general unions, with a more diverse membership and with many activists ideologically opposed to the Labour government's modernization agenda, senior trade union officials feared membership rejection and a further souring of relations with the Labour government that such a result would bring in its wake. The public services union UNISON therefore led the way in instigating a two-stage membership ballot in which it was recommended that members support the piloting of the new pay system in the 12 'early implementer' pilot sites and accept a three year 10 per cent pay deal. Judgement was to be reserved on overall approval of the pay system until a second ballot was held in 2004, following evaluation and possible re-negotiation of any outstanding problems with it. This strategy prevailed and led to successive ballot results in favour of the proposals, allowing final agreement and national implementation of *Agenda for Change* across the NHS from December 2004.

The initial impact of *Agenda for Change* can be gauged by the lessons emerging from the twelve early implementer sites. The review undertaken by the (Shadow) Executive of the NHS Staff Council was very positive suggesting that staff and managers were well disposed towards the system and that it had facilitated better career structures and partnership working. They estimated that over 90 per cent of staff would receive an immediate pay increase (NHS Staff Council, 2004). The Review Body for Nursing and Other Health Professionals suggested that the reforms had helped service delivery by facilitating the creation of new and extended roles and that staff welcomed the removal of artificial demarcations between groups working closely together. It did, however, highlight some serious problems with certain aspects of unsocial payments and concerns that there might be insufficient funding for the implementation process (RBNOHP, 2004). Its second report was much less positive and raised concerns about the workload involved during the lengthy implementation process: 'The general feeling amongst analysts is that the evaluation process is extremely complex and anomalies are experienced at all Trusts' (RBNOHP, 2005: 5). These comments highlight the limited managerial capacity available to implement complex pay reforms. Some staff felt that the scheme focused too much on clinical experience rather than professional skills and in general it was noted that 'staff morale and motivation has dipped at most Trusts during implementation' (RBNOHP, 2005: 8).

One of the most significant findings has been the positive outcome in terms of relations between staff side representatives and managers with improved partnership working. The emphasis in the *Agenda for Change* proposals on partnership working has undoubtedly bolstered forms of co-operative working in the NHS, but the experience of early implementers may be atypical because staff side support within each trust was a pre-requisite for selection as an early implementer (see Foster, 2002). Experience across the public services indicates that partnership working can easily be derailed by unanticipated financial and organizational problems and partnership relations may not penetrate beyond a relatively small group of activists (Tailby *et al.*, 2004; Winchester, 2005).

Trade union policy and practice

Union membership in the public services has been sustained far more successfully than membership in the private sector, which has declined sharply since 1979. Labour Force Survey data indicates that in 2004 trade union density for all public sector employees was significantly higher than in the private sector, being 59 and 17 per cent respectively, although public sector union density has declined by 2.7 percentage points since 1995 (Grainger and Holt, 2005: 3). In the health sector union density was 42 per cent, a significantly lower figure than other areas of the public service, which may reflect the sizeable role of the private sector in the health industry category. Many health service unions, however, especially those representing professional staff have grown in recent years as the size of the NHS workforce increased.

An important feature of trade union structure in the NHS is its complex multi-union character. Several of the most influential trade unions are not affiliated to the TUC and combine the functions of trade unions and professional associations, recruiting only within the health sector. The British Medical Association (BMA) and The Royal College of Nursing (RCN) are the most influential with memberships of 113,711 and 359,739 respectively (Certification Officer, 2004). These organizations have been termed 'professional unions' to signify that they do not rely exclusively on collective bargaining but instead attempt to control labour supply by limiting membership to registered professionals with an orientation towards the defence of job demarcations and long-standing pay differentials (Burchill, 1995).

By contrast UNISON is a general union with 1.3 million members spread across the public services. It has the largest trade union membership in the NHS and was formed in 1993 from the merger of three public service unions. It organizes most of the union members among clerical and administrative staff, the majority of ancillary staff members, and has a substantial membership amongst health care assistants in acute and non-acute settings. UNISON has tried to broaden its membership base by seeking to increase its membership amongst registered nursing staff where it faces intense competition from the RCN, the largest union outside the TUC.

Three of the large predominantly private-sector multi-occupational unions have a membership presence in the NHS. The Transport and General Workers' Union (TGWU) and the General and Municipal Boilermakers (GMB) represent mainly ancillary and ambulance grades and membership has declined in tandem with decreases in the workforce arising from competitive tendering. Manufacturing, Science and Finance (MSF) that became part of Amicus in 2002 represents technical and professional staff, especially amongst hospital laboratory staff, pharmaceutical staff and therapists.

Union organization and renewal

The emphasis on devolving authority to the front line under the Labour government has generated a substantial human resource management agenda at local level. This has confronted the trade unions with an acute challenge because of the need to service a more fragmented bargaining system and develop the capacity to handle a growing and increasingly complex workload. Traditionally, however, union activity has been highly centralized reflecting national systems of pay determination. The smaller health service professional unions have faced this dilemma most forcefully in terms of their ability to represent their members in a more fragmented service; some have affiliated to the TUC, and others have joined the larger general unions (Bach and Givan, 2004).

For professional unions, whose growth and influence has been premised on a strategy of exclusivity, reforms of the workforce with increases in assistant staff and the development of new roles has encouraged the nurses' and midwives' unions to consider whether to open up their membership to a broader range of occupational groups. During October 2000, in a landmark decision, RCN members voted to admit HCAs and nurse cadets with a level 3 national vocational qualification into associate membership; about 40,000 health workers are eligible to be members. This vote, which required a two-thirds membership majority, has important implications. First, it is tangible recognition that HCAs have become central to health care delivery and are undertaking tasks formerly reserved for registered nurses. Second, over a longer time-scale it could provide a substantial boost to membership by opening up a large pool of potential members and enabling the RCN to recruit them early on in their training rather than having to wait until they are registered; when they may already be a member of a rival trade union. It therefore set an open important precedent for the RCN in terms of recruiting beyond its traditional boundaries. Third, the RCN has tried to placate membership concerns that the decision represents an erosion of their professional status. HCAs are to be confined to an associate membership category that prevents them holding any of the top positions or voting on RCN business.

The formation of UNISON in the early 1990s was a direct response to the restructuring of the public services and the anticipated move to local bargaining. Compulsory competitive tendering led to a sharp reduction in the employment of ancillary staff and there were fears that the extension of CCT to white-collar groups would precipitate a similar membership decline. The formation of UNISON sought to economize on scarce resources, reduce inter-union competition between the partner unions, and capitalize on the shift towards decentralized bargaining activity by providing the resources which would ensure continued membership growth across all sections of the workforce. This enabled UNISON to become 'the union for the public services' and to seek a privileged relationship with government and local employers (Terry, 1996). The merger has only partially fulfilled these expectations with UNISON membership stabilizing after a lengthy period of decline. There have been significant internal tensions reflecting the different union structures and conceptions of union purpose which each organization brought to the merger. In common with almost all public service unions, UNISON has confronted problems of workplace organization and the ability of full-time officers to cope with rising workloads (Undy, 1999).

As noted earlier the advent of a Labour government altered the climate of employment relations in the UK by its determination to foster a climate of 'social partnership'. For the Labour government this implies a more collaborative relationship between employers and trade unions orientated to mutually beneficial changes (see Tailby and Winchester, 2005).

A key stumbling block for the trade unions has been the Labour government's support for the private finance initiative (PFI) which has become the dominant system of procuring new hospital facilities using private capital and management. It involves the NHS commissioning and monitoring services, but not providing them. Trade unions have viewed PFI as a form of creeping privatization. They have argued that PFI is unacceptable because it allows private companies to profit from public services and has led to buildings of poor quality alongside sub-standard facilities management services in contracts that are let for 25–35 years (UNISON, 2002). Whilst employees' terms and conditions are legally protected on transfer from the public to the private sector, trade unions have argued strongly that new staff should have the same pay and conditions as protected employees to avoid the creation of a 'two tier' workforce. The government's support for public-private partnerships soured its relationship with public service trade unions during its second term of office, despite granting some concessions to public service trade unions in relation to the rights of transferred staff (Bach and Givan, 2005).

The government's broader public service agenda has therefore made workplace trade unionists cautious about embracing partnership working. The Department of Health has expressed strong support for staff involvement and social partnership, reflecting the government's attempt to gain staff consent for modernization and its broader agenda to improve working lives (Department of Health, 2002b). There is little consensus, however, about the aims and outcomes of these arrangements. Partnership may simply be a new label for employee involvement with outcomes partly related to inter- and intra-union relations (Heaton *et al.*, 2001) whilst Munro (2002) has noted potential opportunities to enhance union influence. Many trade unions have viewed the implementation of *Agenda for Change* as an opportunity to draw more members into active participation in the workplace, an approach that seems to be yielding dividends. Nonetheless, the size and complexity of the national HR agenda has placed constraints on union involvement. Increased workloads and continuing staff shortages has often made it difficult for trade union representatives to undertake their functions. There are relatively few trade union members prepared to be active members, increasing the burden on already over-stretched union activists. Professional staff in particular are reluctant to participate in trade union activities, if they perceive their involvement as increasing the workload for their colleagues and jeopardizing service standards. These difficulties are frequently exacerbated by line managers that are reluctant to release trade union representatives, despite good formal time-off policies (Bach, 2004).

Waddington and Kerr (1999: 187) indicate that UNISON structure and organization is weaker in health than elsewhere and they report high levels of dissatisfaction with local union organization amongst union members. Similar weaknesses in union organization and a shortage of union activists have also been noted in studies of acute hospitals (Carter and Poynter, 1999: 508), highlighting the fragility of union organization. Less is known about other health service trade unions, although a survey of RCN stewards suggested that management support for their role remained strong (Kessler and Heron, 2001). Carter and Poynter (1999: 507) point out that weak workplace union organization has been masked, and at the same time reinforced, by a concentration of bargaining at national level. A similar process may be occurring at present with government expenditure increasing NHS staff numbers and boosting trade union membership levels, whilst disguising the underlying fragility of union organization.

Discussion

In the last two decades the NHS has been subject to a continuous process of reform. In what remains a highly centralized organization, dependent almost exclusively on central government funding, it proved more straightforward for the Conservative government to bring about far-reaching changes in management structures, systems of financial management and accountability than it was to gain the consent of the NHS workforce and their representatives to fundamental reforms of employment practices. Although local pay did not take root in the NHS, health service managers used their increased discretion to alter the composition of the workforce, reform occupational roles and introduce a variety of human resource management techniques.

The Labour government elected in 1997 accepted most of the radical organizational restructuring of the health service whilst extending the scrutiny of organizational performance. It inherited a workforce weary of constant organizational change and the requirement to achieve performance targets, and demoralized by unflattering media scrutiny of the health service. In addition, long-standing problems of recruitment and retention amongst many health care professions reflected a lack of attention to the overall human resource management agenda. For much of its first two terms in office, there has been a tension between the Labour government's attempts to improve the working lives of NHS staff alongside the pressure on staff to fulfil a range of national targets.

Labour government ministers shared the predilection of their predecessors for constant intervention from the centre. The unrelenting steam of initiatives linked to short-term service targets disorientated managers and public service professionals distracting them from longer-term policy and development during a substantial part of the Labour government's period of office. The Labour government has acknowledged some of the limitations of its overall approach to reform in its renewed focus on a patient-led, devolved NHS that supports front-line staff (Department of Health, 2005a). It has attached a high priority to the human resource management agenda and sought to renew the model employer tradition with its ambition to make the NHS an employer of choice. There are signs of significant improvements in the working lives of health service staff and the government is on course to fulfil most of its pledges on staff numbers, alongside substantial improvements in hospital infrastructure and waiting times (King's Fund, 2005).

What remains uncertain is whether this resourcing is sufficient to meet the scale of the government's ambitions and the expectations of employers, employees and patients. Increased expenditure has facilitated the implementation of ambitious pay reforms in the health service and encouraged changes in working practices. A substantial challenge remains, however, in terms of managerial capacity and the degree to which the HR agenda is embedded in the NHS. The next few years will reveal whether an organization that for most of its history has been highly centralized and hierarchical, and that has traded on the commitment of its staff, can shift its culture to embrace staff involvement, professional development for the whole workforce, altered professional roles, and partnership working with trade unions.

References

Arrowsmith, J. and Mossé, P. 2000. Hospital Reform and the Working Time of Hospital Nurses in England and France, *European Journal of Industrial Relations*, 6(3), 283–307.

Audit Commission 2001. *Brief Encounters: Getting the Best from Temporary Nursing Staff*. London: The Audit Commission.

Audit Commission 2002. *Recruitment and Retention: A Public Service Workforce for the Twenty-first Century*. London: Audit Commission.

Bach, S. 1999. 'From National Pay Determination to Qualified Market Relations: NHS Pay Bargaining Reform', *Historical Studies in Industrial Relations*, 8: 99–117.

Bach, S. 2004. *Employment Relations and the Health Service: The Management of Reforms*. London: Routledge.

Bach, S. and Givan, R. 2004. 'Public Service unionism in a restructured public sector: challenges and prospects', in Kelly, J. and Willman, P. (eds) *Union Organisation and Activity*. London: Routledge.

Bach, S. and Givan, R. 2005. 'Union Responses to Public-Private Partnerships in the National Health Service', in Fernie, S. and Metcalf, D. (eds) *British Unions: Resurgence or Perdition?* London: Routledge.

Bach, S. and Winchester, D. 2003. 'Industrial Relations in the Public Sector' in Edwards, P. K. (ed.) *Industrial Relations: Theory and Practice*, Second Edition, Oxford: Blackwell.

Bacon, N. and Storey, J. 2000. 'New Employee Strategies in Britain: Towards Individualism or Partnership?', *British Journal of Industrial Relations*, 38(3), 407–427.

Blair, T. 2002. *The Courage of our Convictions: Why reform of the public services is the route to social justice*. London: Fabian Society.

Bryson, C., Jackson, M. and Leopold, J. (1995). 'The Impact of Self-governing Trusts on trades unions and staff associations in the NHS', *Industrial Relations Journal*, 26(2), 120–134.

Buchan, J. and Seccombe, I. 2002. *Behind the Headlines: A review of the UK labour market in 2001*. London: RCN.

Burchill, F. 1995. 'Professional Unions in the National Health Service: Issues and Membership Trends', *Review of Employment Topics*, 3(1), 13–42.

Burchill, F. and Casey, A. 1996. *Human Resource Management. The NHS: A Case Study*. Basingstoke: Macmillan.

Carter, B. and Poynter, G. 1999. 'Unions in a changing climate: MSF and Unison experiences in the new public sector', *Industrial Relations Journal*, 30(5), 499–513.

Certification Officer 2004. *Annual Report of the Certification Officer 2003–2004*. London: Certification Office for Trade Unions and Employers' Associations. http://www.certoffice.org/annualReport/pdf/Full%20report%202003-2004A.pdf

Colling, T. 1999. 'Tendering and Outsourcing: Working in the Contract State' in Corby, S. and White, G. (eds) *Employee Relations in the Public Services*. Routledge: London.

Corby, S., Millward, L., White, G., Drucker, J. and Meerabeau, E. 2001. *Innovations in Pay and Grading in NHS Trusts*. Greenwich, University of Greenwich.

Department of Health 1989. *Working for Patients*. Cm. 555. London: Department of Health.

Department of Health 1999. *Agenda for Change: Modernising the NHS Pay System*. London: The Stationery Office.

Department of Health 2002a. *Improvement, Expansion and Reform: The Next Three Years. Priorities and Planning Framework 2003–2006*. London: Department of Health.

Department of Health 2002b. *HR in the NHS Plan*. London: Department of Health.

Department of Health 2002c. *A Modernised NHS Pay System* http://www.dh.gov.uk/assetRoot/04/03/49/64/04034964.pdf

Department of Health 2004a. *National Standards, Local Action: Health and Social Care Standards and Planning Framework 2005/06–2007/08*. London: Department of Health.

Department of Health 2004b. *Staff in the NHS 2004*. London: Department of Health.

Department of Health 2004c. *Delivering HR in the NHS Plan 2004*. London: Department of Health.

Department of Health 2004d. *The NHS Improvement Plan: Putting People at the Heart of Public Services*. Cm 6268. London: Department of Health.

Department of Health 2005a. *Creating a Patient-led NHS: Delivering the NHS Improvement Plan*. London: Department of Health.

Department of Health 2005b. *NHS hospital and community health services non-medical staff in England: 1994–2004*. London: Department of Health.

Department of Health 2005c. *Hospital, Public Health Medicine and Community Health Services Medical and Dental Staff in England: 1994–2004*. London: Department of Health.

Department of Health 2005d. *Statistics for General Medical Practitioners in England: 1994–2004*. London: Department of Health.

Edwards, C. and Robinson, O. 2004. 'Evaluating the Business Case for Part-Time Working amongst Qualified Nurses', *British Journal of Industrial Relations*, 42(1), 167–183.

Elliott, R. and Duffus, K. 1996. What has been happening to pay in the public-service sector of the British economy? Developments over the period 1970–92. *British Journal of Industrial Relations*, 34(1), 51–85.

Foster, A. 2002. 'Expressions of Interest in Early Implementation of the New NHS Pay System (*Agenda for Change*), Letter to Chief Executives of NHS Trusts, July 2nd. Available at www.doh.gov.uk/agendaforchange

Grainger, H. and Holt, H. 2005. *Trade Union Membership 2004*. London: DTI. http://www.dti.gov.uk/er/emar/trade_union_membership2004.pdf

Grimshaw, D. 1999. 'Changes in Skills-mix and Pay Determination among the Nursing Workforce in the UK', *Work, Employment and Society*, 13(2), 295–328.

Ham, C. 2000. *The Politics of NHS Reform 1988–1997: Metaphor or Reality?* London: King's Fund.

Heaton, N., Mason, B. and Morgan, J. 2001. Partnership and Multi-Unionism in the Health Service, *Industrial Relations Journal*, 33(2), 112–126.

Horsman, M. 2003. Continuity and Change: Public Sector Pay Review Bodies, 1992–2003, *Public Money and Management* 23(4), 229–236.

Incomes Data Service (2001a). 'Pay and bargaining prospects 2001/2002', *IDS Report 842*, London: Incomes Data Services.

Incomes Data Service (2001b). 'Public sector pay in 2001', *IDS Report 839*, London: Incomes Data Services.

Incomes Data Service (2003). 'Pay Modernisation in the NHS', *IDS Report 884*, London: Incomes Data Services.

Kendall, L. and Lissauer, R. 2003. *The Future Health Worker*. London: Institute for Public Policy Research.

Kessler, I. and Heron, P. 2001. 'Steward Organization in a Professional Union: The Case of the Royal College of Nursing', *British Journal of Industrial Relations*, 39(3), 367–391.

King's Fund 2005. *An Independent Audit of the NHS Under Labour (1997–2005)*. London: King's Fund. Available at: www.kingsfund.org.uk/pdf/fullaudit.pdf

Kirkpatrick, I. and Hoque, K. 2005. 'The decentralization of employment relations in the British public sector', *Industrial Relations Journal*, 36(2), 100–120.

Labour Research 2003. 'NHS deal gets nervy welcome', *Labour Research*, 14–16.

Le Grand, J. 2002. 'The Labour Government and the National Health Service', *Oxford Review of Economic Policy*, 18(2), 137–153.

Light, D. 2001. 'Managed Competition, Governmentality and Institutional Response in the United Kingdom', *Social Science and Medicine*, 52(8), 1167–1181.

Lupton, B. and Shaw, B. 2001. 'Are Public Sector Managers the Profession's Poor Relations', *Human Resource Management Journal*, 11(3), 23–38.

Marsden, D. and French, S. 1998. *What a Performance: Performance Related Pay in the Public Services*. London: Centre for Economic Performance.

McBride, A. 2003. 'Reconciling competing pressures for working-time flexibility: an impossible task for the National Health Service (NHS)', *Work Employment and Society*, 17(1), 159–170.

Munro, A. 2002. 'Working Together – Involving Staff, *Employee Relations*, 24(3), 277–289.

NHS Employers 2005. *Independent Sector Treatment Centres: Human resources framework*. http://www.nhsemployers.org/docs/hr_framework_0105.pdf

NHS Staff Council 2004. *Agenda for Change: Review of Experience in the Early Implementer Sites*. http://www.dh.gov.uk/assetRoot/04/08/82/16/04088216.pdf

Nursing and Midwifery Council 2004. *Statistical analysis of the register 1 April 2003 to 31 March 2004*. http://www.nmc-uk.org

OECD 2004a. *Health Data*, 3rd Edition. Paris: OECD.

OECD 2004b. *OECD Economic Survey of the United Kingdom 2004*. Paris: OECD.

Power, M. 1997. *The Audit Society: Rituals of Verification*. London: Oxford University Press.

Procter, S. and Currie, G. 1999. 'The Role of the Personnel Function: Roles, Perceptions and Processes in an NHS Trust', *International Journal of Human Resource Management*, 10(6), 1077–1093.

Public Administration Select Committee 2003. *On Target? Government by Measurement*, Fifth Report of Session 2002–03, HC 62-I. London: House of Commons. http://www.publications.parliament.uk/pa/cm200203/cmselect/cmpubadm/1264/126402.htm

Purcell, J., Purcell, K. and Tailby, S. 2004. 'Temporary Work Agencies: Here Today, Gone Tomorrow?' *British Journal of Industrial Relations*, 42(4), 705–727.

Review Body for Nursing and Other Health Professionals (RBNOHP) 2004. *Report on the key lessons from the Early Implementers of Agenda for Change in England 2003*. http://www.ome.uk.com/

Review Body for Nursing and Other Health Professionals 2005. *Report of findings from follow up visits to the Early Implementers in England 2004*. http://www.ome.uk.com/review.cfm?body=6

Seifert, R. 1992. *Industrial Relations in the NHS*. London: Chapman and Hall.

Tailby, S., Richardson, M., Stewart, P., Danford, A. and Upchurch, M. 2004. 'Partnership at work and worker participation: an NHS case study', *Industrial Relations Journal*, 35(5) 403–416.

Tailby, S. and Winchester, D. 2005. 'Management and Trade Unions: Partnership at Work?' In Bach, S. (ed.) *Managing Human Resources: Personnel Management in Transition*, 4ᵗʰ Edition, Oxford: Blackwell.

Terry, M. 1996. 'Negotiating the Government of UNISON: Union Democracy in Theory and Practice', *British Journal of Industrial Relations*, 34(1), 87–110.

Thornley, C. 2003. 'What Future for Health Care Assistants: High Road or Low Road?' in Davies, C. (ed.), *The future health workforce*. London: Palgrave Macmillan.

Transport and General Workers Union (2002) *Enron NHS? Foundation Hospitals and the backdoor privatization of the National Health Service*. London: TGWU. http://www.tgwu.org

Undy, R. 1999. 'Negotiating Amalgamations: Territorial and Political Consolidation and Administrative Reform in Public Sector Service Unions in the UK', *British Journal of Industrial Relations*, 37(3), 445–463.

UNISON 2002. *PFI: Failing Our Future – A UNISON Audit of the Private Finance Initiative*. London: UNISON. http://www.unison.org.uk

UNISON 2003. *Foundation Hospitals and the NHS Plan*. London: UNISON. http://www.unison.org.uk

Waddington, J. and Kerr, A. 1999. 'Trying to stem the flow: union membership turnover in the public sector', *Industrial Relations Journal*, 30(3), 183–195.

Wanless, D. 2001. *Securing Our Future Health: Taking a Long-Term View: Interim Report* London: The Treasury. http://www.hm-treasury.gov.uk/wanless

Wanless, D. 2002. *Securing Our Future Health: Taking a Long-Term View: Final Report*. London: The Treasury. http://www.hm-treasury.gov.uk/wanless

White, G. 2000. 'The Pay Review Body System: Its Development and Impact', Historical Studies in Industrial Relations, 9: 71–100.

White, G. and Hatchett, A. 2003. 'The Pay Review Bodies in Britain Under the Labour Government', *Public Money and Management*, 23(4), 237–244.

Winchester, D. 2005 'Agreement on implementation of pay reforms in the National Health Service', http://www.eiro.eurofound.eu.int/2005/01/feature/uk0501105f.html

3
Health Labour Relations and the New Zealand Revolution

Kurt Wetzel

Introduction

Between 1984 and 1996, successive Labour and National party governments revolutionized New Zealand's political economy by instituting a public policy regime grounded in neoliberal beliefs. Those governments "marketized" New Zealand by removing obstacles to the efficient operation of capital, product and labour markets.[1] Longstanding social democratic policies and programs, which had regulated financial markets, protected or subsidized domestic production, and encouraged trade unionism, were terminated or sharply modified. Instead of buffering markets' impacts upon citizens, workers and business, the new order called for self-reliance and competition.

The government reformed the state sector, adopting profit sector-like structures and practices. Commercially promising state assets were "corporatized," i.e. made into profit-maximizing state-owned enterprises.[2] Many were subsequently privatized. The core public service was similarly reconceived and restructured. One observer stated:

> ... New Zealand has been more venturesome than any other country in discarding old practices and devising new ones. It has revolutionised public management without going through the protracted pilot testing and cautious implementation that have slowed innovation in some other countries. Measured by their bold objectives, conceptual basis, reliance on statutes, and speed of implementation, the New Zealand reforms have been truly remarkable.[3]

The publicly funded health care delivery service lay within these revolutionary reformers' purview. Salmond *et al.* observed, "What makes the present [health] reforms controversial in New Zealand and of interest internationally are the radical nature of the changes and the speed and manner of their introduction".[4] Market-mirroring mechanisms forced the newly created Crown health enterprises to compete with each other and with the private sector.

Labour policy received similar treatment. Long-standing structures and statutory protections for collective representation were removed. The *Employment Contracts Act* 1991 (ECA) deregulated labour markets by abolishing the statutory basis of trade unions' status, power and legitimacy. Health restructuring and industrial relations reforms empowered health care managers to transform the sector's industrial relations. Management was called upon to implement reform in ways that obliterated the old order.

This era of ideology-driven restructuring reached its denouement in 1996 when the National-New Zealand First coalition government assumed power. The coalition had neither a mandate nor the will for further radical reform.

In 1999, a centre-left minority Labour-Alliance coalition came into power, committed to modifying certain aspects of the New Zealand revolution. Coalition-legislated health and labour policy shifts, along with key administrative changes adopted by executive government, have had substantial implications for health sector industrial relations.

Collective bargaining in New Zealand's health industry involves unions representing domestic workers, a host of support staff and sub-professions, nurses and medical specialists, among others. This chapter looks at how these unions were differentially affected by and adapted to a twelve-year period of radical health reform that was followed by a swing to the political centre. It also examines the unions' survival strategies and their responses to the post-revolution environment.

The New Zealand Revolution

State sector reform

Health sector and industrial relations reforms were products of a carefully prescribed, ideology-driven template that was applied throughout the state sector. While Treasury developed the template,[5] institutional economic theory provided the inspiration.

Under the pre-reform "sector" model of the public service, policy advice to the health minister and service delivery resided in the same department. The sector model presumes that the two roles interact synergistically, with the administrative service experience informing and expediting policy formation. The thinking is that client groups' needs and desires can be ascertained and reflected in programs and policies, and that accountability is provided by linking ministers to program delivery.[6]

Treasury played an important role. It criticized the sector model's failure to provide departments with defined, consistent goals. It considered departments vulnerable to "provider or bureaucratic capture," whereby operational concerns unduly influence policy decisions. To resolve the provider capture problem, Treasury adopted the remedy offered by public choice theory, which is to split policy advice and policy implementation.[7] Treasury's model also introduced competition by making service delivery contestable. It called for multiple sourcing with no preference being given to public versus private sector service providers. The approach drew on both agency theory, which emphasizes the benefits of using carefully negotiated, specific contracts and ensuring compliance with them, and transaction-cost economics, which suggests that contracting out is most appropriate where the quantity and quality of output can be readily determined.[8]

Consistent with these economic theories, Treasury's model embraced "managerialism." Managerialism reflects elements of Taylorism and treats management as a generic activity, with similar approaches being appropriate for both public and private sector organizations. It favours specific limited-term employment contracts over open-term relational contracts characteristic of a professional civil service. It also stresses private sector management techniques such as organizational vision and mission statements, strategic plans, performance-based pay and aggressive cost reduction. Organizationally, managerialism prefers quasi-autonomous units to larger bureaucratic structures.[9]

The *State Sector Act* 1988 brought the Treasury model to the public service. For departments with programs to deliver, the Act anticipated a funder/purchaser/provider split.[10] Thus, some departments were confined to developing policy, advising ministers and funding purchasers. Each department became a distinct entity for all purposes, including employment. This resulted in the State Services Commission's employment relations role being devolved to the departments, which further devolved the responsibility to administrative sub-levels.[11] An integrated public service ceased to exist.

Chief executives, hired on performance-related, limited-term contracts with carefully specified outputs and efficiency objectives, replaced department heads. Performance review and accountability mechanisms were adopted. Managers' remuneration improved substantially and performance bonuses were introduced. Charged with being good employers, the chief executives became responsible for their department's employee relations and bargaining with their employees' representatives.[12]

The Act also ended the Annual General Adjustment, which had provided that an equivalent of the private sector's average wage increase be passed on to state sector workers, leaving the parties to negotiate occupational class pay claims for further increases and sending disputes to compulsory arbitration. The Act terminated arbitration as well.

Labour law reform

Deregulation of the New Zealand labour market came in the form of the ECA in 1991,[13] which enabled public and private sector organizations to undertake dramatic restructurings of their industrial relations. This legislation destroyed the legal underpinnings of New Zealand's trade unions. It proscribed strikes to achieve multi-employer bargaining and, ultimately, turned a highly centralized industrial relations system based on occupational bargaining and a reliance on arbitration into a system centred at the level of the enterprise.

The ECA ended New Zealand's traditional collectivist labour relations policy. It did not mention the word "union" and was neutral on the matter of collective bargaining. The Act was intended to improve organizational efficiency and protect individual rights. Accordingly, it ended compulsory union membership, which became a matter of personal choice, and allowed workers to choose between being covered by collective or individual employment contracts. While employers were obliged to recognize their employees' agents, the ECA did not impose a clear legal duty to bargain in good faith.[14]

Health sector reform

New Zealand's public health service dates from the *Social Security Act* 1938, which provided for universal in- and out-patient care at public hospitals. Except for those without means, most users paid for their visits to general practitioners on a fee-for-service basis. Private health services have been an enduring element of the New Zealand system.[15]

The Labour government initiated a health reform program in 1974. A white paper, *A Health Service for New Zealand*, proposed creating 14 government-funded regional health authorities responsible for providing public health and acute care services, eventually involving them in primary and long-term care as well.[16] Hospital boards and general practitioners opposed the proposal, which was shelved after the election of a National government in 1975. National resurrected the concept in the *Area Health Boards Act* 1983, but it was Labour that established 14 partially elected area health boards after returning to power in 1984.[17]

The National Party returned to power in 1990 with more radical ideas. In a 1991 green and white paper,[18] it called for a system of "managed competition." Inspired by a shelved 1987 task force report,[19] the plan combined structural and managerial emphases. It advocated delineating the funder, purchaser and provider functions and applying private sector methods to public health care organizations.

The *Health and Disabilities Services Act* 1993 embodied the model. The Ministry of Health was designated as the funder and policy adviser to the minister. Four regional health authorities (RHAs) were created. They received population-based funding with which to purchase health services from competing public and private for-profit providers as well as trusts and the voluntary sector. Critics argued that spending public health dollars in the private sector would weaken it, eventually making the public sector the provider of last resort for the poor.[20] There was an initial burst of growth in private sector elective surgery.[21]

Crown Health Enterprises (CHEs) became the publicly owned service providers. The 23 CHEs were typically anchored by a major hospital or group of hospitals. They were expected to be business-like and to be "good employers", and they were to target services to those in the greatest financial need.[22,23] Each RHA and CHE was governed by a board appointed by the minister.[24]

The government encouraged increased individual responsibility. Between 1991 and 1993, it adopted highly unpopular needs-based "co-payments" for in- and out-patient hospital services. The charges were subsequently rescinded.[25] Means tests remained in use for visits to general practitioners.

With the division of the funder and provider roles, oversight of government's ownership interests in public health care institutions moved to Treasury's Crown Company Monitoring Advisory Unit, which oversees government-funded agencies with regulatory, advisory, purchasing or service delivery functions. Health restructuring indeed yielded a faithful rendering of Treasury's model of state reform to the industry.

Implementing change

Anticipating the combined impact of health reform and the ECA, the State Services Commission and the Council of Trade Unions (CTU) agreed to extend health sector collective agreements for one year. The CTU approached health employers about renegotiating national contracts. The Minister of State Services, however, announced that bargaining would be decentralized, a decree that the Association of Salaried Medical Specialists (ASMS) unsuccessfully challenged before the Employment Tribunal.[26] The minister instructed managers to bargain for flexible working hours and changes to penal rates, e.g., call-in pay. He warned against simply renewing existing agreements.[27]

With 23 competing CHEs serving as employers, industrial relations practice came to reflect the government's market. Decentralization created a demand for industrial relations practitioners; staff from other functional areas and people with union backgrounds filled the breach. To accelerate the adoption of private sector practices, government encouraged the RHAs and CHEs to hire private sector managers with no health sector experience. In a number of cases bargaining was contracted to consultants, some of whom assumed near-total responsibility for the industrial relations function.[28] The variety of approaches led to distinct bargaining arrangements, relationships and outcomes, obliterating the legacy of national bargaining.

While some employers were not aggressively anti-union, others viewed reform as an opportunity to weaken the unions. They explored the ECA's frontiers, including the meaning of Section 12(2):

> Where any employee or employer has authorized a person, group, or organization to represent the employee or employer in negotiations for an employment contract, the employee or employer with whom the negotiations are being undertaken shall...recognise the authority of that person, group, or organisation to represent the employee or employer in negotiations.[29]

Arguing that individual contracts facilitate worker and management communication, some CHEs, determined to deal only with workers, initially refused to negotiate with the unions. The Employment Court, however, ruled against one employer for communicating directly with workers during bargaining and violating an understanding reached with the Court not to bypass the union.[30] Such efforts to undermine collective representatives generated suspicion among employees and union hostility.

Although reform replaced state-mandated collectivism with voluntary, contestable collectivism, most CHEs bargained willingly with non-medical workers' unions. They saw collective contracts as efficient vehicles for contracting with large numbers of workers; moreover, strikes were proscribed during the term of the contract.

Managers found individual contracts impractical to negotiate and administer and unnecessary sources of conflict. The individual contracts they "negotiated" with non-union workers mirrored the pertinent collective contracts. Medical specialists, residents and interns were a major exception, and some CHEs encouraged them to negotiate individual contracts.

Labour relations were also influenced by RHA policies. In addition to awarding service contracts on a competitive basis, RHAs pressured their CHEs by cutting funding. (Southland Health, for example, absorbed a $2.5 million cut to provide the same services.) This forced the CHEs, which were commonly in financial difficulty, to seek efficiencies, reduce services, close facilities and engage in concessionary bargaining.[31] One approach they used involved focusing on the core business of providing direct health services. They commonly contracted out cleaning, catering, maintenance and orderly services.

Bargaining structure remained an issue. National bargaining had involved 28 unions negotiating one or more occupation-based awards. Anticipating restructuring, the CTU encouraged health unions to reconfigure themselves. It sponsored meetings to urge the formation of a health industry union or, at minimum, the merger of small unions.[32] The small unions, however, resisted being absorbed, and larger ones objected to giving up members to a new body. The unions' failure to rationalize their structures increased their vulnerability.

The CHEs inherited as many as 31 separate awards, which they undertook to reduce. Although they continued to negotiate with well-positioned small unions, e.g., the boilermakers, they frequently refused to deal with others unions or did so on a *post hoc* basis. Union members were often forced into other unions or onto individual contracts. Different occupational groups represented by the same union were compelled to negotiate a single contract. Composite, or multi-union, contracts became common. The CHEs typically negotiated collective contracts with: medical specialists; interns and residents; nurses; psychiatric nurses; allied professional, clerical and technical employees; x-ray workers; laboratory workers; trades; and domestic staff.

Employers' tactics varied from the confrontational to the pragmatic. For instance, to standardize terms and conditions of local collective contracts, one employer, using principled negotiations, bargained a core conditions composite contract with separate attachments covering 21 non-medical staff unions. By contrast, another unilaterally drafted a collective contract and successfully insisted that each union accept it. Other employers sought to perpetuate the status quo.

Flexibility and cost reduction were a *sine qua non* for improving competitiveness. Concessionary bargaining to eliminate benefits, allowances and work practices inherited from national awards was typical. The more patient or less hard-pressed CHEs negotiated cost-neutral contracts. Not wanting to upset staff, they grandparented existing employees' conditions. This softer approach put them at risk of having uncompetitive labour costs and seeing their funding cut to rates matching those of the lowest cost providers.

Major benefits such as superannuation, sick leave and retirement gratuities were capped, grandparented, bought out, made optional at the employers' behest, or terminated. Penal rates for overtime, weekend, on-call and shift work were eliminated or reduced. Arrangements to eliminate featherbedding and the perceived abuse of sick leave were adopted. Managers found it easier to schedule work to coincide with peak demand and were able to increase the casual workforce. Facility and ward closures as well as service discontinuations resulted in redundancies. Prolonged pay freezes were common, although some CHEs used savings to raise base pay rates. Aggressive employers drove contract terms toward, if not to, the legal minimum entitlements for unskilled workers. Some employers extracted excessive concessions and had to re-institute penal rates to staff night and weekend shifts.

Most technical unions negotiated concessions in order to keep their collective employment contracts. However, some with low membership turnover refused to abandon the 1991 awards. Where turnover was high and unions refused to negotiate concessions, management imposed individual contracts on new hires. As the unions lost members, management refused to deal with them. Those unions representing technical and professional workers whose skills were in short supply took advantage of employers' independence within the decentralized structure by "whipsawing" them, that is, they used other settlements to justify their demand for identical or better terms.

Bargaining proved problematic for the CHEs. Some managers expressed doubt about the effectiveness of the ECA in circumstances of skill shortages. Management negotiators lacked reliable comparative contract data, information on current developments, and means to tap the knowledge of the experienced or learn from each other. They were often forced to rely on the unions' data. The CHEs, whose inclination to act autonomously was manifested in their relationships with government, ignored legislation requiring employers to consult with the State Services Commissioner about the proposed settlements.[33] Not surprisingly, some managers became interested in improving inter-CHE communications and even coordinating bargaining.

Government and employers acknowledged the problem. In 1993, industrial relations directors started meeting quarterly to share information about settlements and recruitment problems. (The chief executives, chief financial officers and board chairs also began holding quarterly meetings.) In the competitive environment, however, industrial relations information was treated as commercially sensitive; some CEOs directed their functionaries to gather but not divulge information. The quarterly meetings were informal and informational. What collaboration there was occurred regionally among practitioners in adjoining CHEs.

Health unions and the New Zealand revolution

Health restructuring, changes in health management and labour law reform had different consequences for four main health unions. The unions' responses to the challenges varied considerably. The responses included pragmatic initiatives to seized unanticipated opportunity, imaginative survival blueprints and demoralized resignation.

Service Workers Union

The Service Workers Union (SWU) is an occupation-based union representing orderlies and catering, cleaning and home care staff. Its membership is 71 percent female, many of them Pacific Islanders and Maori.[34] Unskilled, unassertive workers with low job attachment and fear of employer retribution are often reluctant unionists.

SWU's health sector membership dropped by 30–40 percent as a result of health reform. Local bargaining, the end of compulsory unionism, widespread contracting out of non-core activities (especially dietary and housekeeping work), and drives to rationalize services, close facilities and cut staff undermined the union.

The tendering process posed a serious threat. The initial tenders put out by CHEs required contractors to employ current employees on their existing terms, and most contractors assumed liability for any ensuing redundancy settlements. However, no such obligation was imposed on subsequent contractors.[35] Indeed, some CHEs solicited bids that presumed paying less than the existing levels, e.g., requiring contractors to pay constant wage rates regardless of the day or shift being worked. This effectively eliminated shift and weekend penal rates. The initial contract holders became uncompetitive. Those who could not negotiate concessions and, as a result, lost contracts became liable for redundancy claims from employees not hired on the existing terms by successful bidders.[36]

Equating health sector work to work in the hospitality sector, where penal rates and benefits are not paid, contractors preferred to raise wages slightly while reducing conditions and benefits. SWU found itself in the no-win position of trading wages against penal rates. Either option risked alienating segments of the membership, which could join competing unions or sign non-union employment contracts. In the 1996 bargaining round, contractors generally agreed to employ the existing workforce at commercial rates, but employees lost their right to seek redundancy settlements. Only at large sites where union membership had declined less could SWU defend the 1991 conditions.

The union's situation was perilous. With dues revenues declining and decentralization raising members' demand for services, it could not afford to operate under a "servicing" model, i.e. having union staff address members' needs. Its survival strategy involved fundamental organizational and strategic restructuring. It eliminated its national office, reduced staff by 25 percent, cut staff pay by 10 percent, and embraced the "organizing" model.[37]

SWU split its staff into "advocates," those who address labour relations issues, and "organizers," those who operate at the grassroots level, solidifying and expanding a delegate base, raising members' union consciousness, increasing participation, and developing community and political links.[38] The role of the organizers is to empower the membership to address its own needs. This involves identifying, educating and building the confidence and leadership skills of activists. For the organizers, the challenge was more difficult where contractors discriminated against union activists.

Oxenbridge identifies factors that enabled SWU to undertake this restructuring. These include strong proponents for change, leadership support, financial crisis and traditions of steward education, local representational structure and coalition building. The transition proved difficult for some staffers.[39]

Survival was a challenge for contractors as well. Deteriorating conditions drove experienced workers from the health sector into the hospitality sector. New hires tended to be younger, casual or part-time. They lacked organizational commitment, a health industry identity and union consciousness. Competition shrank profit margins. The Association of Building Service Contractors proposed multi-contractor bargaining, but after exploring likely settlement terms, the union rejected it. Moreover, some CHEs warned that they would disallow tenders from contractors who were parties to multi-employer agreements. They wanted contracts that were adapted to their specific needs.

Public Service Association

The Public Service Association (PSA) represents some 11,500 workers in 30 health occupations.[40] With health reform, its health sector membership declined only marginally. Since membership had been voluntary, there was no exodus of members seeking to become "free riders."

Decentralization and reconfiguration of bargaining groups represented an immense change for the union. Instead of having a single national award, as they had prior to reform, members found themselves covered by 130 contracts, most them composite contracts negotiated in coalition with other unions. Although bargaining involves extensive inter-union coordination, coalitions wield greater power than individual unions. To date, PSA has been satisfied with the coalitions' capacity to negotiate.

The bargaining structure in Wellington's Capital Coast Health (CCH) is typical. PSA participates in four composite contracts. The therapists' contract covers dietitians and occupational, speech and physiotherapists. The coalition includes the PSA, Dietitians Union and non-union workers who have a bargaining representative. A second coalition negotiates the support services collective employment contract.[41] A third involves PSA and New Zealand Nurses' Organization members who provide institutional and community psychiatric nursing services. Finally, there is a clinical services collective employment contract.[42]

Decentralization and staff cuts in PSA expanded the role of local delegates to include first step grievance handling, bargaining and workplace organizing. The union began sponsoring two-day basic and advanced delegate training courses. Burnout, overwork in jobs, fear of employer reprisal, worker turnover, and domestic responsibilities made recruiting and retaining delegates difficult.

PSA found post-ECA health care industrial relations confrontational. CCH aggressively pursued clawbacks. Unions stalled negotiations after 1991, knowing that any settlements would be detrimental to their interests. CCH responded by drafting a collective employment contract that profoundly altered conditions of employment, e.g., eliminated penal rates, incremental pay arrangements, long service benefits, and sick leaves, and imposing it on new employees. However, the new hires often grew dissatisfied, joined unions and reflected their discontent in the workplace. Following a strike threat, a settlement was reached in 1994. PSA found that employers' anti-unionism waned where unions maintained a presence.

The union came to expect problems. It viewed CHEs as sick organizations with poor communications and inept, aloof senior management whose behaviour heightened workers' awareness of the need for collective representation. At the same time, it maintained good relationships with operational-level managers who were attuned to the health industry.

In contrast to the SWU, which began to organize the trusts created to serve deinstitutionalized mental health patients, PSA did not organize in the private sector. It lacked the resources necessary to organize and service small groups of dispersed service providers.

Instead, PSA adopted a strategic plan that acknowledged the legitimacy of the criticism made by the political right that unions had operated both as cartels to control the price of labour and as outsiders who played no role in the work organization. Accordingly, the union decided to de-emphasize collective bargaining in favour of partnering with community groups to build a high quality public health service.[43] It would endeavour to convince the public that employment security and reasonable remuneration were integral to this objective.

At the organization level, the plan called for the pursuit of "strategic partnerships" with management to deliver health services. This involved "seek[ing] agreement with each employer on membership participation in the development of strategic and management plans in that enterprise".[44] The union would attempt to negotiate contracts that were consistent with CHEs' plans.

The strategy also included "maintain[ing] and develop[ing] relations with other unions directly and in conjunction with the CTU's Standing Health Committee"[45] to undertake joint organizing efforts, campaigns to promote a public health care system, and joint CHE-level union committees. PSA aspired to become "the most effective national health industry union".[46]

The union's strategy demonstrated the new order's capacity to delegitimize collective bargaining. Given government's capacity and determination to implement marketizing reforms regardless of public opinion, one could expect it to dismiss lobbying efforts supporting pre-reform programs as expressions of special interests. And since managers were mandated to behave like profit maximizers, it is hard to imagine that partnerships with unions were alluring.

New Zealand Nurses' Organization

When reform began, New Zealand had two nurses' unions. The New Zealand Nurses' Association operated in the public sector – hospitals, large long-term care facilities, Plunket (an early childhood public health program), and the Family Planning Association – where union membership was voluntary. The New Zealand Nurses' Union represented private sector nurses employed by small organizations, general practitioners and clinics. When compulsory unionism ended, membership in the New Zealand Nurses' Union declined drastically. In 1994, the two unions amalgamated into the New Zealand Nurses' Organization (NZNO). With 25,000 members, it is the country's largest health union.

While most NZNO members are registered nurses with polytechnic diplomas, 15 percent are hospital trained, or "enrolled," nurses; the number with university training is increasing. Non-nurse care providers constitute a small part of the union's membership but a growing part of the workforce. Nursing is increasingly a casual and part-time occupation. The demand for nurses remains strong, and they enjoy inter-organizational and international mobility.

Under reform, NZNO negotiated approximately 70 contracts with the 23 CHEs. One contract typically covered the bulk of a CHE's nurses. Other contracts pertained to nurse managers, casuals, midwives, district nurses (home care), and nurses employed at different sites. Because the ECA barred unions from striking to achieve multi-employer bargaining, the union used region-level whipsawing to equalize conditions.[47] Since the three big employers in Auckland draw from the same labour market, their contracts became nearly identical, and nearby Waikato felt pressure to fall in line. It was difficult, however, to extend the same terms to rural and southern nurses. As a result, wage disparities of up to 19 percent in annual salaries appeared.[48]

As a public sector union that negotiated nominal pay increases after 1990, NZNO was exceptional. In 1994, nurses were involved in a wave of strikes and proved to be effective publicists, highlighting concerns about inadequate staffing and patient safety. Employers met their monetary demands. For the 1993–96 period, the union negotiated real increases in four CHEs. Nurses made concessions on penal rates. High turnover rates and the willingness of CHEs to hire new employees on individual employment contracts spurred the union to conclude negotiations without delay.

NZNO preferred collective contracts, but some of its members were faced with negotiating, signing and/or administering individual employment contracts. These members – nurses in managerial positions, who for professional reasons remained members, and nurses offered supplementary individual contracts addressing issues such as job descriptions, "better than collective contract" rates of remuneration or work schedules – regularly approached their union to learn about the processes and/or implications of particular provisions. Bargaining and administering individual contracts could be complex, and considerable staff resources could be expended counseling a member or dealing with management.

NZNO's effectiveness depended on its ability to build a core of local activists. It, too, examined the organizing model. Members proved reluctant to become involved, many citing fear of management reprisal. Family obligations and increasing work pressures absorbed other members' energy and time.

Despite management's perception that nurses wielded influence, NZNO found that mobilizing members was increasingly difficult. Union officials observed that members' faith in the political system, management and the health system had waned, along with their taste for protest. Members were becoming cynical and burned out. They felt impotent and vulnerable. They were keen to have the union staff carry on their protest by proxy.

Although there were job losses, there were no massive contracting out initiatives or concerted deunionization efforts involving nurses. However, working conditions deteriorated as CHEs served more patients with fewer resources.[49] Workloads rose as acuity levels climbed and unpaid work, e.g., late shift completions, expanded. CHEs sought to replace nurses with lower paid staff such as non-nurse care givers, and the union expected to see more health expenditures funneled through private for-profit and not-for-profit providers.[50] As the terms and conditions in the unorganized and alternate provider sector deteriorated, the union anticipated that the CHEs would seek concessions. NZNO's mode was defensive.

Association of Salaried Medical Specialists

Medical specialists employed in public health care facilities are newcomers to collective bargaining. Prior to the *Labour Relations Act* 1987, the Higher Salaries Commission arbitrated specialists' salaries. The legislated end of the Commission led the State Services Commission and health employers to press senior doctors (specialists) to negotiate individual employment contracts. Instead, the doctors formed the Association of Salaried Medical Specialists (ASMS), which registered as a union in 1989.[51] By 1997, membership had risen from 66 percent to nearly 90 percent (1,660) of the country's specialists. Since the other health unions belonged to the Council of Trade Unions and all were subject to the same labour legislation, ASMS also affiliated with the central labour body.

The union's initial bargaining round (1989–90) proved difficult. The State Services Commission, the employers' representative, agreed to bargain a national award. The award reduced restrictions against full-time medical officers engaging in private practice. A memorandum of agreement provided a procedure for individual specialists to negotiate "better than award" conditions for rostered duties such as on call and emergency call in. It also provided for a salary increase, an arrangement whereby remuneration would reflect the results of a "job sizing" determination, and a joint process for deriving job descriptions. The union, however, had difficulty convincing area health boards to implement the memorandum.[52]

The ECA provided a statutory basis for employers to insist that senior doctors go onto individual employment contracts. In the 1993 round of bargaining, nine CHEs refused to bargain collectively. However, a number of CHEs, which together employed 50 percent of all specialists, bargained. Negotiations focused on procedural issues and implementation of the 1990 memorandum. These employers agreed to offer the collective contract to new hires, grant ASMS party status, and recognize the doctors' rights in the competitive environment to conduct research and exchange professional knowledge. While most CHEs eventually negotiated similar settlements, the issue of collective representation remained an irritant.[53]

The 1993 round also saw ASMS and the South Auckland CHE negotiate a breakthrough on the collective coverage issue with a "core conditions agreement." This "virtual collective employment contract," or generic individual employment contract, was signed by members individually. At HealthCare Otago, however, collective representation remained an issue. The CHE considered the specialists inordinately influential but insufficiently accountable and unresponsive to the need to control costs. It tried to reduce their collective power, which extends beyond ASMS to the highly influential profession. HealthCare Otago wanted senior doctors to approach their jobs with a perspective that paralleled that of senior management. Nevertheless, with the exception of Auckland Healthcare, ASMS established the principle of collective representation.[54]

The agreement between South Auckland CHE and ASMS set a pattern in other ways. It raised specialists' pay by 20 percent and implemented the 1990 memorandum's provision to compensate them for rostered duties. Other CHEs negotiated less rich settlements in substantially similar collective employment contracts.[55]

The union's ability to negotiate favourable contracts reflected both market demand for specialists and the doctors' attitude toward collective action. Medical specialists were in short supply. Opportunities to practice privately on a full- or part-time basis and competition for specialist services amongst CHEs created recruitment and retention problems. The doctors were aware of the labour market conditions and mobile. Moreover, they demonstrated a capacity for collective action. Their solidarity and willingness to contemplate job action gave ASMS national and local power.[56]

Decentralized bargaining and the CHEs' reluctance to collaborate enabled ASMS to whipsaw employers.[57] The bargaining structure permitted the union to tailor its approaches to the local situation, arguing for salary parity in those CHEs that were below the average and demanding larger increases from richer CHEs. It also allowed the union to expand the scope of bargaining to matters that could not have been addressed easily at the national level, e.g., parking, sabbaticals, locum entitlements and increased input into managerial decisions. Professional issues such as accountability to patients, the medical council and the employers, as well as intellectual property emerged. ASMS prepared to negotiate penal rates for specialists on shift work.[58]

Performance-related pay became a contentious item. The State Services Commission saw performance appraisal as a managerial responsibility, with salary progression occurring at management's behest. ASMS negotiated collegial salary progression provisions calling for salary committees comprising the chief executive's designate, the medical director and members of the senior medical staff.[59]

Acting like a classic craft union, ASMS fared well in the new order. Despite losing a court case to retain national bargaining, it remained a centralized union, conducting research, publishing a newsletter and developing nationally coordinated bargaining policy.[60] It approached its members' job market as national, if not international, and worked "to maintain nationally competitive and equitable terms and conditions of employment".[61] Ultimately, the end of the national award system and the emergence of local collective bargaining constituted an unanticipated blessing.

Health sector industrial relations and the revolution

The New Zealand health sector demonstrates the different consequences that the revolution's marketizing reforms had for unions. The National Party's labour policy was designed to undermine unionism. The public health care system was restructured to be competitively driven and flexible. Bargaining was decentralized, complicating unions' representational challenges. Managers followed government's lead by infusing the new order's spirit in their organizations.

Health sector unions were forced to contend with problems evocative of those confronted by unions in nineteenth-century Britain and America. They needed to develop means of (re)establishing their viability within a hostile environment. Faced with similar challenges, the four major health unions fashioned different responses.

The SWU, the low-wage, low-skilled workers' representative, had relied most heavily on government's protection of unions and encouragement for collective bargaining. Of the four unions, SWU was most acutely threatened by the revolution. Statutes that had conferred representational rights upon it and institutional structures through which it had bargained were eliminated. Its status as a health sector union diminished as members' work was contracted to private sector providers. Its membership shrank as contractors sought to reduce the cost of employing low-skill workers.[62] The situation portended the de-unionization of health sector support work.

SWU's survival strategy involved an ambitious, innovative grassroots organizing initiative to build union consciousness and solidarity from the rubble of a system lacking traditions of local activism and involvement. It involved identifying, training and empowering rank-and-file activists to address workplace problems and represent the membership at local bargaining tables. It also entailed building ties with working class and social activist communities. SWU maintained ties to the Labour Party. In the environment of the mid-1990s, it was not evident whether this strategy for galvanizing the membership to rescue the union was desperate optimism or shrewdness.

The PSA's membership levels held, but the revolution weakened the union. The situation prompted a visionary response. PSA developed a strategic plan that downplayed traditional unionism. Since collective bargaining was not a promising vehicle in the circumstances, the union de-emphasized it and focused on other activities. The plan called for building strategic labour-management partnerships. In essence, PSA invited management to take up participative industrial relations strategies, which imply workers' commitment to helping management achieve its organizational objectives. The union wanted employers to adopt an element of the high performance paradigm, or human resource management model, instead of an autocratic control approach presumed by Treasury's "managerialism." PSA's strategy also advocated building links with civil society to defend the public health care system.

Metamorphosing PSA into a community leader and industrial partner was a lofty vision.

While SWU restructured and PSA envisioned, the two health sector craft unions took different routes. The NZNO became devitalized and demoralized, but it remained solid. Its members' labour market position and loyalty kept it off the endangered list. NZNO was not invigorated by impending doom to undertake reform. It resolved to ride out the crisis.[63]

By contrast, the country's medical specialists embraced a new opportunity and an old model. The competitive environment encouraged by the revolution enabled them to capitalize on their labour market power. They unionized. The ASMS adopted the ideology, structures and processes of nineteenth-century craft unionism. It saw no need to explore innovative models of collective action. This labour elite's embrace of collective bargaining was wholehearted and effective. Unionization provided a vehicle for galvanizing potentially individualistic members and focusing the profession's bargaining power. The revolution enabled the medical profession to use collective bargaining as a mechanism to advance its interests.

The solidarity for which unions strive came naturally to medical specialists, a group whose training and work experiences are roughly similar. Professional pride, personal independence balanced by group cohesion, and the confidence to stand up to those in non-medical positions of authority define this group. The profession's restricted numbers, exclusivity and common interests gave ASMS bargaining power. The bargaining structure allowed the union to negotiate separately with 23 CHEs that competed against one another and an aggressive private sector for both health dollars and scarce medical talent. ASMS balanced strong central leadership and local autonomy. Other than supporting a publicly funded health system, it avoided partisan political involvement, preferring more discreet, personal approaches to politics.

When government ceased to guarantee workers' capacity to manifest their collective interests, the unions that had relied upon its support foundered. They searched for paradigms that would allow them to restabilize their organizations and exercise collective influence in a market society. Craft unionism proved to be an enduring model for groups with bargaining power.

Swing to the centre

The 1996 election marked the denouement of ideology-driven restructuring that was started in 1984 by the Labour Party and subsequently pursued by the National Party to liberalize New Zealand society. The National-New Zealand First coalition government that assumed power had no mandate or will for further radical reform. In 1999, it gave way to a centre-left minority Labour-Alliance coalition government that was committed to modifying certain features of the revolution.

The Labour and Alliance parties' industrial relations and health policies featured in the election campaign. Both promised to replace the ECA, to make health service delivery more locally accountable, and to supplant the competitive service delivery model with one emphasizing collaboration and cooperation. Following the election, the coalition government legislated health and labour policy shifts, which, along with operational changes adopted by executive government, have had industrial relations implications.

Given a national unionization rate of 17 percent, the public health service is a union bastion. Unions attribute the sector's high voluntary membership rates, conservatively in the 70 percent range, to the rough treatment accorded workers during years of National Party rule. Unions were workers' port in that storm, and they are enjoying higher profiles with the labour-friendly government. Although the emerging order is a matter for future study, a new policy direction is in place.

Employment Relations Act 2000

The *Employment Relations Act* (ERA) came into effect in October 2000.[64] The ERA stipulated that unions are the only bodies that can negotiate collective agreements on behalf of workers. Unions seeking to avail themselves of the ERA's provisions must incorporate as societies and register. The only requirements for registration are that they have 15 members, operate independently of employers, and are governed by democratic rules. Under the ERA, union membership is voluntary. Competing unions are allowed. Employees not belonging to unions can negotiate individual employment contracts.

In contrast to the ECA, which embraced the market ideology and applied a contracting model to employment relationships, the ERA emphasizes human relationships. It encourages "good faith" behaviour, i.e. minimally, behaviour not designed to mislead or deceive. The good faith requirement is not confined to parties involved in the bargaining and grievance resolution processes. It also pertains to relationships between employers and individual employees, unions and their members, a union and other unions that might be bargaining or covered by the same agreement, as well as a union and other unions' members. In addition, employers combining to bargain common collective agreements assume a good faith obligation.

Within the collective bargaining context, good faith means that the parties must recognize each other's bargaining representatives' role and authority, enter into bargaining arrangements, meet, consider and respond to proposals, and provide information to justify their positions. They are not obliged to agree or enter into agreements. Good faith must be demonstrated in consultations where employers' actions could lead to work being contracted out, workers being made redundant, or a business being sold/transferred. Union representatives are allowed access to workplaces to recruit members and to conduct union business.

Subject to ministerial approval, parties may draft a "code of good faith" to guide their relationships. The Minister of Labour is empowered to strike a committee comprising the parties' representatives (and others) to recommend a generic code of good faith. The Minister may impose the generic code on parties that either fail to produce their own code or submit a code that does not receive ministerial approval.[65] Adjudicative bodies can use the codes as standards to ascertain whether parties have satisfied good faith obligations.

The ERA calls for the creation of two government bodies to facilitate good faith relationships. The Employment Relations Service provides mediation services to assist parties in consensually resolving and preventing differences.[66] It uses facilitation rather than the legalistic approach to mediation formerly employed.

The Employment Relations Authority, an investigative and adjudicative body, is empowered to examine disputes not resolved by mediation. It uses the French "inquisitorial" process rather than the Anglo Saxon adversarial model. Counsel does not (cross)examine witnesses; rather, the authority member conducting the investigation asks the questions. Decisions are based upon merit rather than technicalities. The authority hears matters including the application and interpretation of agreements, good faith issues, as well as personal grievances and allegations of unfair dismissal, protections retained from the old regime. The Employment Court remains the tribunal of appeal for these matters.

Health reform

Under the National-New Zealand First government (1996–99), Crown health enterprises were renamed health and hospital services (HHS) and regional health authorities became health funding authorities (HFAs). Neither group's structures or functions changed substantially. The Labour-Alliance coalition undertook a more fundamental change

with the *Public Health and Disability Services (Safety) Act* 2000.[67] Deline-
ation of the funder, purchaser and provider roles ended. The Act disbanded the HFAs and allocated their responsibilities to the Ministry of
Health and 21 district health boards (DHBs). Each DHB oversees an
HHS. The DHBs' purchasing role involves negotiating service contracts
with private and community providers.[68]

The government has indicated that seven DHBs might be appropriate; small health units could be amalgamated or absorbed by their
larger neighbours. Government expects DHBs to cooperate and explore
service-sharing arrangements rather than competing. Specialized services such as forensics and blood are increasingly being provided
regionally. There have been moves to explore ways to regionalize the
delivery of mental health services, perhaps including the creation of
distinct DHBs for that purpose. Although DHBs have created a national
association, remnants of the culture of competition persist. Finally, as
part of the drive to devolve some decision-making authority, government has implemented a process whereby seven DHB members are
elected locally and four are appointed.

Health industry code of good faith

In 2000, industry representatives drafted an interim health sector code
of good faith for the public health care sector and its contractors.[69] In a
number of areas, it exceeds or is more specific than the generic code.
While the generic code focuses upon processes related to negotiating
agreements, the draft health industry code concentrates upon the
parties' ongoing relationships.

The draft health sector code calls for unions to be treated as partners.
Union delegates and organizers are identified as unions' workplace representatives. Union and worker participation at all organizational levels
is to be encouraged and resourced. This includes the strategic planning
and resource allocation processes. Employees and unions can initiate
workplace change. Management of change should proceed on a "no
surprises" basis, with unions being consulted in a timely manner. The
code recognizes unions' and workers' interests in providing quality
health service and commits the parties to engage in workforce planning and development, including upgrading employees' skills and education levels. Health professionals are deemed to have a legitimate role
as patient advocates.

The industry's draft good faith bargaining principles are not as
extensive as those found in the ministerial/generic good faith code. On
these matters, the industry code largely defers to the generic code.

However, the industry code calls for negotiations that are intended to reach settlements using reasoned arguments backed by information. Parties are urged to avoid positional bargaining and tabling "final offers" prematurely. They are expected to behave courteously, avoiding intimidation and personal threats. And they should agree to bargaining processes and agendas prior to beginning negotiations. All bargaining issues are to be considered.

At least one voice in the employers' ranks takes exception to the industry code.[70] It objects to the code's coverage of behaviours occurring beyond the context of bargaining collective agreements. It questions whether the code should extend to contractors. It challenges the idea of giving unions the right to be involved in strategic planning, particularly when no reciprocal responsibilities are specified.

Management's attitudes toward unions have softened with the advent of the Labour-Alliance government. HR managers commonly concede that it is more convenient to deal with unionized workers, as they require less individualized attention. This softening includes encouragement of union membership and a widening acceptance of the value of mature traditional relationships. Some managers routinely consult their unions when drafting policies. Some HR managers profess that unions can facilitate workplace relations. Shop floor delegates and supervisors are being encouraged to address workplace problems promptly.

Health unions in the emerging environment

Unions have been uncritically positive about the ERA and the Labour-Alliance government. The contrast with National Party rule is so profound that they are loath to do anything that might undermine the government. The CTU contends that the ERA is what could realistically be attained. Although it would like successor rights, the CTU does not advocate compulsory union membership. Labour and the Alliance delivered what they promised, which did not include a return to the past. Thus, the ERA should be allowed to operate for three or four years, after which it can be reassessed. The CTU believes that, in the meantime, labour should organize new members and explore ways to advance members' interests within the new framework.

The ERA may be a low common denominator. While there is debate within the trade union movement and management about the partnership model, employers recognize that dealing with collectives is practical and convenient. As such, this is legislation that management can accommodate. Some health employers even like it. They have not attempted to evade its promotion of collective bargaining.

Public Service Association

The PSA's response to the political and legislative changes is in character. The union has modest bargaining and structural reform aspirations. It wants to combine agreements covering clericals, occupational therapists, social workers and psychologists into one for each DHB. Although it sees opportunity for negotiating improved wages and benefits, it is cautious lest it provide the National Party with political fodder.

The ERA provides opportunities that are in line with PSA's goal of promoting collaborative industrial relations to public and private health care organizations. The union's recently developed "Partnership for Quality" program originated as an understanding with the State Services Commission and is consistent with PSA's strategic objective of forming partnerships with management.[71] It calls for open, cooperative relationships that enhance organizational effectiveness and employment quality. It also stresses the parties' shared interests in building worker support for management decisions, ensuring employee input into those decisions, improving job satisfaction and providing high quality health services. The health industry's good faith code appears to mirror this program.

The guidelines and principles of the partnerships are intended to reflect individual parties' needs. They involve regular and open dialogue, which permits either party to table issues. PSA members are expected to participate collectively in decision making. Partnership for Quality presumes that the range of joint decision making will broaden and that consultation will feature prominently in it.

Although strategy development, quality improvement and service provision decisions are expected to be participative, PSA will not encroach on areas of chief executives' accountability. The partnerships will be based on agreements about how specific types of decisions are to be made. The program will raise employers' training costs as employees develop participation skills. PSA is obliged to recruit members actively, maintain a democratic organization and build a delegate base.

While other unions have attacked PSA for becoming too close to management, PSA contends that it defends members, including taking industrial action, and will maintain that capacity. PSA represents 60–80 percent of its potential health sector membership, attributing this high level to chronically poor management whose actions have prompted workers to join the union.

PSA expects that the human resources management philosophy which involves workers in decision making will supplant managerial fiat. Whereas health sector employers were reluctant to reveal business plans, they now ask union members to help draft and comment on them. PSA hopes to build an organization with relationships that serve both its members and employers. If successful, it will be insulated from the effects of political change.

Service Workers Union

The determination of publicly funded health care organizations to focus on their core business resulted in private contractors becoming the employers for 75 percent of the workers who provide dietary, cleaning and laundry services. This figure ranges from 40 percent for orderlies to nearly 100 percent of housekeeping staff. Contractors see health sector service work as comparable to work found in the largely non-union hospitality and private health sectors. For SWU, this created a highly fragmented bargaining structure and presented on-going organizing challenges.

SWU recognized that it would take an array of actions to achieve its bargaining, organizational and representational goals. Accordingly, it has pursued a three-pronged strategy. First, it sought growth and stability by amalgamating in 1997 with the United Food and Beverage Workers Union to form the Service and Food Workers Union (SFWU). The merger added between 5,000 and 6,000 members from the relatively stable food processing industry.

Second, the union tries to capitalize on activists' energies to establish a workplace presence and to organize new members. It has continued to focus on building an organizing union. SFWU relies on delegates and activists to help service and organize workplaces. It tries to allocate 20 percent of its staff's time to new site organizing and training delegates and activists. SFWU's intensive member-organizer program is designed to develop a cadre of activists for organizing drives. The union is also looking to break into the private health sector and to organize contractors in the public health sector.

SFWU claims to represent 90 percent of public health sector support staff and attributes its continued strong presence to its restructuring, refocusing and organizing initiatives. A residual culture of public health care service unionism and the fact that members work on site alongside other unionized staff have enabled SFWU to retain members.

The union's third strategy is to be politically active. SWU's plight eased after 1996 with the less stalwartly anti-union National/New Zealand First coalition government. SFWU subsequently negotiated members' first real pay increases (around 2 percent) in six years. The election of the Labour-Alliance government brightened the union's prospects significantly. Through its predecessors, SFWU has been affiliated with the Labour Party since the 1930s. Four cabinet members and five backbenchers are former union employees.[72] SFWU attempts to influence government's legislative agenda, its health funding priorities, and the ways that DHBs approach their labour relations.

This government and the enactment of the ERA have occasioned attitude changes among a number of contractors and DHBs. Rabid anti-unionism has been replaced by an increased willingness to bargain. The ERA allows unions to push for multi-employer bargaining, and SFWU wants to coax DHBs and contractors to the same bargaining tables.

While SFWU values ERA provisions giving organizers access to workplaces, it is not entirely satisfied with the legislation. As a union operating in a sector characterized by high workforce turnover, SFWU feels the need for a "union shop" provision to end "free ridership," i.e. nonmembers being given the same terms and conditions of employment as dues-paying union members. A union shop would preclude the union from having to recruit each newly hired worker. Given the prevalence of contracting, SFWU is also lobbying for successor rights legislation that extends existing collective agreements to new contractors and for a proposed Minimum Code of Employment Rights. Failing these, it is seeking to have government require DHBs to adopt tendering provisions that impose pre-existing terms and conditions of employment on succeeding contractors.

Changes in the labour market and bargaining developments give the union hope. Employers in Wellington and Auckland, regions that set bargaining patterns, are having difficulty recruiting experienced cleaners. SFWU wants to negotiate pay increases that track the nurses' settlements.

Moral and legal victories over hostile employers have also heartened the union.[73] In 1993 and 1994, Capital Coast Health (CCH) contracted out the work of 181 employees and declared them redundant. Their employment contracts required CCH to consult on matters of mutual interest, but neither the union nor the employees were consulted. SFWU brought a $9 million breach of contract and wrongful dismissal suit against CCH. Although the contractor had employed the workers, they testified to their pain and anguish. In April 2000, the court ruled that the employees' distress might have been avoided or mitigated had CCH adhered to the industrial democracy clause contained in its contracts. CCH apologized and negotiated a $1 million settlement.[74] Having survived what it regards as "the government from hell", SFWU is optimistic.[75]

New Zealand Nurses' Organization

The 1991 ECA and health reform combined to end the system under which the NZNO had negotiated a national agreement prescribing uniform conditions of employment and entitling nurses to bid on job postings across the country. Those arrangements had satisfied nurses' equity concerns and met their needs for career/professional development and geographical mobility. After a period of feeling powerless and adrift, NZNO has regained its bearings and confidence. The union represents 57 percent of public sector nurses and, as a result of the worldwide nursing shortage, has new clout. Moreover, it has developed an agenda.

NZNO contends that bargaining at the level of fragmented, competing health units is a dysfunctional artifact of an old regime. Issues requiring industry attention, shortage of registered nurses and workforce development, are not amenable to local solutions. The union is encouraging the Labour-Alliance government to restructure the decentralized/fractured industrial relations system. It is pushing for a staged return to centralized bargaining.

NZNO believes that regional multi-employer collective bargaining would better enable it to address its members' professional and financial interests. Furthermore, multi-employer collective agreements (MECAs) would improve the industry's capacity to plan and develop the nursing workforce. MECAs would end nurses' disruptive practice of shopping for health units that offer the most attractive terms of employment.

The union proposes starting with common table negotiations involving two or more adjoining DHBs. Other DHBs could join the talks or opt for coverage under MECAs. NZNO has found employers, who had resisted the multi-employer bargaining for ideological reasons, to be increasingly receptive to it. The DHBs, however, lack strategic vision, mindsets and organizational structures that would allow them to act collectively. Most focus on activities that do not require cooperation. The ministry is providing a strategic impetus. Since broader-based bargaining is consistent with government's plans to reduce the number of DHBs to seven or eight, NZNO's initiative is being encouraged.

Following the lead of HHS chief executives and board chairs, human resources managers have begun meeting quarterly at a national level to discuss issues related to workforce, bargaining structure and new legislation. They exchange bargaining information and organize conferences. While the government has asked managers to consider negotiating a national settlement with NZNO, employers tend to favour an incremental return to central bargaining.

Multi-employer negotiations will be complex and settlements potentially expensive. DHBs are faced with fiscal constraints, incompatible payroll and human resource information systems, and differing operational requirements. Provisions contained in the 21 HHSs' collective agreements have diverged. Because MECAs involve negotiating common contract language, compensation rates, scheduling arrangements and so forth, a supplementary tier of local negotiations will likely be required.

Predictably, NZNO will insist upon incorporating the most generous provisions into MECAs. While the union acknowledges that the initial MECAs will have to be fiscally neutral, its members are showing an incipient willingness to take job actions to achieve monetary objectives. In December 2000, nurses at CCH gave notice that they would hold three one-day strikes. The job action was called off after the employer met the union's terms.[76] Persuaded by this bargaining experience and recognition of the impending problems of negotiating MECAs with employers who are unaccustomed to reaching interorganizational accommodations, NZNO has acknowledged the value of being able to call upon the government's new mediation service.

As both a union and a professional body, NZNO is increasingly interested in the partnership implications of the health industry's good faith bargaining code. It welcomes the opportunity to be involved in day-to-day decision making and strategic policy making.

Association of Salaried Medical Specialists

The trajectory of ASMS has not changed. It developed as a craft union in the harsh environment of the early 1990s, representing a labour elite in dealings with an empowered, ideology-driven management cadre charged with introducing private sector ways into the health system. It has brought collective representation to 1900 senior doctors and dentists in all HSSs. Strong demand for medical specialists' services, high unionization rates and membership solidarity, combined with employers' determined fragmentation *vis-à-vis* the centralized union, have allowed ASMS to be effective.[77] While other unions have struggled to hold their own, ASMS has improved its members' terms and conditions of employment. Indeed, members' mean full-time base salaries increased 36 percent between 1993 and 2000.

Recent political, market and health sector changes, which have invigorated the other health unions, have had a minimal effect on ASMS. With a modus operandi that enabled it to thrive under the old regime, it has not felt compelled to restrategize or restructure to take advantage of new circumstances. It remains focused on improving members' terms and conditions of employment. Its bargaining objectives include subsidized pension plans, premium pay for on-call work, six weeks' annual leave,[78] and provisions allowing members to claim a minimum of 30 percent of the hours spent attending to patients for other duties, e.g., administration, department meetings, audit/quality assurance activities and professional development.[79] The union has expanded membership to practitioners who work outside of the DHBs.[80]

ASMS members hold a variety of political views. Some have substantial private practices. Lack of consensus precludes the union from taking a stand on how to reform the health care system.[81] It can address professional concerns,[82] the implications of medical students' debt loads and costs associated with training, recruiting and retaining specialists in New Zealand.[83] It asserts the importance of professional rather than managerial control over the process of credentialing doctors[84] and the value of professional unity in the face of "commercial-style bosses" and managers who behave like "institutional psychopaths".[85] ASMS is a formidable traditional craft union.

Conclusion

New Zealand's neoliberal revolution created hostile political, policy, fiscal and organizational climates for health sector unions. It forced health care unions to rethink their strategies and, in some cases, reorganize in order to adapt to the environment. Three unions – ASMS, SFWU and PSA – fashioned distinct strategies to address the challenges. The relatively stable NZNO waited for market and political changes to revive its fortunes.

The unilateralist ambience eased after the National Party's ideology was diluted in 1996 by its less dogmatic coalition partner. Government's anti-union animus ended with the election of a cautious centre-left coalition in 1999. The Labour-Alliance government's ideology, labour and health policies, and administrative practices combined with strengthening labour markets to benefit the unions. Health sector unionism is undergoing a nascent renaissance.

The Labour-Alliance government delivered on its electoral promise to repeal the anti-union ECA. To avoid outraging business interests, which could smother the country's economic recovery prospects, it enacted less than bold labour legislation supporting the negotiating model. The ERA does not bestow rights on workers and unions that a subsequent anti-union government would necessarily deem anathema. The health sector unions' rekindled confidence is probably more a function of the repeal of the ECA and the change in executive government's approach than the enactment of the ERA.

Depending on how the judiciary interprets the ERA's good faith provisions, New Zealand's unions may be in the same situation as the unions in US "right-to-work" states, where union membership is also voluntary and employers have a good faith obligation. Although the Act confers status on minority unions and competing unions in the same workplace, it does not provide for successor rights. It is still too early to ascertain the consequences of this pioneering legislation.

The coalition's health reform legislation envisions the end of a fractured public health care system driven by a competitive model. Health managers have been advised to end the use of anti-union practices. Partially elected health boards are in the offing. Union representatives can more easily access government officials to discuss their concerns. The coalition government is not opposed to good compensation for public employees.

The health unions seem to accept that this is as much as they can expect from governments that can range from beneficent to malevolent. They have implicitly embraced a modern variant of the conclusion reached by the American Federation of Labor's founding president Samuel Gompers: Building stable, self-reliant unions is preferable to relying upon government. The unions have struggled in their own ways to achieve stability; they have adopted different approaches for coping with change.

ASMS and NZNO are operating like traditional craft unions, relying on their labour market power to protect members' interests. NZNO is committed to resurrecting national bargaining, and, of note, ASMS announced in late 2002 that in the future its negotiations would be conducted at the national level.[86] Clearly, the hyper-decentralization of health care industrial relations is ending.

SFWU seeks to become an organizing union, which uses rank-and-file activists as workplace representatives and organizers. The job of representing low-wage health sector workers involves more than bargaining collectively. SFWU has built alliances with like-minded community groups, amalgamated with another union, and fought for its members' rights in the courts. However, its salvation lies in its ties to the Labour Party.

PSA's strategy includes collective bargaining and employee/union involvement in health organizations' decision making. It embraces the ERA's vision of collaborative good faith. PSA is committed to helping improve health organizations' effectiveness and making them better places in which to work. It remains to be seen how management will receive this initiative. Highly stressed New Zealand health care organizations cannot easily rebuff offers of cooperation and good will from a key union. This could herald the complete abandonment of "managerialism" and the movement toward human resource management in the health sector.

It would be convenient to attribute the unions' recrudescence to changes associated with market forces and to a government sympathetic to unionism. The government's ideology, administrative emphases and legislative action prompt a simple, if not simplistic, explanation of health unions' growing confidence. However, hard times have made the unions innovative and durable, and they may be better equipped for the upcoming phase of health industrial relations restructuring than their management counterparts.

Afterword

Enactment of the ERA in 2000 signalled a new policy direction, a departure consolidated and amplified by amendments made in 2004. The new direction reflects a vision of management operating efficiently and compatibly with workers, who enjoy safe, satisfying work and union representation. The government is endeavouring to cultivate trust-based relationships characterized by good faith in bargaining and other employment-related dealings. The vision eschews legalistic, bureaucratic and adversarial arrangements in favour of ones intended to encourage participatory and adaptable relationships and to promote responsible, reasonable behaviour. It uses the language of partnership.

The amendments give teeth to unions' rights. The law enables the parties to negotiate the adoption of an array of bargaining structures including multi-employer and multi-union arrangements. It curtails "free riding." In other words, management cannot "pass on" the terms of collective agreements to employees who are not covered by an agreement without first negotiating "bargaining fees" to be levied on those workers whose employers adopt identical terms. Union membership is not compulsory as under a "union shop" arrangement, but unions are recompensed for expenses they incur in negotiating these bargaining fees. Otherwise, non-unionized workers must negotiate their own individual contracts with their employers.

The amendments also specify conditions under which the Employment Relations Authority may be approached to facilitate non-binding resolution of bargaining impasses and the process it will use. They strengthen the "duty of good faith" obligation and empower the Authority to impose settlements where serious breaches have occurred.

In 2004, ASMS, representing 92 percent of senior doctors, achieved a long-sought goal when it concluded a MECA with all 21 district health boards, represented at the table by District Health Boards New Zealand (DHBNZ), the health board employers' group. This is the union's first national agreement since the early 1990s. The Resident Doctors' Association (NZRDA) followed suit by also negotiating a national MECA with DHBNZ.

In 2005, NZNO negotiated a national MECA, which improved pay relativities with teachers, police and overseas nurses through a 20 percent pay increase over 12 months. The agreement included a provision for a ballot of non-NZNO nurses to determine whether to require payment of a bargaining fee from those adopting the settlement. With union membership dues marginally more expensive than the bargaining fee, NZNO acquired 1500 new members. Those opting not to assume the MECA's terms and conditions are required to negotiate individual contracts with their employers.

Unable to persuade DHBNZ to negotiate a national MECA, PSA is negotiating three MECAs covering allied health, mental health and clerical workers in four regions (Auckland, midlands, lower north island and south island). It is possible that some agreements may be transformed into national agreements.

Having adopted the "Partnership for Quality" strategy as its key program, PSA is encouraged by developments on the partnership front. A bipartite steering group comprising representatives from DHBNZ and New Zealand's Council of Trade Unions (CTU) has arranged funding for joint management/union delegate training on participation/partnership, or, as some unions prefer, "bi-partite engagement." The group also negotiated and ratified the health sector's Code of Good Faith, which is a schedule to the ERA and, hence, enforceable.

The most contentious issue currently before the DHBNZ-CTU steering group involves staffing arrangements to provide essential or emergency services during disputes. Although there have been no recent health sector strikes, the ERA recognizes the inevitability of disputes leading to strikes/lockouts and does not deny the right to strike. With clerical workers in Waikato and psychologists in Wellington threatening to take industrial action, the steering group may be called upon to develop protocols governing such eventualities.

An independent Mediation Service, employing 40 mediators, is being established inside the Department of Labour. Its role will be to help resolve workplace grievances and mediate contract disputes. The Employment Relations Authority can investigate those matters that mediators fail to resolve. The Employment Court will hear cases referred to it by the Authority as well as appeals of the Authority's decisions.

SFWU is reconfiguring itself and attempting to capitalize on the ERA. In 2003, the union commissioned a consultant's report to assess the organization. While the report, "Running on Empty," praised SFWU's application of the organizing model, it observed that internal reform aimed at helping the union survive the right wing revolution had outlived its usefulness. In particular, the extreme organizational decentralization, which made the union's national secretary job a half-time position, had reduced SFWU's capacity to wage national campaigns. The union is currently going through an extensive consultation exercise with members to gain support for a $1-per-week dues increase to rebuild national capability.

SFWU lobbied extensively for the 2004 ERA amendments. Having achieved its ends, it is working to make use of the legislation before the government changes. It wants to consolidate bargaining units. With members currently covered by 50 disparate collective agreements in the public hospital system and the agreements typically running for 12 months, the union's bargaining costs are high. Decentralized bargaining also precludes SFWU from establishing national pay rates – some members earn only slightly more than minimum wage – and re-establishing relativities with nursing aides, which have seriously eroded over the past decade. The union's push mirrors the CTU's policy of consolidating union power in each sector.

SFWU has approached the government, DHBNZ and the four major dietary and housekeeping services contractors to request a national MECA. The large contractors, three of which are multi-national corporations, are reportedly not unsympathetic to the overture. If the employers reject its application, the union will petition the Employment Relations Authority to declare a breach of the employers' good faith obligation. SFWU believes that a MECA would unify its public hospital group and repair splits that have occurred where small groups of members have joined non-public health sector unions.

The ERA and the Code of Good Faith offer other protections that are particularly valuable for SFWU members. Something approaching "successor rights" is guaranteed to workers made vulnerable when their jobs are contracted out or a new contractor becomes their employer. Under these circumstances, workers are entitled to retain the same jobs under identical terms and conditions. This includes hours of work, individual arrangements and union representation. Workers cannot be forced to reapply for their jobs.

SFWU is positive about the ERA's requirement for management to consult about workplace changes or restructuring that affects employees. While the right to a voice does not guarantee the union's desired outcomes, it does provide a forum for discussion about how change is managed.

Finally, the 2004 ERA amendments entitle union members to take leave from work to participate in union training programs. This enables an organizing union such as SFWU, which relies upon activists and is dealing with a legacy of anti-unionism, to build grassroots support by identifying and training activists. The labour-friendly New Zealand government is providing SFWU with an opportunity to regenerate.

It is also worth noting that in 2001, New Zealand moved from fully appointed district health boards to a governance model combining elected and appointed members. In 2004, to produce more representative health boards, i.e. results more proportionate to the district's voting pattern, elections were carried out using the "single transferable vote" system rather than "first past the post". District health boards consist of up to 11 members, seven elected (every three years) and up to four appointed by the Minister of Health. The minister appoints each board chair from among either elected or appointed members.

Acknowledgements

The author would like to thank the Industrial Relations Centre at Victoria University of Wellington for both collegial and material support. An earlier truncated version of this paper appeared as: K. Wetzel, "The Labour Relations of New Zealand's Health Reform," *The Journal of Industrial Relations* 41,1 (1999): 53–71.

Notes

1. L. Evans, A. Grimes and B. Wilkinson, "Economic Reform in New Zealand 1984–95: The Pursuit of Efficiency," *Journal of Economic Literature* 34 (December 1996): 1856–1902.
2. P. Walsh and K. Wetzel, "Preparing for Privatization: Corporate Strategy and Industrial Relations in New Zealand's State-owned Enterprises," *British Journal of Industrial Relations* 31,1 (1993): 57–75.
3. A. Schick, *The Spirit of Reform: Managing the New Zealand State Sector in a Time of Change*, A Report Prepared for the State Services Commission and Treasury, New Zealand, 1996, p. 2.
4. G. Salmond, G. Mooney and M. Laugesen, "Introduction to Health Care Reform in New Zealand," *Health Policy* 29 (1994): 1.
5. New Zealand, Treasury, *Government Management: Volumes 1 and II* (Wellington: Government Printing Office), 1987.
6. J. Boston, J. Martin, J. Pallot and P. Walsh, *Public management: The New Zealand Model* (Auckland: Oxford University Press), 1996, pp. 72–73.
7. Public choice theory assumes that humans are primarily self-interested "rational utility maximizers". It likens voters to consumers and advocacy groups to consumer associations. Bureaucrats are viewed as motivated to maximize departmental budgets while politicians seek to maximize votes regardless of the implications for the commonweal; constituents and interest groups endeavour to grab disproportionate shares of the wealth, and the state's role expands. The theory has yielded remedies to prevent such distortions. *Ibid.*, 17–18.
8. Transaction-cost economics focuses upon ascertaining the governance arrangements most suited to producing and exchanging services and goods while minimizing both production and transaction costs. The concept is closely tied to agency theory. As it might pertain to the employment relationship, contracting would be preferred with contestable services and where transaction costs are low, i.e. where the behaviour risks are less because moral and selection hazards are not great. This is appropriate where the quantity and quality of the output can be easily ascertained and potential suppliers are numerous. In-house provision within a hierarchical arrangement may be preferred where markets are not contestable, transaction costs are high and the product quality is characterized by uncertainty. *Ibid.*, 21–25.
9. *Ibid.*, 23–24.
10. The provider/purchaser split idea was popularized by Professor A. Enthoven, a former US government official and economist. It is a feature of UK health reform. S. Harrison and C. Pollitt, *Controlling Health Professionals: The Future of Work and Organization in the NHS* (Buckingham: Open University Press), 1994, p. 114.
11. Boston *et al.*, p. 11.
12. *Ibid.*, 204–259.
13. New Zealand, *Employment Contracts Act*, 1991, No. 22.
14. If workers authorize unions to represent them, employers must recognize those unions and may not negotiate contracts directly with individuals. Employers may, however, refuse to negotiate with unions. Court of Appeal, *Eketone v. Alliance Textiles* [1993] 2 ERNZ 783.

15. "If there are people in the community who prefer to make arrangements for themselves as there are in the educational world – they are entirely free to do so." Ministry of Health, *A Health Service for New Zealand* (Wellington: Government Printer), 1974, p. 45.

16. M. Laugesen and G. Salmond, "New Zealand health care: a background," *Health Policy* 29 (1994): 15.

17. C. D. Scott, "Reform of the New Zealand health care system," *Health Policy*, 29 (1994): 28.

18. Minister of Health, *Your Health and the Public Health* (Wellington: Government Printer), 1991.

19. A. Gibbs *et al.*, *Unshackling the Hospitals: Report of the Task Force on Hospitals and Related Services* (Wellington), 1987.

20. Public Health Coalition, *Destination Privatisation* 1 (August 1996): 2.

21. Inadequate funding to meet the demand for service resulted in lengthy wait lists for elective surgery. This encouraged those with the means to purchase supplementary private health insurance. Coverage under those schemes grew from 40 percent of the population in 1991 to 55 percent in 1995. *Consumer* 295 (July 1991): 3; *Consumer* 338 (June 1995): 26.

22. It is particularly noteworthy that the 1996 coalition agreement between the New Zealand First Party and the National Party to form a government provided for removing the competitive profit focus from health and replacing it with the obligation to operate in a businesslike fashion. New Zealand Government Executive, *Coalition Agreement*, 1996.

23. Laugesen and Salmond, p. 17.

24. Scott, p. 31.

25. *Ibid.*, 30, 33, 36.

26. Employment Tribunal, *Association of Salaried Medical Specialists v. State Service Commission*, WT 34/92, 18 June 92.

27. S. Oxenbridge, "Health Sector Collective Bargaining and the Employment Contracts Act: A Case Study of Nurses," *New Zealand Journal of Industrial Relations* 19,1 (1994): 20; I. Powell, "The Experience of Collective Bargaining for Salaried Senior Doctors Under the Employment Contracts Act," *New Zealand Journal of Industrial Relations* 20,2 (1995): 199.

28. The Association of Salaried Medical Specialists bargained with consultants in nine Crown health enterprises.

29. New Zealand, *Employment Contracts Act*, 1991, 12(2).

30. *New Zealand Medical Laboratory Workers Union Inc. v. Capital Coast Health Ltd.* (1994) E.R.N.Z., 2, p. 93 (E.C.); R. Harbridge, *et al.* (1996), *Employment Contracts: Bargaining Trends & Employment Law Update 1996/96* (Wellington: Victoria University of Wellington), 1996, pp. 54–55.

31. "Crown Health Enterprises Sink Further into Debt," *The Dominion* [Wellington], March 12, 1997.

32. New Zealand Council of Trade Unions, *Unions in the Health Sector: Common Issues, Future Strategies*, 1994, pp. 1–10.

33. New Zealand, *Health and Disability Services Act*, 1993, No. 22, Sec. 43(2).

34. S. Oxenbridge, "Organising the Secondary Labour Force: The New Zealand Experience." Paper presented to the Association of Industrial Relations Academics of Australia and New Zealand (AIRAANZ) Conference, Melbourne, 1995, p. 5.

35. The major exception occurred at Capital Coast Health. The Service Workers Union struck to win an agreement that barred the CHE from accepting tenders that did not carry forward the 1994 terms and conditions. Two other CHEs acceded to a similar arrangement.

36. In one case, employees refused the successful bidder's terms, choosing instead to claim redundancy. However, the unsuccessful bidder was forced into bankruptcy, and the employees lost their redundancy pay. A number of contract holders approached employees requesting their accession to voluntary reductions in the terms and conditions of their employment. Where workers agreed, the contract holders of the day – whether successful or unsuccessful in their subsequent bid – were able to stay in business.

37. Similarly imperiled US unions in the 1980s had resurrected the organizing model from their 1930s experience. SWU was inspired by the Service Employees International Union's "Justice for Janitors" campaign. SWU officials visited the US and a US union educator went to NZ to train staff. K. Brofenbrenner and T. Jurvavich, "It Takes More than Housecalls: Organizing to Win with a Comprehensive Union-Building Strategy." Paper presented to the AFL-CIO/Cornell Conference on Organizing, Washington, D.C., 1996, pp. 1–25.

38. Links were established with Maori organizations, Pacific Island churches, health consumer groups, mental health community trusts, and women's groups.

39. S. Oxenbridge, "Organising Strategies and Organising Reform in New Zealand Service Sector Unions," *Labour Studies Journal* 22,3 (1997): 3–27.

40. The Public Service Association, *The Health Union: A Strategy for the Future in Partnership with the Community and Management*, May 1996, p. 2.

41. Signatories to this coalition include the Public Service Association (clericals, telephonists, sterile supply), Building Trades Union (electricians, plumbers, carpenters), Service Workers Union (orderlies), Engineers Union (wheelchair mechanics), Amalgamated Workers Union (drivers and stores); Clothing Laundry & Allied Workers Union, and an independent bargaining agent representing some switchboard operators.

42. This coalition includes the Association of X-ray Workers, the National Distribution Union (dental technicians) and the Public Service Association (audiologists, child psychotherapists, orthotists, pharmacists, psychologists, scientific officers and social workers, as well as biomedical, medical radiation, anaesthetic, laboratory and cardio technicians).

43. The Public Service Association, *The Health Union: A Strategy* ... , p. 5. PSA has been an active supporter of the Coalition for Public Health, a public interest publicity and lobby group.

44. *Ibid.*

45. *Ibid.*, p. 6.

46. *Ibid.*, p. 4.

47. The *Employment Contracts Act* has made it difficult for the New Zealand Nurses' Organization to act for nurses employed in small private health care and long-term care organizations. It currently negotiates a national multi-employer collective employment contract with the New Zealand General Practitioners Association on behalf of 2000 nurses and receptionists employed by medical centres. Plunket and family planning negotiations are also national.

48. "Pay Rates Differ Significantly," *Kai Tiaki: Nursing (New Zealand)*, (October 1996): 12.
49. Coalition for Public Health, *Nursing and Medical Staffing Trends 1990–94*, 1995. This study found decreases of 1,077 full-time equivalent (FTE) registered nurses and 1,073 FTE enrolled nurses resulting from service cuts.
50. "Enrolled Nurses' Review Under Way," *Napier Daily Telegraph*, January 21, 1997; "Nurses to Lose HB Jobs," *Hawkes Bay Herald*, November 26, 1996.
51. I. Powell, "The Experience of ...," pp. 195–6.
52. *Ibid.*, 197.
53. *Ibid.*, 201.
54. Situated in an active private health market and operating the country's largest teaching hospital, Auckland Healthcare had fewer recruitment and retention worries. It opposed collective employment contracts, preferring "letters of understanding" and individual contracts.
55. *Ibid.*, 205–6.
56. I. Powell, "The Experience of ...," pp. 204–5.
57. Association of Salaried Medical Specialists, *Annual Report* (Wellington), 1996, pp. 4–5.
58. *Ibid.*, 2–3.
59. I. Powell, "The Experience of ...," pp. 207–08.
60. *Industrial Relations in New Zealand: Where Now?* Proceedings of the 25th Anniversary Seminar of the Industrial Relations Centre, Wellington, November 1995, pp. 39–40. Edited by K. Hince.
61. Association of Salaried Medical Specialists, *Annual Report*, p. 2.
62. Crown Company Monitoring Advisory Unit figures showed a marginal drop in the percentage of Crown health enterprises' total aggregate operating costs that go to defraying personnel costs, from 66 percent in 1993/94 to 64 percent in 1996/97.
63. The survival of the New Zealand Nurses' Organization was aided by the requirement of the *Labour Relations Act* 1987 that unions register democratic constitutions. The union was forced to change its governance structure, which had given senior nurses disproportionate power. NZNO's size gave it critical mass, and its medical indemnity insurance program helped attract and retain members.
64. New Zealand, *Employment Relations Act*, 2000, http://rangi.knowledge_ basket.co.nz/gpacts/public/text/2000/an/024.html
65. New Zealand, Ministry of Labour, *Code of Good Faith for Bargaining for Collective Agreement* (Wellington), September 22, 2000, pp. 1–3. The ministerial code reiterates, amplifies and clarifies the *Employment Relations Act*. It provides that parties must recognize and bargain terms and conditions of employment with the representatives rather than their principals. Parties are barred from undermining the bargaining or authority of others and are obliged to seek agreements expeditiously. The code urges parties to consider a number of procedural matters to facilitate the bargaining process, and requires them to meet with reasonable frequency to bargain and explain their own proposals or reasons for opposing others'. Negotiators are to adhere to agreed-upon bargaining processes, which include provisions for considering and responding to proposals. Parties must work to identify barriers to settlement and consider alternatives solutions. Perceived breaches of

good faith should be raised by the parties and addressed. The code was drafted by the New Zealand Employers Federation, the New Zealand Council of Trade Unions and the State Services Commission.

66. New Zealand, Employment Relations Service, *Employment Rights and Obligations in the Employment Relations Act 2000 Environment.* Wellington: Ministry of Labour, October 2000, pp. 68–9.

67. *Public Health and Disability Services (Safety) Act* 2000, No. 93, http://www.gp.co.nz/wooc/bills/public_health/health.html.

68. The much-discussed emergence of US-type private health service provision has not grown to the degree anticipated or feared. Users of private hospitals come predominantly from HHS overflow, queue jumpers and supplier-created demand.

69. Regional HR/Unions Forum and National HR Managers' Group Sub-groups, *Draft Health Sector Code of Good Faith,* August 24, 2000, pp. 1–5. Unions were represented by CTU, PSA and NZNO.

70. Steven Fraser, "Hutt Valley Health Comments on The Draft Health Sector Code of Good Faith," 2000, pp. 1–7.

71. State Services Commission and New Zealand Public Service Association, *Partnership for Quality, Guidelines for Departments* (Wellington), September 2000, pp. 1–11.

72. "Record number of SFWU unionists in Parliament," *Our Voice* (March 2000): 6. One minister is a former national secretary.

73. *Spotless Services (NZ) Ltd. v. Service and Food Workers Union Inc. in Respect of Walker [125],* (1999) WC84/99, November 25; December 22 (E.C.). The Employment Court upheld an Employment Tribunal ruling that the employer, a health sector contractor, had breached its collective employment contract by unilaterally terminating four employees it claimed to be redundant. SFWU hopes this case will deter management from treating employees cavalierly.

74. *Mihi-Turangi Andersen et al. v. Capital Coast Health Ltd.* (2000) WE25/00, April 14, 2000 (E.C.).

75. Darien Fenton, "Welcome to our future," *Our Voice* (March 2000): 2.

76. "Nurses' Pay Boosted, Strike Off," *The Dominion* [Wellington], December 6, 2000, p. 3.

77. Ian Powell, "Lest We Forget! Early Life Under The Employment Contracts Act," *The Specialist* 43 (June 2000): 4–5; Henry Stubbs, "The Employment Relations Act 2000," *The Specialist* 44 (September 2000): 6–7.

78. Ian Powell, "Self-defining Collective Bargaining Priorities In Public Hospitals," *The Specialist* 45 (December 2000): 8–9.

79. Henry Stubbs, "Non-Clinical Activities – A Vital part of any Job Size," *The Specialist* 43 (June 2000): 10–11.

80. The Association of Salaried Medical Specialists represents practitioners employed by the Family Planning Association, Sexual Health Service of Capital Coast Health, Hokianga Health Enterprise Trust and three health centres of the Wellington Regional Union Health Services.

81. Pippa MacKay, "Unity in our Profession – The NZMA can help," *The Specialist* 43 (June 2000): 8–9.

82. *The Specialist* 43 (June 2000): 9. With respect to professional concerns, the Association of Salaried Medical Specialists carries out representational, advisory and informational roles.

83. Adrian Skinner, "Costs and Effects of Student Loan Scheme and Student Debt," *The Specialist* 43 (June 2000): 1–2; Peter Roberts, "Tomorrow's Specialists – Our Piece of the Puzzle," *The Specialist* 43 (June 2000): 6–7. Fewer medical students can afford a year off for research or, particularly in the case of females, to do a residency and look for employment, often overseas, which offers high pay.

84. Alastair Macdonald, "Recent Developments in Credentialing," *The Specialist* 45 (December 2000): 1–2.

85. Peter Roberts, "Correction: Institutional or Organisational Psychopathy," *The Specialist* 45 (December 2000): 4–5.

86. *The Specialist* 53 (December 2002): 1.

4

The Canadian Context

Kurt Wetzel

Canada's health care system

Canada has a population of some 32 million people, spread unevenly over nearly ten million square kilometres. In 2001, the country spent approximately C$89.5 billion on the provision of health services, or roughly C$2,982 per capita.[1] Approximately 73 percent of this amount was publicly funded by the federal and provincial/territorial governments, while 27 percent came directly from individuals receiving specific services.

Canada has no single, integrated national health system. Rather, it has a collection of ten provincial and three territorial health systems that share a number of common service features and are linked together by a web of joint federal-provincial funding, regulatory and administrative relationships, and broad public support for the idea of national health standards as reflected in the *Canada Health Act*. The federal and provincial governments play key but different roles. Over time, however, provincial/territorial governments have assumed primary responsibility for funding, regulating and managing the direct delivery of health services to their citizens. While small differences exist, provinces allocate roughly 40 percent of their annual budgets to health care.

In the 1990s, rising costs and decreased revenues led to major changes in provincial health delivery systems. Eight provincial governments significantly restructured the governance and organization of their health services. Although differences occurred among the provinces in terms of the scope and pace of these "reform" initiatives, the organizational consolidation and integration of services was a common objective.

In the mid-1990s, as part of an effort to deal with its own budget deficit, the federal government unilaterally announced changes in how and how much it would fund the provincial/territorial governments for health care. The provinces reacted strongly, arguing that their health expenditures had increased 343 percent between 1977 and 1996–97, with an average annual growth rate of 7 percent. Moreover, not only had the federal government's cash transfers not increased commensurately, but they had, in fact, decreased from 26.9 percent of overall provincial/territorial health expenditures in 1977–98 to 12.9 percent in 1996–97.[2] Faced with the choice of reducing health services, increasing patient charges where possible, or increasing their own spending to replace the drop in federal funding, most provinces did some of each.

Given sustained political debate, improving government finances and growing public concern about the adequacy of funding for health services across the country, the federal government again changed its policy regarding health funding to the provinces. It started increasing cash transfers and reached an accord with the provincial/territorial governments specifying that future changes to federal transfer payments would not be made without prior intergovernmental consultation. Perhaps more importantly, in 2001 it established the independent Royal Commission on the Future of Health Care in Canada and charged it with recommending policies and measures "to ensure the sustainability of a universally accessible, publicly funded health system that offers quality services and strikes an appropriate balance between investments in prevention and health maintenance and those directed to care and treatment".[3] The commission's report, released in November 2002, emphasized the need for strategic investment in Canada's medicare system, more planning and accountability, and enhanced cooperation between the two levels of government. It focused on the supply and distribution of professionally trained providers as well as their roles and responsibilities. In the area of primary care, it recommended greater emphasis upon training health professionals to operate collegially in integrated teams.[4]

Industrial relations in Canada's public sector

The topic of public sector industrial relations in Canada has received considerable attention in recent years, although there has not been a specific focus on the health sector.

Swimmer *et al.* examine provincial public service sector industrial relations in the 1990s, "an era of restraint and restructuring".[5] The decade, the most tumultuous in the public sector's bargaining history, saw the federal government adopt "off-loading," i.e. reducing transfer payments to the provincial/territorial governments, as one means of reducing its budget deficits. Provincial governments, in turn, trimmed their expenditures by reducing services, restraining wages, cutting workforces and restructuring service delivery. This period of restraint and restructuring coincided with the emergence of the neoliberal political agenda. This line of thinking questions government's traditional role in providing public services and advocates the adoption of business-like management practices throughout the public sector. The era of restraint and the rise of neoliberalism coincided with health restructuring in Saskatchewan and Alberta.

Roberts explores the OECD-wide phenomenon of "new public management" (NPM), which is particularly prominent in neoliberals' public sector restructuring schemes.[6] NPM has been touted as a vehicle that can be used to reduce bureaucracy, to select pragmatic mixed means – private, quasi-public and public – for delivering public services, and to introduce market principles into the public sector. The author discusses NPM's implications for the public sector's "human capital crisis," which resulted from staff cuts, overwork and pay restraint. Health reform has clearly been affected by the NPM paradigm.

While the Romanow Report looks at the human capital crisis within Canada's health sector, it does so only from the macro level. That is, it addresses broad workforce issues in terms of training programs for skilled workers, changing patterns of practice for service providers, and databases pertaining to the workforce. It does not deal with the sector's management issues or its industrial relations.[7]

Writing in the mid-1990s, Warrian highlights the implications for public sector industrial relations of both adverse economic contexts and NPM, with its emphasis on measuring organizational effectiveness, establishing accountability mechanisms, and improving operational flexibility. He notes that while private sector unions have transformed themselves to survive globalization, public sector unions have balked at accommodating change, behaving like obdurate progeny of traditional private sector mass production industrial unions. Within the public sector, Wagnerism has yielded such ill-adaptive characteristics as fragmented bargaining unit structures, job control unionism typified by narrow job classifications and seniority-based pay, and adversarialism. Warrian suggests that unless these unions change profoundly, they can expect government to curtail its role as a chief public service provider in favour of more market-responsive providers. He presages deregulation, wage cuts, and bargaining that includes employee, community and client interests.[8]

Governments' approaches to public sector industrial relations are the focus of work by Panich and Swartz.[9] In the 1980s, the federal government started using state fiat to tackle inflation by controlling public sector wages. In the 1990s, federal and provincial governments drew on their extraordinary powers to attack deficits. The authors see this program of "permanent exceptionalism," which involves the use of *ad hoc* legislation to exempt governments from labour laws that guarantee free collective bargaining, as a "coercive assault on trade union rights."

Canadian governments' tendency to embrace *ad hoc* legislation to resolve public sector labour disputes unilaterally instead of engaging in collective bargaining is also examined by Swimmer and Bartkiw.[10] Until the mid-1980s, governments typically used interest arbitration to shield themselves from public accountability for public sector strikes and costly settlements. Strikes were proscribed and arbitrators were blamed for rich agreements. Governments, however, lost control over wage budgets. By contrast, Quebec centralized bargaining, legalized strikes and routinely ended massive job actions by union common fronts by imposing back-to-work legislation. This prompted the labour movement to politicize bargaining by working in elections to defeat unfriendly governments. Throughout the 1990s, governments increasingly relied upon legislation to address contentious bargaining situations. The electoral costs proved to be manageable. By 1997, most governments had eliminated their budget deficits and, using NPM, had trimmed their workforces. The authors anticipate a pattern of *ad hoc* legislation and increased centralization. Public sector workers' bargaining rights have eroded.

Reshef and Rastin consider the responses of provincial public service employees and teachers to two powerful neoliberal political agendas: Ontario's "Common Sense Revolution" and Alberta's "Klein Revolution." Each involved cost reduction following NPM tenets. Both governments restructured the public sector and trimmed social services. Looking at these provinces' institutional and political cultures, the authors proffer a model for analyzing union leaders' decisions to pursue collective action to respond to their political attackers. Such decisions reflect cost-benefit analyses that weigh such factors as the degree of the government's threat, union leaders' beliefs about collective action, and assessments of both the internal context (union members' fears and political support, and union solidarity) and the external context (labour law, labour market and political culture).[11]

Unlike the aforementioned public sector studies of Canada's industrial relations, which focus upon tumult, Thompson's assessment of the same period concludes that the sector has been relatively stable.[12] Contracting out has not become pervasive, and collective representation, compensation and bargaining systems have remained largely unchanged. There has been no profusion of innovative regimes. Rather, governments have forced unions to accept settlements that control expenditures.

There is considerable evidence of powerful unilateralist forces at play, forces that are weakening public sector unions in Canada. However, the story may be more complex and subject to change over time and across jurisdictions. All of Canada's provinces have undertaken health reform to some extent. The case studies of Saskatchewan and Alberta suggest that the institutional consequences of health restructuring, its impact upon workers' attitudes as well as changes in the economy and labour markets may counter those forces.

Notes

1. Robert G. Evans, "Raising the Money: Options, Consequences, and Objectives for Financing Health Care in Canada," discussion paper #27, prepared for the Commission on the Future of Health Care in Canada, October 2002, p. v.
2. Provincial and Territorial Ministers of Health, *Understanding Canada's Health Care Costs: Final Report*, August 2000, pp. i–v.
3. Canada, Privy Council, P.C. 2001–569, 3 April 2001.
4. Canada, Commission on the Future of Health Care in Canada, *Building on Values: The Future of Health Care in Canada – Final Report* (Ottawa), 2002.
5. Gene Swimmer, ed., *Public-Sector Labour Relations in an Era of Restraint and Restructuring* (Toronto: Oxford University Press), 2001.
6. Alasdair Roberts, "Altered States: Public Sector Restructuring and Governmental Capacity," in Richard P. Chaykowski, ed., *Globalization and the Canadian Economy: The Implications for Labour Markets, Society and the State* (Kingston, Ontario: School of Policy Studies), 2001, pp. 105–30.
7. Commission on the Future of Health Care in Canada, pp. 91–114.
8. Peter Warrian, *Bargain Hard: Transforming Public Sector Labour-Management Relations* (Toronto: McGilligan Books), 1996.
9. Leo Panich and Donald Swartz, *The Assault on Trade Union Freedoms: From Wage Controls to Social Contract* (Toronto: Garamond Press), 1993.
10. Gene Swimmer and Tim Bartkiw, "The Future of Public Sector Collective Bargaining in Canada," *Journal of Labor Research* 24 (Fall 2003): 579–95.
11. Yonatan Reshef and Sandra Rastin, *Unions in the Time of Revolution: Government Restructuring in Alberta and Ontario* (Toronto: University of Toronto Press), 2003.
12. Mark Thompson, "Public Sector Industrial Relations in Canada: Adaptation to Change," paper presented to the 11th Congress of Industrial Relations, Bologna, Italy, 22–26 September 1998.

5
The Labour Relations of Saskatchewan's Health Reform

Kurt Wetzel

This chapter describes and analyzes the labour relations of health reform in one province: Saskatchewan. Located in the heart of the Canadian Prairie, Saskatchewan covers 651,000 square kilometres and has a population of one million people. While two thirds of its people live in urban centres, the largest city has just over 200,000 residents. Agriculture, the service sectors and natural resources drive the province's economy, although the resource riches are not as bountiful as those of its western neighbour, Alberta. Since 1991, the province has been governed by a social democratic government committed to the goals of maintaining a viable, affordable health care delivery system and respecting workers' collective rights. However, fiscal constraints, both real and enduring, have made the government's negotiating approach to labour relations difficult to sustain.

The provincial context

When the New Democratic Party (NDP) returned to power in 1991 after two terms in opposition, Saskatchewan was burdened by mounting deficits, a $15 billion debt and dismal economic prospects brought on by low commodity prices and drought. The NDP, heir to the province's social democratic legacy, undertook two major initiatives. First, it addressed the fiscal crisis by cutting spending and raising taxes. Although the government brought in a balanced budget in 1995, debt reduction, debt servicing and revenue problems, cuts to federal transfer payments, kept it focused on fiscal matters. Second, it reformed the province's unaffordable, fragmented and outdated publicly funded health care system.

Making a virtue of a necessity, the political descendants of those who had pioneered Canada's Medicare system and administered it into maturity in the 1970s undertook to save it. The NDP set out a vision for refocusing and improving the delivery of health care in the province. That vision entailed shifting from a preoccupation with treating illness and delivering institutional care to an emphasis on "wellness," i.e. promoting and maintaining good health. It also involved extensive restructuring to regionalize and integrate service delivery.

The government adopted a health policy regime propounded in the *Ottawa Charter for Health Promotion*.[1] The charter emerged from the First International Conference on Health Promotion (November 1986), a collaborative initiative of the World Health Organization, Health and Welfare Canada and the Canadian Public Health Association to examine issues and actions linked to improved health. It advocates wellness as opposed to the clinical, or curative, approach associated with the medical model. Wellness links health status to the quality of life that flows from an array of environmental, economic, social, political and policy factors. It calls upon individuals and communities to take greater responsibility for and control over their own health. Wellness presupposes a knowledgeable, involved citizenry and envisions an active research function to enable decision makers to make informed choices.

In Saskatchewan, movement toward health reform began in 1989, when the Progressive Conservative (PC) government struck the Commission on Directions in Health Care (Murray Commission) to investigate issues affecting the health care system. The commission endorsed the principles of Medicare enshrined in the *Canada Health Act, 1984*[2] – accessibility, comprehensiveness, universality, portability and public administration – and concluded that current health system operating assumptions were outdated and reform was overdue. It recommended incorporating greater local ownership and management and a systemic focus on maintaining good health. It proposed integrating and coordinating health service delivery, fostering personal independence by providing more health services/education in homes and communities, focusing on service outcomes, and making the health system affordable. And it advocated establishing locally elected, provincially funded regional councils to provide health services.[3]

In January 1992, the NDP health minister initiated the "Wellness Project." *A Saskatchewan Vision for Health: A Framework for Change* became the reform blueprint.[4] It envisioned shifting resources from acute and long-term institutional care, which consumed 60 percent of health dollars in 1992, to community-based services and the promotion of healthy lifestyle choices. It advocated changing the public's expectations of the health care system. The plan involved massive restructuring. Henceforth autonomous facilities and service sectors (home care, community health, mental health, public health, acute care, long-term care and ambulance services) would be consolidated and integrated into health districts, which would administer service delivery.

The *Health Districts Act* [5] enabled the creation of health districts to provide a wide array of integrated services and specified district boards' powers, duties and composition. Communities defined the districts' boundaries, constrained by the requirement that a minimum population of 12,000 in a contiguous geographical area be served by each one. The government set up interim health boards, appointing trustees with an assortment of affiliations, backgrounds and perspectives. These board members would stay in place until October 1995, when the first district health board elections were held. With these elections, Saskatchewan implemented a hybrid model of district governance: eight members elected from wards within the district and four members, also from within the district, appointed by government. (For the province's two largest districts, Saskatoon and Regina, the government has the authority to appoint six members, two of whom may be resident outside the districts.)

The Act required union hospitals (i.e. hospitals formed by the "union" of towns and municipalities) and ambulance boards to amalgamate with the newly formed districts. Because the government did not want to engage in expropriation, home care boards, for-profit organizations and non-profit municipal and denominational corporations, including nearly all long-term care facilities, were not compelled to amalgamate.[6] Nonetheless, all 45 home care boards in the province and many long-term facilities did so voluntarily. By early 1994, 29 (later 32) district health boards had replaced some 400 independent acute care, long-term care, home care and ambulance boards. This participatory approach to district formation proved to be slow and yielded a relatively large number of districts as compared to neighbouring Alberta, where that province's government specified boundaries for 17 regional health authorities (RHAs) and appointed boards composed of its supporters.

Health reform in Saskatchewan, while consolidating governance and service management at a district level, included a strong element of democratic decentralism. In April 1995, mental, community and public health services were devolved, or transferred, from the provincial and municipal governments to the districts, bringing to an end the government's role as a direct provider of health services. Districts, in consultation with their communities, were responsible for identifying local needs, specifying priorities and providing services on an integrated, coordinated basis across service sectors, emphasizing community-based health services.

The government's fiscal objectives drove the timing and pace of health reform. It cut the health budget by $45 million (3%) in 1993, and funding was to remain constant at $1.56 billion after 1994–95, with no increases planned through 1998.[7] Savings were to be achieved by consolidating and de-institutionalizing services. Simultaneously, the government was calling for improved system effectiveness. In 1992, it had created the Health Services Utilization and Research Commission (HSURC) to study utilization patterns and health outcomes of programs and practices, and to encourage and fund research and disseminate the findings.

Restructuring the health delivery system meant building larger, more complex, integrated organizations. The wellness model challenged existing organizational cultures, operations and philosophies. Managers and employees were urged to change their attitudes and behaviours. Early in the process, HSURC CEO Steven Lewis opined, "The traditional hierarchical approach with rigid roles, formal education and territorialism will be replaced by a contemporary model with democratic decision making, more flexible roles, modular and continuous education processes and a sense of community".[8]

Throughout the long and difficult process of health reform, the government demonstrated both leadership and forbearance. In April 1993, the Department of Health set the tone and created momentum for restructuring by converting 52 small rural hospitals and integrated facilities into "wellness centres." Budget cuts forced district boards to follow this lead by rationalizing service delivery and reallocating resources. The Department also implemented a contentious "one-way valve" policy, which permitted districts to move resources out of but not into costly acute and long-term institutional care.

Within this environment of fiscal restraint, reform had organizational and personal consequences for virtually everyone in the system. The industry's high political profile, labour intensity and heavy unionization complicated the process. The fundamental organizational changes brought about by the restructuring affected workers' employment security, job status and content, promotion opportunities, work intensity, work location and union representation. It was also evident that the requisite cost savings could not be achieved without workforce reductions. Reform affected unions' certifications and collective agreements, the size of their memberships and their survival in the health sector. It also inflamed endemic inter-union rivalries.

The NDP has long had close ties to organized labour. Its labour relations policies and practices fall within the realm of traditional orthodox pluralism. *The Trade Union Act*,[9] originally enacted in 1944, embodies provincial labour relations policy. It constitutes an early and complete embrace of "Wagnerism," allowing any public or private sector union that proves majority support in an appropriate bargaining unit to be certified by the Saskatchewan Labour Relations Board (SLRB) as the exclusive bargaining representative for all employees in that unit. An employer must recognize the certified bargaining representative and bargain with it in good faith. All workers have the right to strike.

Industrial relations in the province's health sector were highly developed in the early 1990s. The system was replete with parallel structures, separate and often competing employer associations, union rivalries, collective agreements providing dissimilar terms and conditions of employment, and occasional strikes.[10] Health labour relations ranged from tumultuous to accommodating. Acute and long-term care bargaining had been centralized in the 1970s, a model that home care later adopted. Two multi-employer associations represented employers and government (the funder) in negotiating provincial agreements under a government "observer's" gaze. Public, community and mental health workers bargained directly with the provincial or appropriate municipal government.

Although industry players had long been calling for changes to the health care delivery system, successive governments had sidestepped the complex and politically volatile task of restructuring health labour relations. In 1991, the PC government urged the unions to rationalize their representational structures voluntarily, warning that if they did not, it would be done for them. The government sponsored mediation to encourage voluntary change. However, with an election looming, the unions declined to participate, choosing instead to take their chances with what they hoped would be an NDP government.

The unions got their wish, but health reform forced and expanded the issue. The creation of districts led managers to push for greater flexibility to deploy their workforces as needed. Unions had to find a way to accommodate the new organizational structures while looking out for their members, who were feeling the impacts of budget cuts – job loss, work intensification and reduced work status. Unfortunately for everyone, health reform was being implemented in a fiscally inauspicious environment by parties used to mature adversarial industrial relations and inexperienced in massive restructuring.

The NDP's approach to health labour relations restructuring was participatory, low key and deferential rather than prescriptive or visionary. Government did not encourage the parties to adopt approaches that might complement the wellness model (for example, building collaborative relationships). Instead, it facilitated processes that enabled those affected by restructuring to provide input. It also established and sought advice from an external health labour relations review committee, encouraged the districts to embrace an industry association to represent them (and government) in collective bargaining, and urged both unions and employers to pursue voluntary solutions to restructuring problems. If necessary, piecemeal SLRB decisions could be sought.

Government facilitated the resolution of labour adjustment issues raised by workforce reductions. When voluntary means proved inadequate to the task of addressing issues related to rationalizing union representation and restructuring bargaining, it created, at the parties' behest, a commission to resolve those matters. Only when the parties had begun to negotiate collective agreements did government manifest a taste for exercising its fiat.

The actors in the health industrial relations system

Structuring an industrial relations system to meet the actors' needs involves pursuing an illusive and delicate balance. Government's legislative and executive powers allow it to pursue fiscal, political, policy and labour relations objectives unilaterally by fiat. The challenge for a government concerned with democratic niceties is to pursue its agenda without marginalizing the other actors. Management has an abiding interest in being able to address issues that have operational implications and to achieve flexibility. Unions want the capacity to represent their members and themselves in dealings with government and management at the workplace and through collective bargaining and political processes.

Government

Aware of the potential political and fiscal implications of health labour relations, NDP governments in the 1970s devised structures to enable them to influence the cost of settlements, depoliticize, or professionalize, negotiations and let management address operational issues. These mechanisms were designed to keep Cabinet abreast of bargaining developments, enable it to set monetary bargaining mandates, and ensure that its interests were represented by reliable, professional, industry-based negotiators.

A Cabinet committee on collective bargaining, composed of the Minister of Finance and other key ministers, authorized negotiators' mandates and informed Cabinet about public sector bargaining developments. A personnel policy secretariat (PPS) served as emissary for the Department of Finance, communicating or, in some cases, negotiating mandates with the bargaining representatives for the industry's employers and the government. As added insurance, government physically manifested itself – the "ghost" at the bargaining table – by detailing an "observer" from the PPS to monitor negotiations, participate in management caucuses and listen to the unions.[11] These arrangements were intended to keep the unions' attention focused on the bargaining tables, thereby minimizing "end runs" to the government, which frustrate and discredit management spokespersons.

Government policy reflected the belief that politicians' desire to be viewed positively, their lack of a detailed understanding of bargaining issues, and their impatience with the tedium of bargaining make them less than ideal negotiators. Ministers and department officials were cautioned neither to meddle in the conduct of bargaining nor to make themselves available to unions seeking to end run management negotiators. Although the policy was retained by the PC government in the 1980s, adherence to it deteriorated when PPS officials started meddling in the conduct of bargaining and failed to provide management negotiators with clear mandates.[12]

Aware that health reform was fraught with labour relations pitfalls, the new NDP government moved on a variety of fronts. In 1992, the Department of Health appointed the Labour Relations Review Committee to consult with stakeholders and recommend changes and approaches to industrial relations consistent with health reform. The chair's report suggested that the wellness-based reforms be reflected in the sector's industrial relations, with government's encouragement. It observed that wellness lends itself to building collegial, trust-based relationships that could replace hierarchical authoritarianism in the workplace. At the collective bargaining level, the report urged the government to take the lead in lessening "adversarialism" and moving relationships in the direction of labour-management partnerships, and to avoid direct involvement in negotiations.[13] Government, however, did not use health restructuring as an opportunity to encourage the parties to move away from traditional adversarial industrial relations.

Reform seemed to commit government to arrangements for devolving, decentralizing and sharing decision making. By vesting responsibility for service delivery in health districts, government had created entities requiring the capacity to plan and make decisions affecting themselves and the industry within clear policy and funding parameters. It was therefore incumbent upon government to remove major obstacles and help develop structures that would allow the districts to operate as cost efficient, integrated organizations.

Reform substantially altered the size and role of the Department of Health. Budgeted staff cuts and the devolution of 1,400 mental, public and community health services workers to districts left the Department with 600 staff in 1999, down from 2,200 in 1990. Its Pay Negotiations Unit was disbanded, leaving the Department of Finance to monitor the financial aspects of health bargaining. The Department's role was to allocate resources, develop policy and legislation, evaluate programs, assess population health, and establish and monitor provincial standards to ensure that appropriate services are being delivered. It also engages in health promotion and provides consulting services to the districts.

The Department was restructured to address districts' routine concerns. However, on matters pertaining to broad policy and funding, the initially emboldened, partially elected district boards, acting through their industry association, the Saskatchewan Association of Health Organizations, were inclined to address their issues directly to the Minister of Health or Cabinet. An ongoing concern was with minimizing government interference in politically sensitive operational issues. This concern was well founded, as the temptation for the government/funder to "micro-manage" the districts has, on occasion, proved overwhelming.

Aside from structural and operational considerations, a number of industrial relations issues required the government's attention. Displaced health workers' adjustment to job loss had to be eased. Health unions' representational rights had to be realigned in ways that were consistent with the new district structure. Bargaining structures had to be reworked to reflect the new order. Government had to ensure that its interests and those of the industry would be well represented in bargaining and that health and fiscal policy objectives were achieved. Finally, relationships with unions and unionized voters had to be protected. The potential pitfalls were enormous.

Health districts and their management

Reform changed the health delivery system's structures, governance and reason for being. Instead of the wide array of defined services provided on a stand-alone basis, health districts were delivering integrated services regionally, driven by the wellness philosophy. The enormity and complexity of restructuring at the district level depended upon the district's size, the variety and sophistication of the services it provided, and the vagaries of the local politics. Overall, it was a huge organizational and political undertaking.

Health reform was undertaken to make the system more affordable. It was premised on the assumption that health spending was adequate but the resources needed to be used more effectively. Districts were expected to find efficiencies and savings in their reduced budgets to fund reform initiatives, new/increased community-based services. There was no transition funding for building the local or provincial infrastructure needed to support these larger, more complex organizations. Enabling technology for payroll, information and communication systems materialized very slowly. (Indeed, it was not until efforts to address the Y2K problem generated a budgetary appropriation that much of the aging information system was upgraded or replaced.) Within these constraints, the statutorily autonomous and accountable districts were expected to implement health reform as community needs dictated except for one restriction: They could not allocate additional resources to institutional acute or long-term care.

Labour relations presented a major obstacle to the health reform process. Existing structures were incompatible with the tasks facing the districts. Unions had been certified to represent bargaining units in organizations that no longer existed as legal entities. And although bargaining units were no longer appropriate, the unions were keen to protect their turf and the sanctity of collective agreements that had not anticipated the changes accompanying health reform. Districts were barred from restructuring their workforces until severance arrangements could be reached between the payer and the unions.

Meanwhile, management faced profound administrative problems. In order to close or merge facilities and reconfigure services, management needed the capacity to redeploy staff. It was difficult to transfer workers along with their seniority to similar jobs in another bargaining unit, regardless of whether the receiving unit was represented by the same or a different union. Collective agreements covering employees in the various health sectors and unions had distinct provisions. Consequently, employees working side by side and doing the same job could be paid at different rates. Districts devoted considerable effort to negotiating transfer arrangements with unions and seeking guidance on specific cases from the Labour Relations Board. Health districts urged the SLRB and government to reconfigure bargaining units to reflect the district structure and awaited government action on the labour adjustment issue.

Many health districts faced an additional structural challenge that affected their capacity to rationalize and integrate service delivery. The "affiliates," mostly denominational acute and long-term care facilities, had been permitted to retain their organizational identities and autonomy, i.e. separate boards, managements, collective agreements and certifications. It was not clear how these independent entities were supposed to fit into the integrated district structure. Resistance and apprehension were high, so, in 1995, the government commissioned a report to address district-affiliate relationships. While stressing the value of allowing affiliates to maintain their unique identities, the report recommended that districts act as "lead partners," with the affiliates becoming "part of the whole." The partners were urged to coordinate service delivery to ensure efficient resource use.[14] Except where an affiliate is the key provider of a district's acute care services, districts and their affiliates have been largely successful in building accommodating and mutually respectful relationships.

In the field, the management of health reform at both the senior and middle levels was problematic. Few of the high profile, experienced managers who had worked in the old regime survived the transition. Many were seen as unadaptably wedded to a narrow or institutional focus and were not given opportunities to compete for positions in the new structure.[15] Accordingly, the composition of senior management changed. Most districts had difficulty attracting and retaining qualified managers with health experience to lead the reform process. In more than one case, a high-ranking provincial bureaucrat assumed a senior district management role.

Through the 1990s, senior managers found themselves in a particularly difficult role. They were increasingly expected to be politically astute as well as operationally proficient. Elected board members pursuing political/single-issue agendas or failing to appreciate what had been accomplished prior to their arrival were often sources of frustration. There were ongoing concerns about real and potential conflicts of interest resulting from doctors or union-backed trustees, including district employees, sitting on district health boards. Managing was further complicated by periodic politically inspired initiatives undertaken by government without adequate consultation or due recognition of districts' operational concerns and priorities. Moreover, budgetary processes within the Department of Health were such that districts did not receive their budgets until very late in the fiscal year. Not surprisingly, turnover among district CEOs, who were subject to the vagaries of district politics, was high.

At the same time, however, health reform provided an opportunity for strategically placed managers wanting to be part of visionary change. Those individuals were empowered to question ossified practices, introduce new programs and pursue the goals of wellness albeit without adequate resources or time. The fact that many health boards embraced the policy governance model, which treats industrial relations as an operational concern to be addressed by management, also led to a higher profile for labour relations practitioners, who are defining the shape of health industry labour relations for the next generation.

Many middle managers, however, believe that health restructuring has come at their expense, requiring them to adjust to repeated reorganizations that shuffled people and responsibilities. Through much of the process they felt overworked, undervalued, overwhelmed, excluded from the planning process, burnt out, insecure and skeptical about their organization's capacity or will to implement promised change. Professional development opportunities, whether formal education or short courses, were limited by resource constraints or a lack of time or energy. The most critical management skills include the capacity to react and adapt, but there was scant time even for reflection.

From the outset of reform, districts strove to cut costs in ways that minimize negative reaction from the public and the workforce. The public's concern about the quality and availability of services made it important for districts to be seen as trimming "fat" rather than front-line care. As services were rationalized, merged and focused away from the administratively intensive institutional sectors and toward the community sector, management itself became the favoured downsizing target. According to the best estimates, approximately 15 percent of managerial positions were eliminated in the first two years of restructuring and only 3 percent of in-scope jobs. Indeed, while reform significantly increased the complexity and scope of the management function, district boards often announced the elimination of administrative positions as a matter of pride. Coordination and cooperation across sectors became a key focus.

While in-scope personnel, medical staff and middle managers elsewhere in Saskatchewan's public sector have organizations that defend their collective interests,[16] health managers have no collective voice. Their workloads have risen sharply, while their pay increases have been modest and slow in coming. Unionization is anathema to this group, which ranges between the dedicated and the cynical. They pride themselves on not having what they see as a union mentality, a fact that is evident in the unassertive Saskatchewan Association of Health Services Executives.

In 2002, the government further refined the system's delivery and governance structures. Opting for a model closely resembling that in Alberta, it consolidated the 32 health districts into 12 regional health authorities and moved from partly elected back to fully appointed health boards. It is too soon to know what, if any, impact these changes will have on the realization of the government's ongoing reform agenda, the role/workloads of middle managers, or CEO turnover rates.

Saskatchewan Association of Health Organizations

In the early 1990s, spurred by resolutions from their respective memberships, two members from each of the Saskatchewan Health-Care Association, the Saskatchewan Association of Special Care Homes and the Saskatchewan Home Care Association began meeting to lay the foundation for a new, single industry association. Wanting to avoid problems that had hampered their organizations, this steering committee brought in external facilitators and consulted other provincial bodies, including those representing urban and rural municipalities and school trustees. With health reform just around the corner, the committee concluded that an effective association would need access to policy makers and, in turn, that government would be more responsive to an organization representing district boards rather than a coalition of interests, affiliates, or management.[17] The government, tired of dealing with three separate associations with redundant services/ activities and overlapping memberships, supported and facilitated the amalgamation discussions.

The Saskatchewan Association of Health Organizations (SAHO) came into being in July 1993, an equal merger of its predecessors. It established a board of directors comprising 12 non-employee district health board members and, starting in 1998, one non-employee affiliate representative, all elected by the membership.[18] Many other health agencies, for example, educational and licensing/regulatory bodies, also belong to SAHO, and while they often participate on committees, they are not represented at the SAHO board table.

SAHO is a full-service industry association that facilitates communication, cooperation and the pooling of members' resources. Nearly 80 percent of its funding comes from fee-for-service revenue and interest revenues, with government grants and membership fees accounting for 8 percent and 13 percent, respectively.[19] It has a staff of approximately 90.

The primary role SAHO has sought to fashion for itself includes acting as the bargaining representative for its members and government, administering benefit plans (pension, group life insurance, disability income, dental) for industry employees, and serving as the health districts' voice to government and external groups on health system matters. In addition, it provides a group purchasing program, payroll services for most districts and training/education opportunities for health managers and employees. SAHO strives to build industry consensus and reflect a reasonable, well-informed perspective on key issues. It communicates regularly with its members, and can quickly poll them and act on their behalf. SAHO has also gained respect for two premiere educational events: the annual conference (which it combines with its annual business meeting) and the annual orientation/continuing education institute for board members.

Initially, individual health districts were ill equipped to address the enormous variety of complex challenges facing them, and they recognized the importance of acting collectively to deal with government, external groups and common internal issues. Districts were ready to accept SAHO as their provincial association, provided it took direction from the membership and delivered good value for their membership fees.

In January 1994, SAHO established quarterly meetings of district board chairs, vice-chairs and CEOs to provide a forum for joint discussion, problem solving and networking. A sense of optimistic collegiality gradually emerged as trustees and managers became comfortable with one another and examined the challenges and opportunities. External presentations and a discussion with the Minister of Health became standard components of these non-decision making forums, which, by the end of the decade, were being held semi-annually. The regular "in camera" portions, however, excluded everyone other than the district representatives, SAHO board members and senior SAHO staff.

While *The Health Districts Act* set out in broad terms the responsibilities and powers of district health boards, policy and relationship matters remained to be worked through. In 1995, the Department of

Health invited the districts to participate on an advisory committee to explore policy issues and define districts' relationship with government. Acting on behalf and with the support of the districts, SAHO accepted the invitation. Characteristically, it appointed its board chair, CEO and six board members, but no district managers, as representatives on the Health District Advisory Committee. An early and important achievement of this committee was the development of *A Framework of Accountability*,[20] which spelled out in detail the specific relationships and accountabilities of the Minister of Health and the health districts *vis-à-vis* the legislature, the public and each other. (The document eventually became a bone of contention for a government wanting tighter control over district boards.) The SAHO Board has also met on several occasions with Cabinet members.

SAHO has no board-level labour relations committee, its predecessors' oversight committees having proved cumbersome and meddlesome. Indeed, policy concerns, lobbying and industry politics initially preoccupied the board. Instead, a strategic advisory committee composed of senior SAHO staff and eight practitioners from large, medium and small districts was established for informal consultations on pressing labour relations issues. SAHO also struck a committee to examine amalgamations, certifications, transfers and mergers.

SAHO staffers serve as spokespersons in provincial negotiations, assist with contract administration and arbitrations, consult on SLRB matters, conduct labour relations training, and provide training and seminars on occupational health and safety, labour standards and issues like discipline and absenteeism. SAHO regularly brings together the districts' HR representatives to examine current issues. Toward the latter part of the decade, the association began working with the unions on a joint province-wide job evaluation and pay equity system, and with its members on a much-needed human resource management information system.

From the outset of reform, the larger districts were able to draw on their own experienced labour relations staff to deal with the volume and complexity of the industrial relations issues confronting them. Because smaller districts lacked those resources, SAHO devoted considerable time and effort providing training and backup support. This prompted some complaints about small districts' dependence upon SAHO, a dependence cultivated by the ready availability of competent staff committed to serving the members. Gradually those districts' independence and professionalism improved. By 2000, every district had a full-time human resource person. Unions no longer had to deal directly with the district CEO, whose understanding of industrial relations issues might have been limited and unsophisticated. Problems now more commonly occur with affiliates that lack dedicated human resources HR staff.

In SAHO's early years, its labour relations professionals exercised considerable discretion, free from health district politics and government interference. Staff morale was high. The board and senior management identified organizational values and broad goals, but enunciated no labour relations philosophy. Although government was loath to advocate a vision for health industrial relations, SAHO staff quietly did. From their predecessor organizations they adopted best practices that could be used for transcending traditional adversarialism, an approach that required some previously hard-line staffers to undergo personal transformation. They built positive relations centrally by resolving problems. It became routine to share information previously regarded as privileged with union leaders to garner their input and keep them informed. Cooperative, trusting relationships with unions emerged, reflecting staffers' personalities and beliefs.

The unions responded favourably to this openness. The contempt that union leaders had expressed for their pre-SAHO counterparts disappeared. Unions value a strong, central industrial relations function and interpret SAHO's existence as evidence of a commitment to province-wide bargaining. However, SAHO's lack of authority over the districts, whose attitudes, experiences and resources vary considerably, frustrates those unions that prefer to operate centrally. Restructuring issues, for example, which generate enormous pressures for unions (layoffs and transfers), are within each district's purview. Some districts are comfortable engaging in open dialogue with unions, while others are reluctant. Some managers actively seek union input, while others avoid it. As a result, the tone of local union-management relationships depends largely on the personalities involved.

SAHO engages in the same intra-organizational processes as unions, informing, consulting and building consensus before acting. HR staff seek to provide districts and unions with prompt, informed service. Each labour relations consultant services a specific geographic area, backs up another area, and serves as a specialist in the affairs of one union and as a backup for another. Consultants meet regularly with practitioners in their respective regions. Issues are addressed locally unless they have provincial implications, in which case the union specialist is likely to be involved.

SAHO has been active in health system restructuring from the start. In 1993, it represented the industry in negotiating a labour adjustment mechanism, the Transfer/Merger Agreement (TMA). To its dismay, it was not involved in determining the terms under which the Department of Health's direct service employees were devolved to districts in 1995. Subsequently, however, SAHO bargained supplementary issues with the Department and represented the industry throughout the process of restructuring union representation.

Government defines its own and, consequently, SAHO's role in collective bargaining. From the start, SAHO was apprehensive that government might choose to meddle in negotiations or be receptive to end runs by the unions. It endeavoured to build good working relations with government and to be a cohesive, politically attuned body on which government could rely. It wanted its bargainers to have clear mandates and be left alone to work out the details of settlements. The arm's length relationship SAHO espoused would be undermined if government attempted to call the plays or dealt directly with the other team. Union leaders, on the other hand, while recognizing the value of having a credible employers' organization, would rather politicize bargaining if they see this approach as potentially more rewarding than dealing with the industry negotiators. This could entail bypassing SAHO to deal directly with the funder on major monetary and non-monetary items and discussing only the less critical issues at the table with SAHO.

The health unions

Although the basic structures and objectives of health system reform had been specified, the processes and rules for health care labour relations restructuring had not. For health workers and their unions, reform became a perilous journey through uncharted waters. In an industry that had provided stable full-time employment, workers found themselves employed by new, rapidly evolving organizations characterized by mergers, reorganizations and unit closures. Management's push to deploy labour more flexibly and effectively led to transfers and lay offs. Some workers' employment status was reduced to part time or casual, and workloads generally increased. Workers turned to their unions, concerned about issues such as severance benefits and the transfer of seniority rights.

Institutional issues loomed as large. Health organizations draw from an assortment of labour markets. They create labour forces of hierarchically arrayed occupational groups, each proclaiming its unique identity. Similarly, health unions have distinct organizational cultures, approaches to bargaining and politics, and their own institutional concerns and aspirations. Health workers value the right to select their union, and they ardently oppose being separated from those whose goals and professional identities they share.

Regionalization and service integration had implications for unions' representational rights and the structure of bargaining. The enormity of the stakes strained union relationships, which, in some cases, were historically distrustful, even hostile. Union leaders entered the restructuring process prepared to protect or seize opportunities to expand their territory. Indeed, the commissioner who ultimately addressed these representational issues was struck by the intensity of the union and personal rivalries.[21] Government's exhortations for health unions to explore consensual solutions to their differences fell on deaf ears. Ultimately, reform would require restructured unions to bargain new, consolidated collective agreements to replace those that had applied to particular sectors.

Health care labour relations are highly political. The NDP has traditionally supported collective bargaining and comprehensive, publicly funded health care. While unions do not thrive under non-NDP governments, health unions do not necessarily support the party. Their politics range from active support, for example, affiliating with the party, providing cash and campaign workers and canvassing members to vote NDP, to tacit endorsement or support for individual candidates, to eschewing partisan activities. Their political action can also be manifested at bargaining tables, in lobbying activities and on picket lines. Health reform offered the unions another political venue, particularly once district health boards had elected members.

The Saskatchewan Union of Nurses (SUN), the only health craft union in the province and with a history of three provincial strikes, represented 7,800 registered nurses in acute, long-term and home care at the outset of representational restructuring in 1997. Strong, highly centralized, militant, female dominated and strategically positioned in the workplace to wield enormous bargaining power, SUN has come increasingly to include "professional" issues, particularly staffing, on its bargaining agenda. The union has not been active in provincial partisan politics, although individual members may be. (A notable example is a former SUN president who became the associate health minister in the mid-1990s). After the onset of health reform, SUN affiliated with the Saskatchewan Federation of Labour (SFL). When health board elections were implemented, the union began dabbling in local electoral politics.

The Canadian Union of Public Employees (CUPE), the largest health union, represented 9,800 members, or 30 percent of the workforce, including dietary, maintenance, housekeeping, clerical, laboratory and patient aide workers in long-term and acute care. Municipal public health workers and staff in two provincially run mental hospitals, including 445 psychiatric and public health nurses, belonged to CUPE. The provincial organization is active on behalf of the national union's bargaining and social agendas and maintains a discrete distance from the NDP, although locals have supported the party or certain candidates. CUPE has traditionally taken an aggressive approach to bargaining.

The Service Employees International Union's (SEIU) membership roughly mirrored CUPE's and included staff of one home care board. Its 7,800 members comprised 24 percent of the health workforce. SEIU is a business union that has had strong NDP ties. SEIU and CUPE have a history of rivalry and ideological differences. In the 1970s, they bargained one provincial agreement in coalition, but differences over bargaining strategy ended that relationship.

Also clashing with SEIU is the Health Sciences Association of Saskatchewan (HSAS), whose 750 members largely include university-trained professionals, for example, physiotherapists, social workers and pharmacists, some of whom once belonged to SEIU. HSAS, which has made efforts to expand its representation of laboratory technicians at SEIU's expense, is regarded as a raiding union. It avoids partisan political action and is the only health union not affiliated with the SFL.

At the start of health reform the Saskatchewan Government Employees Union (SGEU) had 3,300 health sector members. These included employees of three provincially owned long-term care facilities, the Wascana Rehabilitation Centre and the Cancer Foundation, as well as 480 provincially employed public health nurses and workers employed by 23 newly organized home care boards. SGEU's roots are in the provincial public service, and it avoids direct involvement with political parties.[22]

Restructuring

Health labour relations restructuring evolved in three distinct phases: labour adjustment, representational restructuring and negotiations carried out under the new bargaining structures. Each phase was a high-stakes undertaking involving not only the parties, but senior ministers and bureaucrats as well.

Labour adjustment

The first major restructuring issue to confront health unions involved establishing a labour adjustment program to define the rights of workers who were affected by the creation of health districts. As services were integrated and workplaces merged or closed, some workers had to change work sites, jobs and unions. Workers faced situations in which employees from workplaces belonging to other locals of the same union, a different union or no union entered their work units. Questions emerged about the seniority rights of workers in closed and merging units, the status of collective agreements in amalgamated units, and the treatment of workers who were being laid off. These issues became the subject of negotiations involving the unions, SAHO and government, and were addressed by the Transfer/Merger Agreement and Career Adjustment Assistance Program.

When health reform began, government wanted to cultivate cooperative, sensitive approaches to restructuring to allay employee apprehension. It encouraged SAHO and the unions to negotiate protocols for handling staff changes associated with the creation of integrated health districts. Accordingly, CUPE, SEIU, SUN and SGEU, all SFL affiliates, formed the Provincial Council of Health Unions. The price for securing these SFL affiliates' cooperation was the exclusion of HSAS from the discussions. So, without HSAS input, the parties negotiated part one of the labour adjustment strategy, the 1993 Transfer/Merger Agreement (TMA). Addressing issues related to the movement of employees between bargaining units, the TMA was intended to maximize employment opportunities and obviate local bargaining of adjustment issues.[23]

The TMA allowed seniority rights to accompany workers into the receiving bargaining unit, specified job posting requirements, created recall lists for those laid off, and guaranteed the transferability of benefits.[24] It clarified employees' rights, reduced confusion, and lowered resistance to restructuring, and its language was ultimately incorporated into collective agreements. The TMA was not universally adopted, however. Parties in each district could negotiate agreements that tailored TMA principles to their needs. Some districts negotiated agreements with each union.

Policy makers assumed that health restructuring would reduce health sector employment. Part two of the labour adjustment strategy, the Career Adjustment Assistance Program, addressed that eventuality. The Provincial Joint Union-Management Adjustment Committee was created, again without HSAS, to negotiate and oversee a safety net for employees who were either laid off or had their hours reduced by 20 percent or more. Safety net services included career counselling and job placement, (re)training, relocation assistance and enhanced severance.[25] Over $5 million was made available to fund the program.

The program did not work as intended, and, by August 1998, less than $2 million had been spent. The payouts were too meagre to entice workers into leaving the health care sector. Instead, laid-off workers opted to go onto recall lists (which still allowed them to access program funding for retraining), take part-time or casual positions, and draw unemployment insurance benefits. Considerable work was available for other-than-full-time employees because the volume of work did not decrease as full-time positions were cut. Thus began a trend toward a more highly "casualized" workforce.

Representational restructuring

The second major undertaking involved restructuring and rationalizing unions' representational structures. The creation of districts and integrated services found employees from different unions, each with its own collective agreement, working side by side in the same occupation and in the same workplace. Sectoral compensation differences also existed, for example, between home care and acute care. In 1997, 25 collective agreements covered 29,815 health workers who were members of 538 appropriate bargaining units. This multiplicity of agreements interfered with districts' ability to plan, administer the workplace and use labour flexibly and effectively. Moreover, negotiating multiple agreements involved an avoidable cost.

The aim of representational restructuring was to reduce the number of unions and collective agreements, thereby enabling management to deploy workers where they were needed. This undertaking entailed identifying categories of workers that were suitable for district-wide, multi-sector bargaining units, amalgamating existing bargaining units, and certifying (or, in the language of the report, "designating") unions to represent them.

Government had been pressing the unions to reach consensual arrangements that would preclude or, at minimum, guide any statutorily or administratively imposed solutions. At government's urging, SAHO met with the unions individually and collectively to explore voluntary restructuring options. For the unions, however, the risks were not evenly distributed. Some stood to gain members at other unions' expense or from the 8 percent of the workforce that was hitherto unrepresented. The winners would acquire more resources and be able to exercise greater bargaining power. Those unions with a smaller health sector presence recognized that they were likely to fall prey to the larger, better-entrenched unions and be eliminated from the sector. After two years of discussions, it was apparent that the unions, having spent years establishing their turf, were unwilling to cede their members voluntarily to other unions.

Three separate reports that examined this issue recommended that the SLRB be tasked with the job of representational restructuring.[26] The SLRB, however, made decisions that embraced case-by-case incrementalism, and it therefore preferred voluntary, or *ad hoc*, settlements to rulings that might provide guiding principles for redefining bargaining units.

Pressure for comprehensive third-party action mounted. In Saskatoon, HSAS and SEIU petitioned the SLRB to create district-wide bargaining units, a move that would carve out and transfer segments of each other's membership. The district applied for the creation of three district-wide units composed of, respectively, registered nurses, allied health professionals and support staff.[27]

Apprehensive about the precedential implications of any SLRB action prompted by Saskatoon's application, CUPE, SGEU, SUN and SEIU, with SAHO's concurrence, jointly approached the government. They urged the appointment of a commission to reconfigure bargaining units in a way that would respect existing bargaining units, where possible, and ensure provincial bargaining. They also requested that the process permit all who might be affected by representational restructuring to provide input.[28.]

Government complied and acted swiftly. In July 1996, it enacted *The Health Labour Relations Reorganization (Commissioner) Act*, which empowered a commission to reorganize health sector labour relations. The commission was directed to consider relationships emerging from health reform, the goal of integrating service delivery, the need to move toward consistent sector-wide terms and conditions of employment, and the history of union representation.[29]

The commission's powers were enormous. It would determine bargaining units, designate exclusive bargaining agents for the employees, and establish rules for integrating employees into those units, including seniority rights for unionized and unrepresented employees. Where a unit's employees were covered by multiple agreements, the commission would decide which would pertain. It would also define a multi-employer bargaining structure and designate the employers' representative, set common contract expiry dates and assume additional responsibilities pertinent to the Act's intent. In addition, the Act placed a three-year moratorium on any SLRB rulings that might interfere with the commission's findings.[30]

After consulting the parties, the government named James Dorsey as commissioner. He undertook his duties on September 1, 1996, and produced his report on January 15, 1997. The report, *Reorganization of Saskatchewan's Health Labour Relations,* rejected multi-union bargaining, defined three employee units and designated the unions that would represent the workers in each unit:

- The Nurse Unit is provincial and is composed of registered nurses. SUN, the unit's designated representative, grew by 800 members.
- The Health Support Practitioner Unit, also provincial, includes occupations that typically require registration under an Act conferring exclusive right to an occupational title, notably, chiropodists, physical, occupational and dental therapists, social workers, dieticians, pharmacists, and speech pathologists. The Commission directed that a vote be taken to determine majority support. HSAS won that certification vote.
- The Health Services Provider Unit is district wide and includes the remaining non-managerial and non-confidential employees such as lab technicians and dietary, housekeeping, clerical, patient aide and maintenance workers. In all but one district, either SEIU or CUPE was designated to represent these workers, depending on which union already represented the large majority in the district. In the one district where a vote was held, SGEU won.
- The Regina Laundry, represented by the Retail Wholesale and Department Store Union, and for-profit employers, Extendicare, were left as separate units.

The report designated SAHO as the employers' exclusive bargaining representative, i.e. the health sector's "accredited" bargaining representative, and made association membership mandatory for all districts and most affiliates. It also stipulated that SAHO's governance structure would have to be adjusted to permit affiliate participation on its board.[31]

Under the Dorsey Commission, the four main health unions (CUPE, SEIU, SUN and HSAS) consolidated their hold on the right to represent the province's health workers, while SGEU was nearly eliminated as a health sector union. The 25 collective agreements would decline to ten, and the parties were to determine which agreement would pertain to previously unrepresented workers. Seniority, including non-unionized workers' years of service, was made portable into the new units.[32]

Anticipating the next phase of the health labour relations restructuring, the Dorsey Report provided:

> There will have to be negotiation of the merging and melding of collective agreements. The creation of new units does not automatically extend existing 'unit' rights to the scope of new units. Benefits do not automatically move to either the highest or lowest among the agreements. Consistency and any cost to achieve it are to be incurred over time – probably a number of years and rounds of collective bargaining.[33]

The creation of district-wide locals reshaped intra-union political dynamics. Some long-standing political fiefdoms were successfully challenged, shifting power to different groups. Now, with their bargaining power increased and future bargaining agendas already set, the major health unions turned their attention to standardizing the terms and conditions of employment in merged units.

Collective bargaining

With the TMA and representational restructuring concluded, the third health labour relations restructuring phase, negotiating new collective agreements, began. Centralized bargaining between individual unions and multi-employer associations in the home care, long-term care and acute care sectors had been the norm. The new regime consolidated negotiations involving these three sectors along with the community and mental health sectors. There would be four major multi-sector agreements.

The first post-Dorsey bargaining round began in the spring of 1999. Negotiations included a focus on settling upon common terms and conditions of employment for each union. The key issues involved standardizing contract language, pay, benefits and hours of work, for example, statutory holidays and vacations. For management, these issues were fraught with operational, administrative and cost implications. The unions argued for adopting the best existing provisions as the norm.

Monetary issues were also important. Driven by the province's perennially tenuous fiscal situation, government insisted that unions in Crown corporations and the public sector sign three-year agreements providing for increases of no more than 2 percent in each year. Government's determination to win these terms had been exemplified in 1998, when it took the extraordinary step of legislating SaskPower workers, who had been locked out, back to work and imposing a collective agreement with the 2-2-2 percent provision. The government, with its electoral mandate nearing expiration, wanted to create favourable conditions before calling an election.

Health workers were not in an accommodating mood. Restructuring had affected many negatively, creating a sense of grievance and militancy. Health districts were larger, more impersonal organizations. They required employees to work more intensely and with less supervision. Workplace conditions were often more stressful. The loyalty most workers felt to the pre-existing smaller, more narrowly focused and personally managed work organizations had waned. Layoffs, understaffing and the changing composition of the workforce, as less than full-time status became more common, had also weakened their organizational commitment. They did not find government's guidelines compelling.

Restructuring had increased unions' bargaining power. Bargaining unit amalgamation meant that health workers across all sectors could bargain and take job action simultaneously. The new bargaining structures would make it more difficult for districts to deliver skeletal and essential services during strikes. The integration of health services meant that managers from other sectors could not replace the strikers. Furthermore, heath reform had significantly thinned management ranks, and the acuity levels of individuals in hospitals, long-term facilities and home care had risen markedly.

Government and SAHO experienced intra-organizational problems that undermined SAHO's effectiveness as the employers' representative before negotiations began. Their relationship had soured a year earlier over a matter involving the disposition of a sizeable surplus in the SAHO Retirement Plan. The cash-strapped government felt that it had not been adequately consulted before SAHO acted. Coincidentally, the incoming Minister of Health brought experience from the Department of Education, where government has long exerted direct control over teacher negotiations and marginalized the Saskatchewan School Trustees' Association.[34] To make matters worse, SAHO suffered the untimely departure of the vice-president in charge of labour relations and two key staff negotiators.

The Minister and Deputy Minister of Health began to meddle in the initial set of negotiations, those involving CUPE. The unions learned that they could end run SAHO and pitch their case directly to government. Dismayed SAHO negotiators encountered union counterparts who knew more about the government's thinking on key issues than they did. They also found health districts' operational concerns being given short shrift in the politically charged environment.

Government's involvement in the SUN negotiations was extreme. SAHO negotiators conferred directly and extensively with senior officials including the ministers of Health, Labour and Finance, assorted deputy ministers and a representative of the Personnel Policy Secretariat. SAHO's board chair assumed a high-profile labour relations role despite his lack of expertise in the area. The most visible intervention was the premier's abortive, last-minute attempt to negotiate the settlement.

In April 1999, SUN struck over a myriad of monetary and non-monetary issues, including a contentious proposal for independent assessment committees composed of nurses to make binding decisions about workplace staffing. Warned by the large districts that they would not be able to deliver essential services, the government promptly enacted back-to-work legislation. The legislation imposed an agreement that paid nominal obeisance to but in a variety of areas substantially exceeded the 2-2-2 percent guideline. The outraged nurses defied the legislation as well as an ensuing court order directing them to return to work.

Except for the scope of the strike and health organizations' heightened sense of vulnerability, little had changed from previous SUN strikes. During the 1988 and 1991 strikes, hospitals had been forced to rely upon SUN locals to provide essential services. In neither case had management/government capitulated; nor had there been situations that were construed as medical emergencies. In 1999, SUN implemented protocols identical to those used in 1991 with similar results. It adopted a "contingent services" strategy:

> A roving emergency services team of union nurses decides where real emergencies exist and calls in help; this help is removed as soon as the situation has been stabilized; management receives no guarantees from the union other than emergencies will be dealt with.[35]

The strike's impact was severe and cumulatively more disruptive. Health districts were at local nurses' mercy. Local nurses decided what essential service coverage to provide. All but the most urgent services were interrupted. Although some of the most seriously ill were sent out of the province, the needs of seriously ill patients were met.

After ten days, the nurses returned to work, negotiations resumed and an agreement was concluded. (SUN was subsequently found in contempt, fined $120,000 and ordered to pay $30,000 in costs.) Plans for a spring election were dashed. The NDP's relations with its labour constituency had hit a low.

The experience of the three SUN strikes is revealing. Health strikes are difficult for managers who are ordinarily accountable for service delivery to abide. The situation requires them to surrender control over the provision of essential services and to trust the nurses. The degree of cooperation that local management received during these strikes reflected the tone of the parties' local relationships. Units with trusting relationships typically enjoyed a more generous accommodation and weathered the strikes better than those with conflictive relationships.

The strikes also highlight the importance of decentralizing decision making regarding essential services coverage. While provincial-level bodies can develop guidelines, operational decisions are best made at the site and service levels by locals who understand the workplace, what services are essential, patients' needs and the out-of-scope staff's capabilities. Nurses' locals have generally acted responsibly, knowing that the strike would collapse unless union members and the public were satisfied that essential services coverage was being maintained.[36]

Finally, the 1999 strike suggests the inadvisability of unilateral government action to end a legal health strike in the absence of a demonstrable medical emergency. SUN values its right to strike and prides itself upon acting responsibly. The government's decision to curb collective rights based on fear of what could happen provoked an illegal backlash.

By exercising direct control in the first round of post-Dorsey bargaining, government reversed a well-established NDP labour relations tradition and the devolutionary philosophy of its own health reform program. Its hands-on approach undermined and humiliated SAHO's professional negotiators and cast doubt on the association's future. Some union negotiators openly sympathized with their counterparts' plight. When SAHO members recognized that their association had lost the capacity to direct bargaining, the organization's standing deteriorated. Other weaknesses also manifested themselves during negotiations, notably the inadequacy of the SAHO payroll system for generating the figures and information required by negotiators. The 1999 bargaining round was a low point for SAHO.

The government and SAHO subsequently recognized and addressed their problems. Three senior government bureaucrats, one from each of the Health and Finance departments, and the Personnel Policy Secretariat, were added to SAHO's Strategic Advisory Committee to discuss strategy and evolve bargaining mandates. SAHO and PPS representatives meet frequently, and SAHO meets with the Cabinet Committee on Collective Bargaining if there is an impending crisis. The association coordinates its communication strategy with that of the Department of Health to ensure that confusing or contradictory information is not issued. Otherwise, SAHO is being left alone to negotiate and deal with the unions.

The most promising development of the first post-Dorsey bargaining round was interest-based bargaining initiatives undertaken by SAHO, SEIU and HSAS. These were joint efforts to explore the complex problems associated with merging pre-existing agreements in ways that considered the needs of both parties. Talks on non-monetary issues were conducted collaboratively. However, SEIU reverted to adversarialism and threatened to strike before concluding a monetary deal directly with government. That deal was based on the SUN settlement. (SEIU has since ended its affiliation with the NDP.)

In 1999, the Department of Health commissioned a report to examine health sector human resources challenges, including the shortage and dissatisfaction of nurses. The report noted that both labour and management faulted government's failure to offer vision and leadership. Providers raised concerns about the quality and quantity of management. The report urged SAHO to provide more management training on operating under collective agreements. It also suggested that the parties search for operational innovations and agreement language that address the industry's human resource problems and clients' needs.[37]

The second post-Dorsey bargaining round began in 2001. CUPE struck for six days. Health districts did not request government intervention and government did not meddle. SAHO helped to prepare districts to deliver essential services during a strike. When the strike appeared imminent, units pared services and put volunteers in place. Health districts withstood the strike while SAHO and CUPE bargained workload, monetary and pension issues. The government and SAHO had learned from their mistakes. Finally, problems associated with unions making decisions about providing essential services at the provincial level became evident.

SEIU and SAHO settled following CUPE in bargaining that again was interest based until monetary issues were addressed. A strike was narrowly averted. However, a willingness to resort to job action resurfaced in the fall of 2001, when laboratory technicians in Regina covered by a valid CUPE agreement struck to demand higher wages. The impact of recent Alberta settlements, especially for those groups with a strong national or international labour market, was evident. In the spring of 2002, SUN settled for a 20 percent wage increase over two years, plus additional sweeteners. Moreover, the traditionally non-militant HSAS began contemplating job action.

Analysis

Saskatchewan's health reform is rooted in a social democratic government's commitment to preserving publicly funded universal health care. The incremental reformist approach was heavily influenced by the need to control costs. The initial budget cuts and the creation of HSURC were intended to catalyze more effective resource use. The emphasis on wellness was designed to move the system's focus beyond high-cost institutional care to the more cost-effective areas of health promotion and illness/injury prevention. Structural changes devolved responsibility to and consolidated service delivery in health districts. The districts assumed the obligation of identifying local needs and delivering the most appropriate mix of integrated health services within the available resources. While government remained accountable for the system as a whole, the Department of Health's formal roles were largely confined to funding, legislation and policy development, and establishing broad program and service standards.

In 1993, the government identified labour relations restructuring as a component of health reform. It struck the Labour Relations Review Committee to examine issues related to this undertaking. In light of the health industry's high labour intensity and unionization, and a wellness policy objective that seemed to suggest the need for consensual rather than adversarial industrial relations, the committee chair observed:

> The system cries for leadership from a more activist, involved and visionary government that understands the kind of labour relations that should accompany "Wellness" and that can sustain its larger vision of how health care should be provided. The potential to build more cooperative, participative and productive employee relations exists, but it requires a persistent and consistent champion. At least in the short term, that must be government.[38]

The NDP government was prepared to negotiate labour relations restructuring and demonstrated degrees of patience, sensitivity and forbearance uncharacteristic of governments implementing major change. It developed collaborative approaches to restructuring using its ties with labour as well as its fiscal, administrative and legislative powers. The government, however, has been satisfied with traditional approaches to industrial relations and not inclined to explore or promote innovation.[39]

The government brokered and modestly funded a labour adjustment scheme to assist workers affected by mergers, closures and the rationalization of service delivery. When it became evident that unions' fractured representational structures could not be rationalized voluntarily, government, at the parties' behest, created the Dorsey Commission. By amalgamating local unions and bargaining units, the commission rationalized representational structures to be consistent with the health organizations' structures. Three district-wide bargaining units replaced myriad units based on five distinct service sectors and hundreds of employing agencies. Health districts got greater flexibility to deploy their workforce. At the same time, the dominant unions emerged larger, more comprehensive and stronger; the impact of strikes would be district-wide across all health sectors as well as multidistrict, or even province wide.

With government's encouragement, the health districts built a collective provincial presence in the form of a multipurpose employers association (SAHO) to represent and serve industry. Its role is also to liaise. SAHO assumed that its role in collective bargaining would be to carry on much as its predecessors had under previous NDP governments, distancing government from and linking it to the monetary side of provincial multi-employer negotiations. Representing both government and the employers, it anticipated professionalizing and depoliticizing bargaining by negotiating operational and monetary issues with its union counterparts.

This NDP government, however, did not initially share its predecessors' preference for keeping politicians out of the industrial relations fray. Driven by a number of factors, including suspicions about SAHO's loyalty and competence, government responded to union enticements to politicize bargaining. Indeed, in the first post-Dorsey bargaining round (1999), the professional industry negotiators became bystanders, or government functionaries, and health districts' operational concerns were relegated to second-order status.

Saskatchewan's health reform on a shoestring budget took its toll. Local management was overwhelmed, under-resourced and unprepared for the enormous restructuring challenge. Repeated workplace disruptions, work intensification, diminished job status, inadequate management support, loss of security and wage restraint made it difficult for workers to transfer the commitment that they had for their old organizations to the new health units. Many ceased being grateful just to hold jobs. Militancy grew, especially in rural areas, where maintaining health facilities was (and remains) a particularly contentious issue. Workers and their unions became increasingly determined to win parity with other health workers and those in other jurisdictions.

Restructuring went relatively smoothly until the point of bargaining the first post-Dorsey collective agreements. The parties faced the formidable task of aligning disparate provisions of previous agreements from different unions and health sectors; they also had to address monetary issues. Both CUPE and SUN used strategies that combined traditional adversarialism and political bargaining.[40] They bypassed SAHO when possible and negotiated with the politicians. SUN negotiations culminated in a confrontation of historic proportions. After high-profile negotiations failed, the government quickly intervened with legislation to prevent strike action and imposed a settlement. Regardless, the nurses, despite a court injunction ordering them back to work, remained on an illegal strike until government consented to negotiate a settlement. By contrast, SEIU and HSAS entered into interest-based bargaining with SAHO to address myriad complex bargaining issues. SEIU, however, followed its cohorts' adversarial leads in bargaining monetary issues.

The bargaining debacle with SUN contributed to the NDP's nearly losing the election later that year. Before the 2002 bargaining round, government rethought its role. It worked with SAHO to refine mechanisms for interaction and abandoned direct involvement in bargaining, leaving SAHO to conduct negotiations in consultation with senior government officials. The government refrained from intervening in disruptive legal and wildcat CUPE strikes. SUN negotiated a 20 percent pay increase that reflected the Alberta nurses' settlement, plus a number of sweeteners. The previously quiescent HSAS struck for four weeks to win its version of the favourable pattern for health professionals.

Saskatchewan has used a mixed approach to health labour relations restructuring. Its experience demonstrates the utility of negotiated settlements, the value of judicious use of third-party action, and the perils of unilateralism. Considerable experience was gained. The government is implementing Commission on Medicare (Fyke Commission) recommendations that the number of health districts be substantially reduced and that human resources planning and management be approached provincially.[41] The move from 32 to 12 districts has not been excessively disruptive, and a province-wide joint job evaluation system, which will reduce the number of job classifications from 900 to fewer than 300, will facilitate a provincial approach to managing human resources.

Nonetheless, the challenge of negotiating agreements without disruptions remains. Cash-strapped health organizations have not proven conducive to building healthy or happy workplaces. The province is not fiscally situated to absorb expensive out-of-province settlements sought by health professionals. The unions have emerged from health reform with militant memberships and a structure that permits them to mount devastatingly comprehensive and disruptive job actions.

Health employers question the efficacy of the unions' unfettered right to strike, but recognize the lack of clearly satisfactory alternatives, particularly where unions'/workers' willingness to undertake illegal action is manifest. Management's concern is well based. Despite their experience in dealing with strikes, the parties have not reached understandings to protect the public. This leaves managers feeling extremely vulnerable. The old way of providing essential services, i.e. using out-of-scope staff from unaffected sectors plus whatever the union supplies, leaves management with little control during province- and industry-wide strikes. The futility of unilateralist action to coerce unions willing to defy back-to-work legislation and injunctions is obvious.

The public, government, unions, union members and management have a common interest in ensuring that service disruptions are minimized and that essential services are provided during strikes. The right to strike must be made contingent upon unions explicitly accepting responsibility for providing essential and emergency services. This seems to call for the parties to negotiate protocols guaranteeing those services.[42] They should be up to the task.

The frustration felt by government, management, labour and the public regarding health sector strikes is understandable. The desire for "a better way" is discussed, by some, in terms of technique, for example, final-offer selection arbitration. There is a tendency to fixate on conflict without examining its causes and to overlook what has been accomplished. The sector's entire industrial relations structure and processes have been reorganized and rationalized with minimal transitional funding. The number of collective agreements has been reduced to a handful. A province-wide joint job evaluation system has been completed. Restructuring has been an enormous undertaking characterized both by a considerable degree of cooperation and by a predictable level of conflict. The parties have learned to address complex issues. Perhaps the conflict should be viewed as a normal outcome in an environment of free collective bargaining rather than as the essence of a new order.

Concern about conflict might more productively be refocused on creating more worker-friendly work organizations. It might also be useful to consider whether collective bargaining for registered nurses and health professionals should occur nationally, at the level of the labour market, instead of provincially. This may also be the time for government to lead the parties in the direction of partnerships, as the New Zealand government has tried. Unions' institutional security and their members' welfare are linked to a viable publicly-provided health care delivery system.

Afterword

Pursuant to a report authored by Michael Shaw in July 2003,[43] Saskatchewan undertook further health labour relations restructuring. Entitled *Organizational Review of Health Sector Collective Bargaining (Employer-side)*, the report contains recommendations intended to identify: 1) "the most effective model for employer representation" in "bargaining and labour relations administration" and 2) "the most appropriate role for government". The Shaw Report reflects observers' inferences to the effect that the employer's side of the system has been "stressed tested" and found wanting. It notes concerns about power imbalances, lack of an appropriate defined role for government, ill will among the parties, and the structure's failure to align interests and accountabilities.

The report summarizes the interests of the RHAs, SAHO and the government. It observes that although government can delegate responsibility for service delivery, it remains accountable. In the past, it finds, employer bargaining representatives were not provided with proper mandates, direction or adequate resources. Henceforth, the report concludes, government must provide health bargainers with strategic direction and make tactical decisions. SAHO should operate under government supervision as well as serve its members.

The report recommends an RHA/health partnership model which government subsequently adopted. Under it, government eclipses SAHO by assuming centre stage. The Department of Health is assigned the role of planning and directing negotiations *via* the newly created Health Labour Relations Council. The department names three members to the Council, which also includes a representative from each of the two largest RHAs and two selected by the others. The RHAs designate a co-chair. (This seat has been vacant for eight months preceding the current bargaining round.)

Department representatives sit at bargaining tables. The department has hired five industrial relations persons. The Department of Finance's Personnel Policy Secretariat, the Cabinet Committee on Public Sector Compensation and Cabinet still oversee health sector bargaining. SAHO staffers continue to act as the employers' bargaining spokespersons.

With government in such a prominent position and SAHO's labour relations role minimized, unions are better positioned to pursue their agendas through political bargaining. If they do not like what they hear at the negotiating table, under a labour-friendly government they can lobby politicians charged with overseeing bargaining. Operational concerns at the RHA's operational concerns are less likely to receive strong advocacy under this arrangement.

Acknowledgements

The author acknowledges the assistance of Raeanne Obrigewitsch in researching this paper and the Saskatchewan's Health Service Utilization and Research Commission for funding.

Notes

1. World Health Organization, Health and Welfare Canada and Canadian Public Health Association, *Ottawa Charter for Health Promotion*, First International Conference on Health Promotion, Ottawa, 1986.
2. Canada, *Canada Health Act*, R.S.C. 1985, c. C-6 (Ottawa: Queen's Printer).
3. Robert Murray, *Future Directions For Health Care In Saskatchewan* (Regina: Department of Health), 1990.
4. Saskatchewan, Department of Health, *A Saskatchewan Vision for Health: A Framework for Change* (Regina), 1992.
5. Saskatchewan, *The Health Districts Act*, S.S. 1992, c. H-0.01 (Regina: Queen's Printer).
6. Walter Podiluk, *Partners in Health Care: District Boards – Affiliate Agencies* (Regina: Department of Health), 1996. The unique character, mission, beliefs and historical status of faith-sponsored organizations provided a rationale for avoiding amalgamation. Instead, some 65 chose to "affiliate" with the districts and retain their own boards and management.
7. Saskatchewan, Department of Finance, *Delivering the Promise*: Budget Address (Regina), 1994; *A New Day Dawning for Saskatchewan*: Budget

Address (Regina), 1995; *Preparing for the New Century*: Budget Address (Regina), 1996. Figures from the Department of Health reveal actual health expenditures (in billions) and the percentage they represent of overall spending excluding debt repayments: 1990–91, $1.530 (33.9%); 1991–92, $1.581 (36.2%); 1992–93, $1.548 (36.6%); 1993–94, $1.464 (35.9%); 1994–95, $1.534 (36.4%); 1995–96, $1.555 (36.5%); 1996–97, $1.608 (37.4%); 1998–99, $1.775 (39.4%); 1999–00, $1.915 (39.5%) (budgeted).

8. Steven Lewis, presentation at Health Education Forum, Saskatoon, 1993.

9. Saskatchewan, *The Trade Union Act*, R.S.S. 1978, c. T-17 (Regina: Queen's Printer).

10. K. Wetzel, C. Maxey and D. Gallagher, "Management and Union Assessments of Multi-Employer Bargaining in Health Care: A Canadian Example," *Journal Of Health And Human Resources Administration* 7, 4 (1985): 445–459.

11. K. Wetzel and D. G. Gallagher, "The Saskatchewan Government's Internal Arrangements to Accommodate Collective Bargaining," *Relations Industrielles* 34, 3 (1979): 452–469; K. Wetzel and D. G. Gallagher, "Management Structures to Accommodate Multi-Employer Hospital Bargaining in Western Canada," in G. Swimmer and M. Thompson (eds) *Conflict or Compromise: The Future of Public Sector Industrial Relations* (Ottawa: Institute for Research on Public Policy), 1984, pp. 499–514.

12. K. Wetzel, *The Labour Relations of "Wellness,"* Report of the Chair of the Labour Relations Review Committee (Regina: Department of Health), 1993, pp. 7–8.

13. *Ibid.*, 1–38.

14. Podiluk, 1996.

15. Exclusion occasioned resentment on the part of overlooked senior managers. They believed that they had been doing what their roles required, i.e. competing with each other for status and resources, and that this should not have precluded their being considered to lead health reform.

16. Physicians belong to the Saskatchewan Medical Association, a vocal and effective interest group. Government has not attempted to rationalize the delivery of physician services, restructure the fee-for-service payment system, or modify physicians' role as the system's gatekeepers, even though health reform's wellness and fiscal objectives are unachievable without the active involvement of the medical community. Physicians continue to enjoy autonomy not afforded to other groups.

17. The Saskatchewan Health-Care Association Board of Directors included representatives of the Catholic Health Association and the Saskatchewan Association of Health Service Executives. The board of the Saskatchewan Association of Special Care Homes comprised roughly equal numbers of trustees and managers, and the Saskatchewan Home Care Association's board also had management representation.

18. In the fall of 2002, in response to the move to 12 regional health authorities, SAHO increased its board size to include 14 regional health board members and one affiliate representative. Under the new arrangement, each health authority selects someone from its own board to sit on the SAHO board. In recognition of their size, the two largest authorities have two seats each.

19. Saskatchewan Association of Health Organizations, *Annual Report, 1997–98* (Regina), 1998, p. 20.

20. Saskatchewan, Department of Health, *A Framework of Accountability* (Regina), 1995.
21. Saskatchewan, Health Labour Relations Reorganization Commission, *Reorganization of Saskatchewan's Health Labour Relations* (Regina), 1997, Appendix I, pp. 34–35.
22. The Professional Institute of the Public Service (PIPS) represented 11 registered nurses employed at the Veterans' Home, and the Retail Wholesale and Department Store Union (RWDSU) represented the Regina Laundry.
23. Health Reform Transition Coordinating Committee, "Transfer/Merger Agreement," in *Labour Adjustment Strategies* (Regina: Department of Health), 1993, p. 3.
24. *Ibid.*, 4–11.
25. Provincial Joint Union Management Adjustment Committee, *Career Adjustment Assistance Program: Employer's Manual* (Regina), 1994.
26. Health Providers Human Resource Committee, *The Education, Regulation and Utilization of Saskatchewan Health Providers: Adapting to Health Reform and Changes in Society* (Regina: Department of Health), 1996, pp. 23, 26; R. Reavley and R. Sentes, *New Directions For Healthcare Labour Relations in the 1990s* (Regina: Department of Health), 1993; Wetzel, 1993.
27. "Proposal for the Establishment of an Independent Health Labour Relations Commissioner," as cited in Health Labour Relations Reorganization Commission, *Reorganization of Saskatchewan's Health Labour Relations* (Regina), 1997, pp. 40–43.
28. *Ibid.*, Appendix B, 95–105.
29. Saskatchewan, *The Health Labour Relations Reorganization (Commissioner) Act,* S. S., 1996, c. H-0.03 s.5(6)(a)–(e) (Regina: Queen's Printer).
30. *Ibid.*, s.6(2)(a)–(i).
31. Saskatchewan Health Labour Relations Reorganization Commission, 62–63, 66–83.
32. *Ibid.*, 80–84.
33. *Ibid.*, 84.
34. D. G. Gallagher and K. Wetzel, "Centralized Multi-Employer Negotiations in Public Education: An Examination of the Saskatchewan Experience", *Journal of Collective Negotiations 9*, 4 (1980): 281–95.
35. Larry Haiven and Judy Haiven, *The Right to Strike and the Provision of Emergency Services in Canadian Health Care* (Ottawa: Canadian Centre for Policy Alternatives) 2002.
36. Bernard Adell, Michel Grant and Allen Ponak, *Strikes in Essential Services* (Kingston, Ontario: IRC Press), 2001, 144–181; Larry Haiven, "The Provision of Essential Services During Nurses' Strikes in Canada," paper presented at Canadian Sociology and Anthropology Association annual conference, 1992, pp. 9–14; Larry Haiven, "Industrial Relations in Health Care: Regulation, Conflict and Transition to the 'Wellness Model,'" in Gene Swimmer and Mark Thompson (eds) *Public Sector Collective Bargaining in Canada* (Kingston, Ontario: IRC Press), 1995, pp. 261–3.
37. Allen Backman, *Health Workplace Opportunities and Challenges for Saskatchewan: Job Satisfaction, Retention, Recruitment and Skill Mix for a Sustainable Health Care System* (Regina: Department of Health), 2000.
38. Wetzel, 1993: 38

39. Dan Cameron, "The Crisis in Public Sector Bargaining in Saskatchewan," *Policy Options* (September 2001): 1–7._

40. Coincidentally, nurses in Newfoundland, New Brunswick, Quebec, Manitoba and British Columbia were involved in disputes at about the same time.

41. Saskatchewan, Commission on Medicare, *Caring for Medicare: Sustaining A Quality System* (Regina), 2001.

42. These agreements might specify the means for determining essential service levels and delivering those services as well as ways for dealing with changing situations and emergencies. Government might be left to monitor local situations and determine whether acceptable service coverage is being provided. Only after a strike has demonstrably created medical grounds for declaring an emergency should government intervene to curtail a job action.

43. Michael Shaw, *Organizational Review of Health Sector Collective Bargaining (Employer-side): Recommendations*, report prepared for and submitted to Saskatchewan Health (Regina), July 2003.

6
Health Labour Relations in the Klein Era

Kurt Wetzel

Introduction

From the inception of Alberta's health restructuring in 1993 and into 2003, the province's health system has been driven by a consistent neoconservative agenda. Over this period, the government has not changed and has enjoyed huge parliamentary majorities. Its agenda has been to marketize the health sector. To this end, it has exercised its legislative and administrative fiat to restructure and oversee operation of the public health services delivery system. This paper explores the Alberta government's approach to health labour relations restructuring and the implications of its policies for health sector unions and management. In addition to examining structural and operational issues for the parties, it discusses the industrial climate that has emerged.

Background

The province of Alberta, located in western Canada, takes in an area of approximately 660,000 square kilometres between the western border of Saskatchewan and eastern border of coastal British Columbia. Its population of just over three million people, roughly 80 percent urban and 20 percent rural, represents nearly 7 percent of Canada's total population.

Alberta politics has a pattern of punctuated equilibrium. That is, extended periods of stable, single-party rule have been followed by quick electoral change to a different one-party regime, albeit a regime that was not previously a numerically significant opposition party. These governments' industrial relations and social policies have favoured employers and prized self-reliance. The province's minimum wage, employment standards, per capita health and social spending, and taxes are Canada's lowest as is its unionization rate. Most provincial public employees, including healthcare workers, are barred from striking.[1] Majority representation on union certification applications is determined by ballot, as in the US, rather than by signed cards.

Alberta's economy and politics mirror the petroleum markets. During the oil boom of the 1970s and early 1980s, Premier Lougheed's government spent lavishly on health care, especially on physical infrastructure, and the industrial relations climate was conciliatory. Oil prices, which peaked at US$41 per barrel in 1981, sank to $10 in 1986. Provincial oil and gas revenues declined from C$6 billion in 1985 to C$2.7 billion in 1987. The Getty government, 1985–1992, curtailed public program spending, making Alberta's average annual rate of increase in program spending over this period the lowest in Canada, 2.3 percent versus 6.8 percent nationwide. While health care spending remained steady, as measured in constant dollars per capita adjusted for population growth, expenditures for education, social services, environment and transportation fell by 40 percent. Industrial and agricultural subsidies, however, continued to contribute to the province's fiscal woes, costing a net C$5.3 billion.[2]

In 1987, the government acknowledged the need for health reform by establishing the Premier's Commission on Future Health Care for Albertans. The commission was mandated to examine the health care delivery system and recommend changes that would enable the province to meet future needs. It heard from 200 individuals and 179 interest groups, including health unions. In 1990, it released the *Rainbow Report: Our Vision of Health*, a comprehensive health care review containing 21 major recommendations.

The Premier promptly struck a Cabinet task force:

> ... to ensure that any recommendation accepted and implemented would support the principles of universality and reasonable access, provide for the continued provision of basic health services, support health promotion, take into account environmental and economic factors and not restrict access to health services because of an individual's ability to pay.[3]

The Cabinet report, *Partners in Health: The Government of Alberta's Response to the Premier's Commission on Future Health Care for Albertans*, addressed each recommendation. It noted strong support for a public health care system and endorsed citizen involvement, the principles of the *Canada Health Act*, health promotion programs, going beyond the medical model, and a vision of health that would partner the public, health care providers and government. It indicated a willingness to fund health research, substance abuse initiatives, long-term and acute care facilities and a continuum of care across health units, but it stopped short of recommending regionalized health services.[4] The *Rainbow Report* and the government's response to it paralleled similar undertakings elsewhere in Canada, for example, Saskatchewan's Murray Commission Report. The vision embraced by *Partners in Health* was strikingly similar to Saskatchewan's "wellness" model. However, the *Rainbow Report* proved to be a false start, as it was not used as the basis for health reform.

By 1993, the provincial deficit had surpassed $3 billion and the debt exceeded $11 billion. To avoid being eclipsed in the upcoming election by the surging Liberals, the Tories, led by Ralph Klein, reinvented themselves as a party much further to the right. After being returned to power, they promised to transform the province by fulfilling four campaign commitments.[5]

The first commitment was to eliminate deficit budgets and retire the debt by 2010 without raising taxes or instituting new ones. The *Deficit Elimination Act* (1993) imposed a four-year timetable for balancing the budget and proscribed future deficits. Excessive spending on health, education and social services was cited in the 1993 Throne Speech as a threat to other essential public services. The government pledged to reduce spending by a minimum of 20 percent over four years and called upon every department, agency and government-funded organization to produce three-year business plans reflecting this contingency. Public sector wages and salaries were to be cut by 5 percent.

The second commitment was to create a climate that would encourage private sector job creation. The Alberta Advantage – the lowest taxes and most entrepreneur-friendly climate in Canada – would be promoted to domestic and international investors.

The government's third commitment involved reorganizing, reducing and streamlining government. The Klein Revolution envisioned smaller government devoid of waste and a citizenry that relied more on itself and less on government. Government would set policy, define standards and fund services, which, ideally, would be provided by agencies operating at arm's length from it. Liquor stores, road maintenance, motor vehicle licensing, enforcement of provincial labour standards and land titles registration would be privatized. Regulations would be revised and, where possible, eliminated. The Throne Speech proffered as a goal: "As much as possible, getting out of direct business subsidies ... ".[6]

The fourth commitment was to consult and listen to the citizenry at public roundtables. Government would use this vehicle to identify the most appropriate ways to revamp service provision.

During this period, the neoconservative revolution occurring in New Zealand was being perceived worldwide by right-wing reformers as offering economic and political promise. The Alberta Progressive Conservatists (PCs) were sympathetic to the economic thinking, political goals and bold methods embraced by New Zealand governments in the 1980s and 1990s. Former New Zealand Finance Minister Roger Douglas, architect of that country's restructuring, encouraged the Alberta reformers. Addressing the PC caucus in 1993, he stated that, based on his experience, critics of restructuring could be thrown into disarray if changes were introduced quickly and simultaneously across a broad front. In New Zealand, he noted, the opposition was finding it difficult to coalesce, focus and respond.[7] The Klein government apparently listened.

While the Throne Speech did not identify health reform as a priority, action on that front was quickly undertaken. The Ministry of Health sponsored ten "Public Roundtables on Health" between September 9 and October 30, 1993. Government issued invitations, set agendas and prepared information packages for participants. Some unions were invited after protesting that they had been excluded, but they were viewed as special interest groups.[8]

Union leaders characterized the roundtables as stage-managed events designed to create the illusion of openness and inclusiveness. They likened the sessions to revival meetings scripted by and for people who shared the government's vision. Discussions were directed and limited, precluding debate among strong-willed, well-informed individuals.[9]

The "Summary of Alberta Roundtables on Health" recommended focusing on the customer, restructuring health services by integrating them, and making services more responsive to communities by removing government from the process and establishing accountability. Proposals for balancing the budget included a 5 percent reduction in compensation and health premiums for the elderly.[10]

The roundtable process culminated in *Starting Points*, an action document released in December 1993 that became Alberta's health reform blueprint. Unlike the *Rainbow Report*, which received passing mention, *Starting Points* offered no vision of high quality, publicly funded health care. Although the five principles of the *Canada Health Act* were appended – namely, universality, comprehensiveness, accessibility, portability and public administration – the report did not discuss how health reform related to them. References to financial considerations and opportunities to privatize recurred throughout. For example, the report asked whether savings could be realized by contracting out dietary, laundry and maintenance services. It noted, "The private sector should be allowed to provide services if the services meet or exceed health standards".[11] Indeed, aspects of the reform scheme challenged the traditions of Canada's medicare system, if not the Act itself.

In contrast to the *Rainbow Report*'s vision for partnering users, providers and government, *Starting Points* advocated "putting the consumer first." It recommended specifying basic taxpayer-supported services, leaving consumers to assume the cost of non-funded services. Adults would continue to pay health insurance premiums ($816 for a family in 2001), and all citizens would be responsible for adopting healthy lifestyles.

Roles for those involved in the system were specified. Providers, for example, would pursue cost effectiveness and help integrate service delivery. Regional health authorities (RHAs) would be established to allocate resources, implement programs and provide "affordable health services." The medical model of service delivery, with its emphasis on institutional care, would yield to an approach more directed at prevention and community-based services. The RHAs would promote "wellness" and be accountable to local boards.

For its part, government would distance itself from service delivery and focus on addressing legislative/regulatory issues, developing health policy and setting budgets. The Ministry of Health would set and monitor standards, establish system direction and priorities, fund service providers, advise and inform, and, only if another agency was unavailable to do so, directly provide health services.[12]

The *Regional Health Authorities Act* (RHAA), enacted in June 1994, empowered the Minister of Health to delineate the health regions' geographical boundaries and appoint the boards charged with overseeing them. It also provided for the establishment of community health councils, to be appointed by the regional boards, to reflect local needs and concerns.[13] The RHAs were responsible for determining local health needs, setting priorities and allocating resources in order to provide integrated service delivery. They were obligated to submit three-year business plans indicating, in quantifiable terms, how they intended to carry out their mandate and measure their effectiveness. Future funding would depend upon meeting those objectives.

Budget cuts forced the RHAs to implement the government's program swiftly. Alberta Health's three-year business plans for the 1994/95–1996/97 and 1995/96–1997/98 fiscal periods anticipated cutting $740 million, 17.8 percent below the 1992/93 level, the peak budget year. Controlling for population increase, the projected reductions represented a cut of 23.4 percent, or $368 per capita, over the four years. Given a 1 percent annual inflation rate, the cuts amounted to 27 percent. By 1997/98, net health spending was to be $1 billion below its 1992/93 level, and one quarter of the provincial spending cuts was to be made up for by raising medicare premiums.[14]

It has been noted that Alberta's health reform scheme was not innovative. Rather, it was an adaptation of models pioneered in Saskatchewan, the United Kingdom and New Zealand, designed to address circumstances in Alberta, particularly fiscal concerns.[15] The *Rainbow Report*'s call for an improved and participatory health system was shelved in favour of a program that pursued three objectives: downsized and reorganized health services, reduced compensation for health workers and opportunities for private insurance and service providers.[16]

Government industrial relations policy

Alberta has distinguished itself by enacting legislation that limits the capacity of public sector workers to take action collectively. In 1982, government legislation ended a nurses' strike by imposing arbitration and threatening to decertify the union and bar members from union involvement for two years if they failed to comply.[17] Bill 44 (1983), which amended the *Labour Relations Act,* permanently banned provincial public sector strikes and strike threats. In the health sector, the strike proscription applied to workers in hospitals and long-term care facilities designated by the Minister of Health as "approved." It also mandated arbitration to resolve collective bargaining impasses and directed arbitration boards to consider in their awards general economic conditions as well as wages and benefits found in the private and public sectors for both union and non-union workers. Employers could petition the Alberta Labour Relations Board (ALRB) to suspend union dues payments if strike action was deemed illegal.

In 1983, a court found that provisions in Ontario's *Inflation Restraint Act* restricting the right to bargain collectively and strike violated the guarantee of freedom of association contained in Canada's *Charter of Rights and Freedoms.* Demonstrating the depth of his government's resolve to end public sector strikes in Alberta, Premier Lougheed vowed to invoke the Federal Constitution's notwithstanding clause to override any judicial action that might undermine the province's anti-strike legislation. The government petitioned the Alberta Court of Appeal for an advisory judgment, and the court upheld the legislation's constitutionality.[18]

Union complaints about legislation limiting workers' rights in Alberta, Ontario and Newfoundland prompted the International Labour Organization (ILO) to dispatch a study mission to Canada in 1985. The ILO declared that Bill 44 violated union freedoms as called for by the ILO Charter, to which Canada is a signatory. The declaration proved to be a hollow victory, as it did not precipitate a policy change in Alberta.[19]

Alberta labour policy makes it difficult for unions to mount legal resistance against public sector employers determined to impose the government's agenda. The law, however, did not stop the United Nurses of Alberta from undertaking an illegal 19-day strike in 1988 to prevent rollbacks. The union subsequently negotiated a settlement free of takeaways, but the job action led to 22 firings and a $400,000 contempt fine for "threatening to strike" and "causing a strike".[20]

The nurses' strike suggested that the deterrent value of legislation is limited in the face of militant workers who enjoy broad public support. Moreover, the outcome showed that a union willing to pay the price for violating the law could force public sector negotiators to change their positions.

RHAs and the health reform agenda

Seventeen RHAs were created and charged with implementing health reform in the acute care, long-term care and community health sectors. Approximately 50 private and religiously affiliated health organizations, called "voluntaries," retained their boards and some autonomy. While some voluntaries operate acute care facilities, most provide long-term care services. All negotiate a contractual relationship with the RHA that funds them. The Alberta Mental Health Board and the Alberta Cancer Board are the other main service providers.

Although government provides no operating guidelines for the RHAs, it does circumscribe their autonomy. The Ministry of Health specifies minimum spending requirements for community services and caps on acute care expenditures. RHAs' business plans must conform to the Ministry's plan, and each RHA is assigned a ministry advisor who serves as the routine contact for operational matters. Individuals sharing the government's perspectives are appointed to the boards by the minister. (In one case, a non-conforming board was replaced.)

The atmosphere following the creation of the RHAs was predictably chaotic. The new authorities had until September 1994 to submit business plans indicating how they would deliver services with reduced budgets. Operating under tight deadlines, they worked to eliminate duplication, cut waste and improve efficiency by closing and consolidating operating units, amalgamating programs, contracting out support services (e.g. administration, laundry, dietary, housekeeping and maintenance), centralizing services and downgrading facilities. Over vociferous protests, Edmonton's 500-bed Nuns' Hospital was converted from an acute care hospital to a community health facility.[21]

The RHAs laid off managers and staff, reduced work schedules, negotiated wage rollbacks, increased workloads, restructured workplaces, transferred workers and reorganized work. In the process, some found that the certified bargaining units were no longer appropriate for the emerging organizational structures.

RHAs also sought to make their workforces more flexible, cost-effective and responsive to the new environment. They pushed "multi-skilling," the merging of distinct job categories into a classification with a wider range of duties. Workers at Edmonton's Royal Alexandra Hospital, for example, saw tasks previously assigned to porters, cleaners, auxiliary nurses and dietary workers combined into a service associate category. Jobs were reclassified into lower skill and pay categories. Some long-term care licensed practical nurses became nursing assistants because there was insufficient work in their scope of practice to allow them to retain their professional designation. Ironically, this left the employer with flexibility payoffs that were fleeting.

The University of Alberta Hospital attempted to institute employee involvement programs. The unions were excluded from the program planning process and confined to roles that involved reacting to a barrage of management initiatives. Management ignored the unions' organizational constraints and adopted operating modes that threatened their organizational security, their members' welfare and existing collective agreements. Recognizing that management was not committed to pursuing a partnership, the unions resisted the programs.[22]

Government's control over the regional health authorities was contentious on several fronts. It frustrated health service providers, local governments and backbench MLAs, all of whom sought input into RHA operations.[23] The unions regarded the authorities as well-connected fiefdoms, suspicious of each other out of fear of further amalgamation, and not accountable to the public.

Friends of Medicare, reacting to a government-sponsored "health care summit," conducted hearings to ascertain Albertans' view of medicare. (Friends of Medicare is a coalition formed in 1979 in response to perceived threats to Medicare; it includes individual service organizations, social justice groups, unions, churches, and organizations representing a variety of sectors and communities.) It issued a report stating, "the only way to ensure accountability is through democratic elections".[24] However, despite issuing a news release advising that two thirds of RHA board members would be elected in conjunction with municipal elections beginning in 1998, the government remained disinclined to relinquish control.[25]

Government's concession to citizen input was the 16-member Provincial Health Council, established in 1995 with a five-year mandate to assess the health system's performance and suggest improvements. The council, drawing on an expert panel of health professionals for advice on technical and professional issues, issued 30 reports. At the end of its mandate, it urged the government to offer a vision of health care and establish an independent, representative body with "clear legal status" to gather citizen input, plan, monitor and evaluate the system, and make recommendations.[26]

Employers' associations

In the early 1990s, Alberta had well-developed health industry associations. The Alberta Healthcare Association (AHA), founded in 1919, represented 180–200 acute and long-term care facilities. The Health Unit Association of Alberta served public health and home care organizations. The Alberta Long-term Care Association had as members private operators (for profit and non-profit) and public institutions.

AHA was a multi-purpose association. It represented its members to government, the bureaucracy, professional organizations, unions and the public. It negotiated provincial collective agreements and assisted with the administration of those agreements. The association helped members with strategic planning, human resource management, executive recruitment and internal organizational issues including those with a clinical component. It ran training/education programs and administered payrolls and benefits as well as insurance and group purchasing programs.[27] Members supported AHA on a prorated basis. Large institutions paid up to $300,000 in annual assessments and, as in Saskatchewan, used comparatively fewer services than smaller member institutions, which often lacked in-house industrial relations expertise.

Demand for a multi-purpose industry association collapsed with the creation of regional authorities. The RHAs were mandated to operate independently rather than in concert. Even the AHA's biggest potential clients, the small RHAs, anticipated being sufficiently well resourced to operate independently, and they quickly came to prize operational autonomy.

Treating AHA as a perhaps irrelevant artifact, government encouraged the RHAs to abandon pre-existing associations in favour of arrangements suited to the new order. For their part, RHAs were skeptical about the need for an industry association. Given individual board members' strong personal ties to the government, they felt little need for an intermediary. Critics claimed that AHA was too controlling, had failed to focus on its members' needs, and was stuck in the past. Its services did not entice the RHAs, which shared government's predilection for transformational change. Indeed, early indications were that regionalization might reduce, if not end, centralized bargaining.

At the request of the Ministry of Health, which wanted a mechanism for maintaining dialogue with industry, the Council of Chairs was formed. Comprising the chairs of all RHAs and the mental health and cancer boards, the council was designed as a vehicle for exchanging information, providing support and managing relationships among the RHAs and with third parties. While the council is influential and facilitates unified political action – it was, for example, instrumental in convincing the government to delay regional health board elections – it has no mandate to make decisions that would bind the regional authorities.

Throughout 1994, the leadership of the moribund AHA called for a provincial organization that could provide continuity. The association also reinvented itself. It cut staff from 120 to 75 full time equivalents (FTEs), spun off services such as payroll, and proposed merging with the public health unit and long-term care associations to form one provincial industry association. Initially, the RHAs spurned these gestures. They relented, however, when multi-region, if not provincial, collective bargaining appeared likely and AHA produced a plan for an industry organization based on a "business model." The Provincial Health Authorities of Alberta (PHAA) was established in January 1995.

PHAA is a member-owned consultancy that embraces a "federation" rather than "association" model and focuses on providing value to its customers: the RHAs, the provincial cancer and mental health boards, and more than 30 voluntaries. It is governed by a board consisting of five chairs and three CEOs, elected from and by the regional and provincial boards.[28] The board defines the association's market, approves the budget and business plan, hires the CEO and monitors operations.

With a staff of approximately 30 FTEs, PHAA supports the RHAs by facilitating their joint initiatives and providing services. Customer choice, fee-for-service or subscription revenue (instead of prorated membership fees) and the application of free market principles characterize its approach. After a full year of operation, each service was evaluated to determine if a business case could be made for providing it provincially. Group purchasing services were discontinued.

The organization is structured around business units that function on a cost-competitive, cost-recovery basis and serve distinct customer groups; services are not cross-subsidized. There is no formal educational mandate, but staff members conduct some training sessions. Nor is there an annual convention; rather, the Council of Chairs hosts the Health Authorities Forum, which is purely educational.

To ensure that it addresses matters of greatest concern to its members, PHAA has established between eight and ten councils of peers, each with representation from every RHA. These councils, for example, the Council of CEOs, comprise executives who have the power to commit their organizations to undertakings that reside within their realm of responsibility.

PHAA services are provided to members through seven business units operating within three functional divisions: Secretariat Support Services, Insurance Services and Human Management Resources Services. (See Figure 6.1).[29]

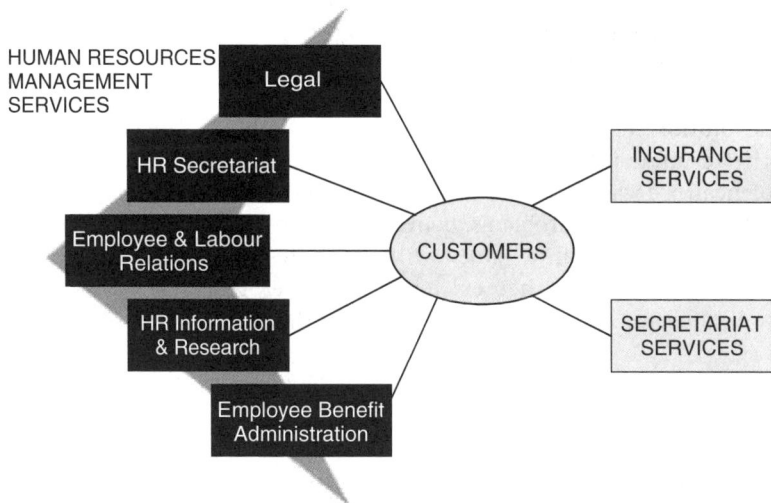

Figure 6.1 PHAA's Business Service Model

Secretariat Services develops policy, conducts research and provides administrative support to health authority councils and industry committees. It facilitates customers' relationships with external bodies and professional associations.

Insurance Services helps customers address their liability and general insurance needs by linking them to insurers.

The remaining five units fall within Human Resources Management Services. The Human Resources Secretariat develops policy, conducts research and assists industry committees addressing industrial relations and human resource issues. These committees include the Human Resources Leaders' Council and the Labour Relations Policy Advisory Council. The latter includes seven labour relations executives and four CEOs from member organizations. It serves the Council of CEOs by providing labour relations strategy advice, nominating bargaining committee members, developing bargaining mandates and overseeing negotiations. The CEOs approve the composition of bargaining teams and, in consultation with government, set bargaining mandates. PHAA staff members serve as negotiators.

Labour Relations supports bargaining and contract administration. It provides advice on grievance handling and works with RHAs on grievances that have broad implications. Human Resource Information and Research conducts salary surveys and analyzes pertinent socio-economic trends. Employee Benefit Management Services consults with customers about benefit plan design and administers the plans. Legal Services offers legal advice and services supporting labour relations activities, namely, labour arbitrations and Alberta Labour Relations Board actions.

PHAA typifies the type of employer organization that the Klein Revolution was eager to create. The unions, however, are critical of it. They claim that PHAA negotiators are remote from the operational side of health organizations and therefore unable to contribute creative solutions to the problems being addressed in bargaining. Rather, they behave like "hired guns" with mandates to fulfil. By generating conflict, they justify their existence. Moreover, the RHAs are not kept well informed about what is happening at the tables.

Health sector unions

In the mid-1970s, the Alberta Labour Relations Board identified standard health service bargaining units for unions representing employees of health organizations, an undertaking which Saskatchewan delayed until the advent of health reform. Hospitals and nursing homes, i.e. "facilities," were parceled into five units: direct nursing (registered nurses); auxiliary nursing (licensed practical nurses); paramedical professional (e.g. dieticians, pharmacists, psychologists); paramedical technical (nondegreed technicals); and general support (maintenance, clerical, housekeeping and dietary workers). Community health services workers were put into three standard bargaining units: nursing; professional; general support. Various unions were certified to represent the same type of employee.

Table 6.1 shows the bargaining units and unions for workers in the facility sector in the early 1990s.[30] The health care sector in Alberta was dominated by six unions. These health unions had no history of co-ordinated action. Nor was their rivalry manifested in enduring, overt inter-organizational enmity.

Table 6.1   Health Unions by Occupational Grouping

Bargaining units	Union
Nursing	– United Nurses of Alberta – Staff Nurses Association – Alberta Union of Provincial Employees
Auxiliary Nursing	– Canadian Health Care Guild – Canadian Union of Public Employees – Health Care Employees Union of Alberta – United Steelworkers of America – Christian Labour Alliance of Canada
Paramedical Technical	– Health Sciences Association of Alberta
Paramedical Professional	– Health Sciences Association of Alberta – Alberta Union of Provincial Employees
General Service Support	– Canadian Union of Public Employees – Alberta Union of Provincial Employees – Edmonton Truck Owners (CLC) – International Union of Operating Engineers – Health Care Employees Union of Alberta – Christian Labour Alliance of Canada – Chemical Workers' Union

The United Nurses of Alberta (UNA) represented 14,000 registered nurses employed in hospitals, community health units and long-term care facilities. UNA is a centralized union with a history of militancy that includes hospital strikes in 1982 and 1988. It is not aligned with a political party or affiliated with the Alberta Federation of Labour (AFL). However, it engages in high-profile, non-partisan political action in coalition with organizations such as the AFL and Friends of Medicare, both of which are committed to defending the publicly funded health care system against encroaching privatization.[31] UNA's rival, the 3,500-member Staff Nurses' Association of Alberta (SNAA), was certified to represent registered nurses in Edmonton's University of Alberta Hospital and in a number of smaller organizations.

The 30-year-old Health Sciences Association of Alberta (HSAA) primarily represents degreed paramedical professionals (e.g. speech pathologists, dieticians and physiotherapists) and paramedical technicals (largely in laboratories). Its members work in acute care and mental hospitals and for the Ministry of Social Services, community health units and Canadian Blood Services. In 1994, the union had 6,500 members. HSAA is not a militant organization or an AFL affiliate, but it is active in health coalitions. Its resistance to government is confined largely to its active participation in the anti-privatization fight.

The Canadian Union of Public Employees (CUPE) represents support staff and licensed practical nurses (LPNs) in hospitals, community health units and long-term care facilities. With its strength in the smaller centres, CUPE is characterized by highly independent locals and is the only national union with major involvement in the Alberta health sector. During the 1980s, under Dave Werlin, a self-described member of the Communist Party of Canada, CUPE was a militant organization. It is currently affiliated with the AFL and the New Democratic Party. In the early 1990s, CUPE had 12–13,000 health sector members. Its major concern has been the privatization of support services.

The Alberta Union of Public Employees (AUPE) (an AFL affiliate until 2001 when it was suspended) is predominately a public service union. At the outset of health reform, it represented between 8,000 and 9,000 support workers in provincially owned hospitals (e.g. University of Alberta, Calgary Children's and Foothills) and in the Ministry of Social Services. Public service downsizing in the early 1990s saw its membership go from 38,000 to 28,000, leading to budgetary problems, an organizational crisis and, in 1994, a leadership change.[32] AUPE was looking for growth opportunities to recoup its losses.

The Canadian Health Care Guild (the Guild) was founded in 1947 as the collective bargaining arm of the Alberta Association of Registered Nursing Assistants, a professional body. At the outset of health reform, this non-militant, province-wide union represented 7,700 LPNs and nursing assistants employed in urban facilities. It maintained a low political profile and was not an AFL affiliate. In the late 1990s, the Guild merged with AUPE.

Prior to health reform, publicly funded hospitals and long-term care homes were represented by the Alberta Healthcare Association in provincial bargaining with HSAA, CUPE, UNA and the Guild. In contrast, community health units bargained individual agreements with the assistance of the Health Unit Association of Alberta. Health unit agreements did not have standardized terms and conditions of employment.

Regionalization had major implications for those unions that had been structured to deal with the myriad local facilities and service units. The creation of RHAs established common regional employers, and unions faced the prospect of restructuring in ways that had implications for their relative size, power and survival in the health sector.

Labour relations restructuring processes

Bargaining unit restructuring and transfer/merger settlements

The creation of RHAs called into question bargaining units certified for specific sites and services. In June 1994, the ALRB issued information bulletin "T-2: Regional Health Authorities Transition," which provided guidelines for bargaining unit determination and representational issues. Henceforth, local boards' bargaining responsibilities would be transferred to the RHAs; voluntaries, however, would retain employer status. The ALRB reconfirmed its policy of having five standard bargaining units for facilities and three for community health units, especially where health units operated separately from active treatment facilities. T-2 also indicated that certifications covering the seven provincially owned hospitals subject to the *Public Service Employee Relations Act* would be transferred to the *Labour Relations Code*.[33]

Regionalization involved integrating services and consolidating facilities. This raised potentially fractious issues associated with intermingling employees from units with different collective agreements and different unions. If bargaining units of different unions were combined, at least one unit would face losing its representation rights and its members would be forced to change unions. Bargaining unit amalgamations within the same union would disrupt locals' internal political dynamics.

The ALRB intended to discourage bargaining unit proliferation. It encouraged parties to explore voluntary bargaining unit amalgamations, suggested that unions jointly apply for "integrated certificates," and agreed to respect majority will on representational issues. Unions representing overwhelming majorities in units being consolidated would be certified without a vote.

If one or the only union represents between approximately 20% and 80% of employees in the consolidated unit, the Board will conduct a representation vote .... A union representing a small percentage of employees will not be included on the ballot .... [34]

Majority unions' collective agreements would govern employees in the new units, and accrued seniority and benefits would be transferable.

Even though bargaining unit restructuring raised potentially critical issues for health unions, it was not preceded by ALRB hearings or a commission to examine these matters. Union input into ALRB policy was confined to an ALRB-hosted conference in September 1996 to address restructuring issues.[35]

Bargaining unit structures did not change as dramatically as might have been anticipated. The regionalization of operations and bargaining units in the community health sector, where services were provided on an area basis, occurred more quickly and more completely than in the site-based active treatment sector. Otherwise, response to the ALRB's guidelines was gradual, with bargaining units emerging from various organic processes. Those processes, the degree to which RHA operations were integrated, and local relationships combined to yield different outcomes.

Region-wide bargaining units emerged from ALRB decisions. Where the ALRB was convinced that an RHA had integrated its regional operations and that intermingling was imminent, it merged bargaining units.[36] The existence of multiple appropriate bargaining units did not pose insurmountable obstacles to parties with viable local relationships. In such circumstances, the parties concluded formal or informal arrangements that allowed the RHA to transfer employees permanently from one bargaining unit to another.

Efforts by Edmonton's Capital Health Authority (CHA) to implement ALRB policy had unintended consequences. In 1997, the authority petitioned the ALRB to consolidate all bargaining units in its active treatment facilities so that there would be one union for each of the five standard units. The CHA's goal was the capacity to assign workers as needed across the RHA.

The ALRB encouraged the parties to pursue a mediated settlement. During mediation, the registered nurses' unions, UNA and SNAA, as well as AUPE and the Guild, reached merger agreements. Henceforth, CHA nurses would have a common collective agreement but remain in 12 appropriate bargaining units.[37]

The parties negotiated the terms under which the employer could reassign nurses. Specifically, if a program were transferred to another site and an insufficient number of nurses volunteered to accompany it, the authority could reassign the least senior nurses for up to six months. Otherwise, nurses could be transferred only in emergency situations. A provincial letter of understanding covering the parties further stipulated that when program transfers were anticipated, management had to discuss the implications for employees with the appropriate unions.[38] CHA did not achieve the flexibility it had sought.

Across the province, parties reached accommodations on merging units and transferring employees between unions. The absence of strongly manifested inter-union rivalry enabled local parties to conclude informal arrangements on intermingling without outside assistance. Two competing support unions, AUPE and CUPE, agreed to set common anniversary dates and work toward common language and compensation provisions to ease transfer/merger problems. The idea of a joint certificate or bargaining council was not pursued. Local party solutions precluded the call for legislative or adjudicative action.

In short, Alberta did not require a commission or ALRB action to address representational issues. The policy of rationalizing representational structures into five distinct groups, an ALRB decision from the 1970s, had prevented an *ad hoc* proliferation of bargaining units. The lack of intense union rivalries, the absence of a universal insistence by unions that they bargain provincially, timely union mergers and informal local accommodations combined to preclude third-party intervention. The result, however, was an arrangement of messy representational structures that would not be addressed by the government until 2003.

Labour force adjustment

The drive by RHAs to reduce costs by reconfiguring services and downsizing the workforce had a significant impact on employees who were laid off or reassigned, or had their hours reduced. The health care workforce was cut from 65,512 to 51,639 (21.2%) between 1993 and 1995.[39] UNA estimates that 5,000 nurses were laid off or moved to less-than-full-time status.

Jobs were cut as large RHAs amalgamated laboratories and contracted out routine diagnostic services. Professional staff experienced work intensification and layoffs as routine elements of their work were assigned to less highly trained assistants. Substantial numbers of full-time professional and technical workers were reduced to less-than-full-time status. Severance pay became a contentious issue because collective agreements had not anticipated such a massive downsizing. Some RHAs paid severance, others could not afford to, and others simply refused.

Initially, government took no position on the treatment of employees affected by the restructuring. In January 1994, the ministers of Health and Labour announced plans for a three-year Health Workforce Adjustment Strategy, intended to reduce adverse reaction to contracting out. The government budgeted $15 million to assist displaced or dislocated workers, and Human Resources Development Canada contributed money for the plan's administration.[40]

The tripartite Workforce Adjustment Planning Committee (WAPC), created to determine how the fund should be administered and distributed, prescribed the terms under which RHAs' adjustment programs would operate. Joint regional committees (JRCs) were established in each region and comprised staff from local Canada Employment centres, the province's Career Development centres, and equal numbers of union and management representatives from which co-chairs were selected. The WAPC evaluated each region's programs and reviewed its activities. It also created a coordinating committee of representatives from management, unions and both levels of government to facilitate information flow, evaluate program implementation and assist the regions.[41]

The Workforce Adjustment Strategy had three primary objectives: to help laid-off employees find work; to assist working employees to remain employed; and to enable employees to leave the industry voluntarily. Program funding could be accessed for tuition, small business training and start-ups, relocation and expenses such as travel to courses/interviews and childcare.[42]

Restructuring was deemed to have affected 14,753 workers, 86 percent of them female and 55 percent in acute care settings. Some 1,800 nurses applied to the program. Of these, 1,054 received assistance averaging $1,800. HSAA members, who accessed the adjustment program in roughly the same numbers as nurses, received an average payout nearly $700 greater.

The Workforce Adjustment Strategy operated as intended. Government recognized the need for the program, unilaterally funded it and devolved its administration in ways that involved the parties in implementing it. A potentially uncomfortable political issue was diffused. The unions' main criticism of the program was that benefits were minimal, but better than nothing.

Contracting out

RHAs have used contracting out, or the threat of doing so, to reduce operating costs, satisfy the government's privatization agenda, intimidate employees and undermine union power. They have brought contractors in to perform housekeeping and dietary work,[43] while moving laboratory and laundry work to contractors' off-site facilities. Urban employers face stronger union resistance to the practice than do non-urban employers. Smaller employers are less inclined than larger ones to contract services out because they realize less savings. When they do contract out, they have a problem attracting suitable bidders.

While workers see contracting out as forcing a choice between losing jobs or working under less favourable terms for union-resistant contractors, unions view it as a threat to their existence. Health unions have had three responses.

The first was to accept the employers' demands for bargaining concessions. In 1994, to save jobs, CUPE broke with the unions' common front and negotiated a "survival contract" which included a three-year, –5;0;0 wage component in exchange for a temporary ban on contracting out. Other unions followed suit.

The second response was to seek to retain the right to represent members whose jobs were being contracted out. *Labour Code* provisions for successor rights offer legal recourse in such matters. HSAA pursued this avenue with mixed results. Privatization has cost it members and its long-term ex-members have lost pay and benefits. Although it has realized some successes, the union has complained of "bizarre" ALRB decisions and intimidation of union members by private sector employers.

The third response was aberrational, taking the form of illegal strikes which were confined to two locales. This occurred in Calgary in November 1995, when CUPE and AUPE members undertook a 10-day wildcat strike, and subsequently in Lethbridge, where CUPE struck the Chinook Health Authority.

Bargaining structure

Prior to health reform, bargaining was relatively centralized. Although the Health Unit Association of Alberta bargained locally, the Alberta Healthcare Association negotiated provincial agreements with six major health unions on behalf of acute and long-term care facilities, including most voluntaries. AHA's members differed enormously in size, with some facilities employing only a few nurses and others more than a thousand.

In 1994, all RHAs and all but two voluntaries remained in centralized bargaining. Afterward, however, the desire to pursue particular objectives, combined with fractured union representation and weak labour markets, prompted some RHAs to reconsider their participation at provincial tables. Ideally, they wanted bargaining arrangements that would allow them to negotiate agreements that were responsive to their specific operational needs, competitive situations and labour markets.

Fragmented bargaining is more common where labour markets are local and the requisite skill sets are relatively low, creating the potential for some employers to pay workers at a lower local rate. CUPE, characterized by highly autonomous locals, saw four locals (Calgary, Edmonton, Medicine Hat, Lethbridge) withdraw from provincial bargaining.

With the labour market for nurses broader and their skill set higher, the parties preferred to bargain centrally. UNA negotiated separate central agreements for acute and long-term care facilities, community health and for-profit facilities. Its strategic objective was to win uniform terms and conditions at the central level for registered nurses throughout the province.

The rationalization of nurses' representation, including mergers of UNA, SNAA and other staff associations, plus organizing drives among the unorganized boosted UNA membership to 18,000. This consolidation eliminated barriers to bargaining standard agreements within and across sectors. In the 1999 round of negotiations, UNA imposed *de facto* industry-wide bargaining on the employers. A subsequent strategy would be to use central bargaining and the threat of militant province-wide action to recoup nurses' losses and improve their lot.

The RHAs did not seek to bargain locally with UNA. They recognized that paying provincial rates to attract and hold nurses was inevitable and that multi-employer central bargaining was prudent.

Bargaining arrangements with HSAA have been fluid. In 1996, the Calgary and Edmonton RHAs withdrew from provincial bargaining, but by 2000, both had rejoined centralized HSAA negotiations. However, their long-term care subsidiaries, CareWest and Capital Care Group, respectively, which they view as competing with for-profit providers, have remained in separate negotiating units.

Collective bargaining

In early bargaining under health reform, management was on the offensive. The government gave health unions until November 23, 1993, to devise mechanisms for implementing "voluntary" 5 percent wage cuts to take effect in 1994. The unions' initial response was collective defiance.[44] Eight health unions formed a coalition, agreeing to discuss wage cuts in exchange for an opportunity to voice their concerns. The government accepted, but the coalition quickly fractured.

CUPE recognized that the RHAs were under budgetary and ideological pressure to cut costs and contract out work. Housekeeping, dietary and laundry jobs were vulnerable to being contracted to operators who would resist abiding by union successorship obligations and hiring existing employees. The union broke ranks and negotiated a three-year, –5/0/0 percent "survival contract" in exchange for a 15-month moratorium on contracting out.

The remaining coalition members convinced the government and the employers to bargain with them. Before discussing wage cuts, however, the unions sought to negotiate both a comprehensive employment security agreement for those affected by reform and a labour adjustment program (severance, early retirement, retraining) for those who lost their jobs. After two days, management and government left the talks.[45] Government subsequently and unilaterally introduced its labour adjustment program.

As a vehicle for bargaining, the coalition was a spent force. In the wake of the CUPE settlement, other support unions acceded to similar agreements. UNA accepted mediated settlements that included 5.38 percent in rollbacks and a severance pay provision, but it avoided granting a number of other concessions sought by the employers.

The coalition continued to discuss common issues, fund activities, engage in political action, meet with government and present briefs until it disintegrated in 1995. In its place came a more activist coalition, the Health Care Alliance. The new coalition, consisting of HSAA, UNA and the Guild, saw its role as coordinating bargaining and building union solidarity.[46]

The Canadian Health Care Guild, a traditionally non-militant organization whose members had resisted being labeled union members, entered the Klein era feeling aggrieved and refused to negotiate the expected –5/0/0 percent package. In 1991, the Guild, representing LPNs, had gone to arbitration seeking a wage adjustment based on a top rate that was 75 percent of what registered nurses (RNs) were being paid. While acknowledging the legitimacy of the union's request, the arbitrator ruled that in view of the prevailing economic climate, the LPNs should be held to a rate slightly under 60 percent.

The Guild argued that as a result of the arbitration award, reduced work hours, layoffs and reclassifications that had downgraded LPNs to nursing assistants (NAs), its members' losses already exceeded the government guidelines. Its membership composition had shifted since 1991, from 74 percent to 44 percent LPNs and from 26 percent to 56 percent NAs. The NA wage rate was 15 percent below the LPN rate. Full-time NAs earned below $25,000 a year, putting them among the "working poor."[47] Regardless, an arbitrator imposed the –5/0/0 percent settlement. As wage rollbacks of 12 to 30 percent were announced, e.g., CUPE and AUPE concessions of 28 percent for Calgary laundry workers, the Guild award seemed moderate.[48]

The first round of health bargaining under the Klein government ended without serious confrontation. The absence of labour resistance was slightly anomalous. Although passivity had typified Alberta's public sector, high-profile strikes at Gainer's Meats in Edmonton and by UNA in 1980s had made national headlines. Under the leadership of Dave Werlin, the AFL had been instrumental in national coalitions (Pro-Canada Network and Action Canada Network) of women's, labour, social and environmental groups opposed to the federal government's plans for the North America Free Trade Agreement, deregulation, social spending cuts and the goods and services tax. But by 1992, this activism had dissipated.[49]

Labour's "quiescence" during this period has been attributed to a combination of factors. Environmental circumstances such as unions' tenuous status in a province noted for its conservatism and hostile labour legislation, the absence of inter-union solidarity, and a pervasive business unionism precluded unions from behaving like agitators or visionaries. The unions were unprepared for debt hysteria and the onslaught led by the highly popular Premier Klein, and they saw no means for resisting. With political protest purportedly beyond their realm of experience, they sought to protect their membership bases, operated within legal guidelines and focused on traditional non-political activities, namely, collective bargaining and ALRB rulings. This passivity enabled the government to implement the reforms of the Klein Revolution and ignore organized labour in the process.[50]

In addition, union members reflected their society. Polling data from 1997 indicated that 53 percent of union respondents would have voted Conservative, and nearly 50 percent would have opposed protests against government policy. Many government workers felt it their civic duty to join the drive to eliminate the deficit, assuming that their sacrifices would subsequently be recouped. Accordingly, members pressured their unions to go along with the reform program and to save jobs. With workers reluctant to take on potentially vindictive RHAs, fear quieted the workforce.[51]

Labour's accommodating spirit, however, had limits. In November 1995, 120 CUPE and AUPE laundry workers in Calgary undertook an illegal ten-day wildcat strike after the RHA announced plans to contract out their work despite the 28 percent wage cut they had accepted to save their jobs. The protest spread to 2,500 workers at six hospitals and nine long-term care facilities. UNA verged on joining the strike. While services at most Calgary hospitals were severely affected, the action attracted considerable public sympathy. This strike, together with one in Lethbridge over the same issue, reflected the strain being put on the health system and workers' desire to end the cuts.

Although the work disruptions in Calgary did not precipitate a political showdown, the government, which had vowed not to waver as it implemented reform, cancelled a $53 million health spending cut scheduled for 1996–97. It also provided funding that enabled the parties to negotiate an 18-month contracting out moratorium and a severance package for future layoffs.[52] No retribution was to be taken against the strikers. The incident demonstrated not only that the rank-and-file would strike when sufficiently outraged, but also that government could not ignore well-timed, high-impact strikes.

In February 1996, the government reported that public sector retrenchment, together with rising oil and gas revenues, had eliminated the 1996–97 deficit. By that time, program spending was down 21 percent, or $3.3 billion, from 1992–93.[53]

This development coincided with a recovery among most mainline health unions. Organizational restructuring, growing restiveness among union members and strengthening labour markets began to bolster the unions' confidence. Workers' taste for further sacrifice subsided as they recognized that they were not net beneficiaries of the low tax "Alberta Advantage."

HSAA has seen its membership grow and diversify under health restructuring. Organizing efforts targeting the unorganized, the long-term care sector, ambulance emergency medical technicians/paramedics and group home workers, plus takeovers of independent staff associations seeking to affiliate with a larger organization, has boosted membership to 10,000, up from 6,500 in 1994.

When restraint made working for RHAs comparatively unattractive, many technical workers left the industry and province, while others took jobs that either did not require shift/weekend work or promised less onerous workloads. The resulting shortage of technical employees, which continues to plague RHAs, gave the HSAA bargaining power and translated into increasingly better collective agreements. Coming off its –5/0/0 percent settlement in 1993–94, the union concluded a 0/0 percent deal for 1996–97, with a 2.5 percent increase provided on the last day of the contract's life. The 1998–2000 HSAA settlement included increases of 3/3/3 percent, and the 2001–02 agreement provided for a 13.5 percent raise, with certain groups receiving an additional 1–7 percent, and overtime paid at double time.

In contrast to the non-militant HSAA, UNA has grown aggressive. Its 1996–97 bargaining round was fractured and protracted. The facilities bargained provincially, while health units and some long-term care employers bargained separately. Facility employers pursued concessions on layoff and recall language, while long-term care employers sought further monetary rollbacks. UNA attempted to recoup earlier wage concessions, improve job security and establish mechanisms that would allow nurses to have input into staffing levels. Neither an ALRB ruling ordering PHAA to bargain in good faith nor mediation catalyzed a settlement. An agreement was reached only after UNA, armed with a mandate of 85 percent, threatened to strike prior to an impending provincial election. The employers did not contest the illegal action and agreed to a 7.11 percent pay raise and local staffing committees. Long-term care homes and the health units, except for the Capital Health Authority, concluded similar agreements.[54] The militancy paid off.

In the 1999 bargaining round, which followed the UNA-SNAA merger, UNA resumed its militant course. It established a single bargaining committee mandated to negotiate agreements containing common provisions. To maintain unity, it deferred ratification votes until all sectors had settled. The round was rancorous. UNA made detailed strike plans and threatened to conduct a strike vote. The ALRB ruled the threat illegal, but the union's militant solidarity yielded standard collective agreements that provided most nurses with a 10 percent pay increase over two years. Two years later, market changes and other circumstances enabled the union to negotiate a two-year agreement that not only made its members the highest paid nurses in Canada, but also provided a plethora of other major contract improvements.[55] UNA has indeed emerged from health reform in excellent condition.

In 1998, the Guild and AUPE bargained jointly with and struck the Capital Health Authority for two days. The resulting settlement gave union members compensation rates more comparable to those of registered nurses, and the strikers and unions received amnesty from legal retribution. In the same year, Guild members employed in long-term care facilities represented by Continuing Care Employers Bargaining

Association staged a four-day wildcat strike. The resulting settlement improved wages but did not provide for a general amnesty. In Calgary, Bethany Care Group issued letters of reprimand to strikers, and CareWest applied to the ALRB for a six-month moratorium on collecting union dues. The ALRB denied CareWest's application on the grounds that the parties would soon be entering a new round of bargaining.

Based on its experiences in the 1990s, the Guild concluded that job action would be required to raise wages and that breaking the law would involve substantial costs. Accordingly, it merged with the better-resourced AUPE. The merger made AUPE a preeminent health union, eclipsing the moribund CUPE, which it raided with impunity until being expelled from the Alberta Federation of Labour for its actions.

In response to the health unions' growing militancy, PHAA drafted a strategic strike policy.[56] The policy suggested that employers continue bargaining during illegal actions, but that, upon learning of impending illegal strikes, they apply to the ALRB for the suspension of dues collection. Other recommended legal remedies included cease-and-desist orders, restrictions on picketing and having the job actions ruled illegal. The strike policy also recommended that disciplinary action, including discharge, be targeted at union leaders and members engaging in inappropriate behaviour. The rank-and-file would be subject to lesser penalties or given amnesty. The policy suggested that employers stop funding benefits (i.e. pension, holidays, sick leave, heath and disability, and life insurance) during illegal actions.

The unions continued their extra-legal action. In April 2000, talks between AUPE (now merged with the Guild) and PHAA regarding 6,700 auxiliary nurses faltered. AUPE had signalled its intentions early by seeking court clarification of the *Labour Code's* proscription on strikes in "approved hospitals." It argued that the Ministry of Health had contravened the *Hospitals Act* by designating nearly half of the province's 300 facilities as approved without specifying the criteria used to make the determinations. Accordingly, the designations should be revoked and workers should be permitted to strike.[57] The court twice declined to rule on the application, making it clear that job action in approved facilities would remain illegal.[58] So when AUPE proceeded with strike plans, PHAA sought a cease-and-desist order, which would allow the court to treat strike threats as contempt.[59] The ALRB found the threat to be bad-faith bargaining and ordered AUPE to call off its planned strike.[60]

The president of AUPE dismissed arbitration as a procedure that demonstrably had not served members' interests. Eight years of near-static wage levels and increased workloads lay behind the decision by LPNs and 3,300 support staff in acute and long-term care facilities and mental hospitals to undertake a two-day strike in May 2000.[61] Patients were discharged and surgeries were cancelled as strikers maintained only essential services, e.g., services on dialysis and cancer treatment units.[62]

Other unions supported AUPE. At three hospitals, 650 CUPE members honoured picket lines until the ALRB ordered them back to work. UNA members worked to rule, refusing extra shifts and additional duties. HSAA members did the same.[63]

The parties subsequently concluded a two-year deal that included a 16 percent wage increase and amnesty for strikers.[64] PHAA petitioned the court to fine AUPE and its president for civil contempt for ignoring the ALRB's cease-and-desist order. In leveling a $400,000 fine, the judge expressed surprise that PHAA had not sought a jail term for AUPE's president since, in his view, monetary penalties alone would not deter others.[65] PHAA had also asked the ALRB to allow employers to stop collecting union dues for six months.[66] In April 2001, the ALRB ruled that dues collection should be suspended for two months.

All in all, AUPE paid a high price for its 2000 settlement and its position as a leading health union in Alberta.

In terms of recovery, CUPE has been the exception. It did not undergo organizational regeneration or experience rejuvenated morale in the wake of health reform. Myriad problems have made it reluctant to confront potentially vindictive RHAs, and the labour market recovery was slow to affect it. Moreover, its decentralized organizational structure has made it vulnerable to raids.

CUPE characterizes its members as dissatisfied with their incomes, angry over workload increases, and prone to both work-related injury and use of sick time; members are described as demoralized and resentful rather than militant. Union membership is equally divided among full-time, part-time and casual workers. Casuals are not covered by the contract's seniority, discipline, layoff, pension, and health benefit (e.g. disability, dental, group life insurance, leave of absence) provisions. High turnover among other-than-full-time workers aggravates the union's fear that employers will use this to justify further contracting out, a fear that may be misguided. Unions have made such a political issue of contracting out that the government allots additional funding to discourage the practice. In 2001, CUPE was able to capitalize on other health settlements to negotiate wage improvements for its members.

Analysis

Health reform in Alberta did not flow from a critique of the province's health care delivery system and a subsequent plan for rectifying identified problems. It was not inspired by an overt desire to improve population health status or the delivery of health services. Rather, it was an element of the Klein Revolution, an urgently pursued, ideologically inspired political agenda brought in by the Progressive Conservative Party in 1993. The Klein Revolution began as a response to an arguably contrived, or at least evanescent, fiscal crisis caused by depressed oil prices in a resource-dependent economy. It provided the pretext for implementing a broad agenda intended to transform the public sector by reducing its role and changing its mode of operation. It endeavoured to "reinvent government" and change the health care system.

The Klein Revolution used implementation strategies pioneered in New Zealand, where a fiscal crisis enabled the government to adopt radical neoconservative change based on a market model. In both jurisdictions, change was far-reaching. Health reform represented only *one* component of a transformative policy agenda. Alberta's health restructuring strategy was centrally conceived and hierarchically controlled.

Reform was implemented using blitz-like tactics, which are the essence of unilateralism. Public input into health care restructuring was perfunctory. Any potential opposition from civil society was overwhelmed and disoriented. Health unions were not consulted despite the enormous implications health reform had for them. This government-in-a-hurry was not concerned about unions effectively challenging its decisions. It treated labour relations as a downstream consideration to be addressed as the need arose. Throughout, the government has enjoyed perennially huge legislative majorities. Having campaigned in the recent election for deep cuts to public spending, the official opposition has provided no resistance.

Structurally, Alberta's reforms have borne some resemblance to Saskatchewan's. Initially, 17 autonomous regional health authorities, the Provincial Mental Health Board and the Cancer Board supplanted more than 200 local boards and government-owned facilities as the organizations responsible for providing health services. The provincial employers' association reconfigured itself to meet the needs of its new membership. The Klein Revolution's health reforms regionalized delivery but firmly centralized power. Government appointed trusted lieutenants to the new regional boards. They, in turn, hired chief executive officers with similar political predispositions (e.g. a former senior cabinet minister) and charged them with decisively implementing the new order according to business plans approved by government.

Senior management had a clear mandate and the authority to act. Health units supervised the implementation of budget cuts and restructuring plans according to tight time lines. Regionalization and accompanying budget cuts prompted managers to merge operating units, rationalize service provision and contract out work. By encouraging the RHAs to act independently rather than in concert, the government ensured that the provincial multi-employer industry association would not evolve into a credible industry voice capable of countervailing or challenging government.

The Alberta government's fiat-driven, fiscally-obsessed health restructuring scheme capitalized on the province's anti-union political climate, a restrictive statutory regime that bans health strikes, and slack labour markets. Its vision presumes that market forces, state-imposed restrictions on collective action, and unions' political impotence will combine to keep labour in check. The government had no need for legislation that further restricted labour's statutory rights. No effort has been made to cultivate collaborative union-management relationships.

For health workers, accustomed to stable environments, the restructuring agenda initially meant layoffs, diminished job status (i.e. lower job classifications; more "casualized" and less full-time work), intensified work, and reduced pay and benefits. Their security was also threatened by the government's commitment to contracting out work to the private sector. Workers were expected to "fall in"; they were not invited to "buy in" to reform.

In the early stages of health reform, workers were too stunned and intimidated by the enormity of change to be inclined to protest. They sought their unions' help in adjusting to health restructuring. However, collective agreements contained no provisions addressing mergers or the transfer of services, and redundancies.

In the absence of inter-union solidarity, rank-and-file militancy, political or community-based allies with whom to protest the direction or pace of reform, and opportunities for input, unions had to accommodate government and management. They were no match for this popular and determined government. Stronger health unions could only delay what weaker ones acceded to quickly. They were forced to accept settlements that initially cut and then froze members' pay.

The unions had institutional and organizational concerns. Some found their existence in the health sector under threat. Local bargaining units represented by the same or different unions faced the prospect of being amalgamated along lines specified by the Alberta Labour Relations Board.

The havoc accompanying restructuring and management's drive for greater flexibility and improved productivity eroded workers' organizational loyalty. Their fears and insecurities turned into resentment and anger. Accommodation yielded to incipient outbursts of rank-and-file defiance. Illegal action was workers' only vehicle for manifesting frustration.

Significantly, the public sympathized with Calgary laundry workers' 1995 wildcat strike, undertaken to protest management's decision to contract out their work despite their 28 percent wage concession to preclude that from happening. The strikers won their immediate demands and an amnesty. Moreover, government cancelled a scheduled cut to the health budget. It had exceeded the limits of what the laundry workers and the public found acceptable. The dispute marked a turning point.

Health restructuring occasioned union reorganizations, mergers, raids and the centralization of collective bargaining that had been spread among competing unions and across different parts of the sector. It had the unintended consequence of strengthening the main health unions, which emerged larger and more capable of undertaking broad-based, strategically coordinated collective action on behalf of increasingly disaffected and emboldened memberships.

The budget deficits and soft labour markets that had enabled government/management to coerce labour faded after petroleum prices recovered. However, once the province's fiscal picture brightened, the government proved reluctant to give health workers recompense for their sacrifices. Health reform had distorted labour markets by driving workers from the health labour force and making health occupations less attractive for new workers. Health organizations found themselves facing personnel shortages in critical areas. This reduced their capacity to negotiate concessionary deals.

In some unions, substantial elements of an aggrieved rank-and-file lost their fear of government retribution and respect for the statutory third-party interest arbitration regime that they perceived as unfair. They became willing to risk taking illegal actions. The prospect of fines, dues suspensions and jail time for their leaders came to be viewed as costs of acceptable settlements. By 1998, there had been three high-profile cases of unions violating the *Labour*

Code. Each case was settled on terms sweetened by an obliging government without legal retribution. At play were two important factors. First, the size and power of the dominant health unions had increased as a consequence of restructuring. Thus, the impact of their jobs actions was likely to be more far reaching than before reform. Second, the public had grown sufficiently familiar with health restructuring problems to recognize workers' grievances as legitimate.

AUPE exercised its newly developed will to resist. It struck in 2000, ignoring the government's warning that the law is the law and must be obeyed. Following the strike and a settlement that it considered equitable, AUPE was fined for civil contempt and the ALRB imposed a two-month suspension of the union's dues check-off privileges. UNA and HSAA reached settlements without job actions. The UNA settlement, however, was achieved in the face of a none-too-subtle strike threat. This rich, pattern-setting agreement has had destabilizing consequences throughout Canada's health sector.

Alberta's record of confrontational health sector labour relations has not prompted a change in labour policy. In April 2003, over labour's protests, the government enacted the *Labour Relations (Health Authorities Restructuring) Amendment Act* (Bill 27) aimed at rationalizing health sector bargaining.[67] The legislation specifies four bargaining units for each of the regional health authorities, i.e. nursing; auxiliary nursing; paramedical, technical and professional services; and general support services.[68] It removes the right to strike from those workers (approximately 10 percent) in the community sector who had that right. The legislation terminates nurse practitioners' right to belong to unions or to bargain collectively. They will negotiate individual employment contracts.

This legislation has irritated the dominant unions while simultaneously consolidating their power. They are apt to continue their periodic proclivity to violate the province's statutory strike ban. The government appears to be cultivating continued confrontational health sector industrial relations. Alberta's restructuring policies and resurgent labour markets have simultaneously strengthened the dominant health unions and given their members sense of grievance. The repercussions have been felt nationwide. The Alberta government's health care industrial relations strategy has contributed mightily to aggravating a national health sector industrial relations problem.

Afterword

In the wake of the Klein Revolution, Alberta's health sector has been on a trajectory characterized by consolidation and adjustment. Structural change has been confined to reducing the number of health regions from 17 to nine. In terms of regional health authority governance, the government has pronounced an 18-month experiment with partially elected boards a failure and returned to the practice of appointing all regional health board members.

Bargaining has been restructured in accordance with Bill 27. AUPE either represented more than the requisite 80 percent of employees or won runoff elections to represent service provider units in six regions. CUPE held two regions but has been raided by AUPE in one of those. Communication, Energy and Paperworkers Union of Canada represents one service provider unit. Runoffs and raids have netted AUPE 7,000 members. UNA has affiliated with the AFL. The two largest health regions negotiate locally with AUPE's service provider units, and four regions negotiate multi-employer agreements. Although some contracting out of dietary and housekeeping services occurs in Edmonton and Calgary, AUPE's willingness to negotiate wage freezes has minimized outsourcing.

Registered nurses (UNA), auxiliary nurses (AUPE), and professional/technical employees (HSAA) now bargain provincial agreements with a renamed but unchanged employers' association – Health Boards of Alberta Services (HBAS), formerly PHAA. Bargaining has been devoid of further confrontations. The health regions receive global funding; government plays no role in negotiations.

Acknowledgements

The author wishes to thank Yonatan Reshef and Herman Schwartz for their comments on earlier drafts of this chapter.

Notes

1. A. Ponak, Y. Reshef and D. Taras, "Alberta: Industrial Relations in a Conservative Climate," working paper, University of Calgary, 2000, pp. 1–3.
2. Kevin Taft, *Shredding the Public Interest* (Edmonton: University of Alberta Press and Parkland Institute), 1997, pp. 15–24, 48.
3. *Partners in Health: The Government of Alberta's Response to the Premier's Commission on Future Health Care for Albertans* (Edmonton: Alberta Health), 1991, p. 2.
4. *Ibid.*, 1–55.

5. Alberta, Legislative Assembly, *Speech from the Throne* (Edmonton), 1993, pp. 6–15.
6. *Ibid.*, 12.
7. Jane Kelsey, correspondence with Auckland, NZ, 2000.
8. Yonatan Reshef, "The Logic of Labor Quiescence," working paper, University of Alberta, 2000, pp. 10–11.
9. Mark Lisac, *The Klein Revolution* (Edmonton: NeWest Publishers), 1995, pp. 144–45.
10. "Summary of Alberta Roundtables on Health" (n.p.) November 1993.
11. Alberta, Health Planning Secretariat, *Starting Points, Recommendations for Creating a More Accountable and Affordable Health System* (Edmonton), 1993, pp. 1–53.
12. Achieving Accountability in Alberta's Health System, November 1998, www.health.gov.ab.ca/public/documents/assnt98. As anticipated by the 1993 Throne Speech, the Klein Revolution created a smaller civil service, down 30 percent by 2000. The Ministry of Health, with *Starting Points* as its blueprint for reform, saw both its role and size diminish dramatically. It went from 2,000 employees in 1993 to 300 in 1995. Five of eight assistant deputy minister positions were eliminated, and computer and support services were subcontracted. Today the Ministry exists to assist the minister, who assumes ultimate responsibility for the provision of health services to the people of Alberta. It recommends health system directions and priorities, drafts policy, monitors population health status, evaluates the system's performance, administers the Health Care Insurance Plan, monitors service delivery, evaluates the RHAs' business plans and budgets, and provides funding. With the exception of air ambulance, drug benefits and communicable disease control programs, which the government continues to administer, the RHAs and the provincial cancer and mental health boards are the service providers.
13. Alberta, *Regional Health Authorities Act*, R.S.A. 2000, c. R-10. Some RHAs initially had as many as 11–13 councils. Most have since consolidated to three or fewer of these advisory bodies.
14. Richard Plain, "The Role of Health Care Reform in the Reinventing of Government in Alberta," in Christopher Bruce *et al.*, *A Government Reinvented: A Study of Alberta's Deficit Elimination Program* (Toronto: Oxford University Press), 1997, pp. 287–8; Alberta Health, *A Three-Year Business Plan* (February 1994), pp. 1–29; Alberta Health, *A Three-Year Business Plan, 1995–96 to 1997–98* (February 1995), pp. 1–35.
15. Plain, pp. 285–86, 29.
16. Simon Renouf, "Chipping Away at Medicare: 'Rome Was Not Sacked in a Day'," in Gordon Laxer and Trevor Harrison (eds), *The Trojan Horse: Alberta and the Future of Canada* (Montreal: Black Rose Books), 1995, pp. 228–31.
17. United Nurses of Alberta, *History Document: The First Twenty Years, 1977–1997* (Edmonton), 1998, p. 11.
18. Leo Panich and Donald Swartz, *The Assault on Trade Union Freedoms* (Toronto: Garamond Press), 1993, pp. 54–6. The Supreme Court of Canada ultimately ruled that the right to strike is not protected under the Charter's freedom of association. Government may remove it. Such government action is "demonstrably justified in a free and democratic society."

19. *Ibid.*, 51–3.
20. United Nurses of Alberta, pp. 13–5; Panich and Swartz, pp. 108–9.
21. Plain, p. 297.
22. Yonatan Reshef and Helen Lam, "Union Responses to Quality Improvement Initiatives: Factors Shaping Support and Resistance," *Journal of Labor Research*, 20 (1999): 111–131.
23. Plain, pp. 298–9.
24. Friends of Medicare, "Healing Health Care: A Report from the Friends of Medicare Health Care Hearings," February 1999.
25. Alberta, Ministry of Health, "Future RHA members to be selected through combination of elections and appointments," news release (Edmonton), 14 February 1996. The first health board elections were held in October 2001. Eight board members were elected to each RHA, with the remaining four appointed by the government. The chairs were appointed by the government from among the elected and appointed board members. In March 2003, the government consolidated the 17 regional health authorities into nine and created new, fully appointed boards.
26. Alberta, Ministry of Health, "Ensuring Ongoing Quality Health Services – Goal of New Council," news release (Edmonton), 1995; The Provincial Health Council of Alberta, *A Legacy Document* (Edmonton), 1999, pp. 1–23.
27. K. Wetzel and D. Gallagher, "Management Structures to Accommodate Multi-Employer Hospital Bargaining in Western Canada," in M. Thompson and G. Swimmer (eds), *Conflict or Compromise: The Future of Public Sector Industrial Relations* (Ottawa: The Institute for Research on Public Policy), 1984, pp. 298–300.
28. Provincial Health Authorities of Alberta, *Bylaws* (Edmonton: PHAA), as amended November 30, 1999.
29. The Provincial Health Authorities of Alberta, http://www.phaa.com/Services/services.htm.
30. Alberta Healthcare Association, Human Resources Department, *A Guide to Employee Relations Implications of Regionalization* (Edmonton), September 1994.
31. United Nurses of Alberta, pp. 1–53.
32. Jeff Taylor, "Labour in the Klein Revolution," in Gordon Laxer and Trevor Harrison (eds), *The Trojan Horse: Alberta and the Future of Canada* (Montreal: Black Rose Books), 1995, pp. 305, 309–10.
33. Alberta Labour Relations Board, "T-2: Regional Health Authorities Transition," Information Bulletin (June 1994), pp. 3–4.
34. *Ibid.*, 10.
35. Alberta Labour Relations Board, "Emerging Labour Relations Issues in the New Health Care Environment," pre-conference papers, September 1996.
36. *East Central RHA v. AUPE and UNA*, [1996], *Alberta Labour Relations Board Reports*, pp. 327–47. In this typical case, the ALRB found that the RHA had centralized many community health operations. Moreover, a region-wide community of interest existed and intermingling among members of the three existing UNA and one AUPE nurses' locals had occurred. Bargaining history favoured a broader unit over one that was fragmented and composed of small units of questionable viability. The ALRB ordered a vote to determine which union would represent the consolidated bargaining unit.

37. Alberta Labour Relations Board, *Bargaining Relationships by Region: Capital Health Authority*, 15 November 1999.
38. *Collective Agreement, Multi-Health Authority (Facility) between United Nurses of Alberta and Provincial Health Authorities, 1 April 1999–31 March 2001*, pp. 226–30; 116–7.
39. Alberta, Ministry of Health, *Health Workforce in Alberta* (Edmonton) 1994, 1995.
40. Alberta, Ministry of Health, *Health Workforce Adjustment Strategy Project Report* (Edmonton), February 1998, pp. 1–2.
41. *Ibid.*, 3–5.
42. *Ibid.*, 1–5, 7–8, 11, 16.
43. Marriot Corporation took over housekeeping services in the Lethbridge Regional Hospital. Except for the supervisors, it brought in its own employees. The supervisors, too, were dismissed after the new staff was trained.
44. Taylor, p. 306.
45. *Ibid.*, 306–7.
46. United Nurses of Alberta, p. 26.
47. *Alberta Healthcare Association v. Canadian Health Care Guild*, [1995], (Dissent), Simon Renouf, January 20, 1995, p. 4.
48. Taylor, p. 308.
49. *Ibid.*, 311–3.
50. Reshef, pp. 1–35.
51. *Ibid.*, 19.
52. Alberta Union of Public Employees, "Backgrounder: Town Hall Meeting on Health Care," Edmonton, 8 January 1996; Reshef, pp. 20–1; Alanna Mitchell, "Alberta Backs Off on Cuts to Health, Reprieve Granted in Wake of Strikes," *The Globe and Mail* [Canada], November 23, 1995; "Ralph Klein blinks: Faced with labor strife, Alberta backs off health cuts," *Maclean's* 108 (December 4, 1995): 41.
53. Jim Dinning, *Agenda '96 Highlights*, Legislative Assembly, Edmonton, 22 February 1996.
54. United Nurses of Alberta, pp. 36–7, 45–7.
55. "Health employers ratify two new agreements for Alberta's 20,000 Registered Nurses," March 18, 2001, www.phaa.com/una_content_full.htm.
56. Provincial Health Authorities of Alberta, "Strategic Strike Policy," (Edmonton) May 1998, pp. 1–19.
57. Tom Barrett, "AUPE Court Application Seeks Right to Strike for Health Staff," *The Edmonton Journal*, March 21, 2000.
58. Gordon Kent and Bob Gilmour, "Court Again Rejects Right-to-Strike Bid." *The Edmonton Journal*, April 29, 2000.
59. Ross Henderson, "Hospitals Prepare for Wednesday's Strike Deadline," *The Edmonton Journal*, May 22, 2000.
60. "Union Told to Ditch Strike Plans," *The Edmonton Journal*, May 23, 2000.
61. Angela Hall and Rick Pedersen, "Wages Key in Hospital Strike," *The Edmonton Journal*, May 25, 2000; Rick Pedersen, "More Surgeries To Be Cancelled," *The Edmonton Journal*, May 26, 2000.
62. Canadian Press, "Health-care Workers in Alberta Stage Illegal Walkout," May 24, 2000.

63. Don Thomas, "RNs to Consider Sympathy Strike," *The Edmonton Journal*, May 25, 2000.
64. "Alberta Health-care Workers Accept Settlement," *The Edmonton Journal*, May 26, 2000.
65. Jill Mahoney, "Judge Slams Alberta Union," *The Globe and Mail* [Canada], May 27. 2000.
66. Jim Farrell, "AUPE Pays $400,000 Fine for Strike," *The Edmonton Journal*, June 23, 2000.
67. "Dark day for labour relations in Alberta," http://ww.afl.org/newsreleases/mar26_03.html.
68. This action followed recommendations put forward by the ALRB in Alberta Labour Relations Board, *Standard Health Care Bargaining Units*, 1 January 2002, pp. 1–49.

7
The Labour Relations of Public Health Care Reform in New South Wales

Nadine White and Mark Bray

Introduction

The Australian health care system has changed considerably over recent years – for patients and workers alike. This paper examines one part – albeit a very important part – of that changing system; namely, the public hospitals in New South Wales. This is the most populous of the Australian states, providing $6^1/_2$ million of the country's total population of around 19 million. The public health system in New South Wales annually accounts over \$7 billion in expenditure, which represents almost one quarter of the state government's budget, and employs around 100,000 staff, approximately 90 percent of whom work in public hospitals operated by NSW Health.

The main theme presented below is that NSW public hospitals have witnessed incremental, but inexorable and significant, reform that has focused mostly on cost reduction. These reforms have generally been achieved peacefully through the mediation of strong and enduring collective labour relations institutions, although cracks are starting to appear under the growing pressure of work intensification.

This theme is developed in three main sections. The data presented in Sections 2 and 3, as outlined below, were collected as part of a larger research project. The data were gathered through documentary and interview sources, as well as statewide quantitative sources from NSW Health. In particular, the data on unions in the NSW health sector, and the finance, labour and activity data for NSW Health was compiled from available data for the period covering the 1990s. In some cases comparable data sets for subsequent periods were no longer available as official data sets.

Section 2 of the paper shows that the politics of health reform has been robust, with the role and operations of the public hospital system becoming the subject of considerable political debate between federal and state governments and between the two main competing political parties at both levels of politics. Yet, despite these political contests, there has been a growing consensus amongst the opposing players – albeit a consensus that is rarely acknowledged – towards a neo-liberal agenda for the public sector generally, and for public hospitals in particular. This new agenda has placed severe limits on the willingness of governments of any political persuasion to provide increases in public funding to hospitals at exactly the time when the costs of hospitals were increasing significantly as the result of new demands upon them, new technologies and new labour costs. The result has been enormous pressure, mostly delivered through the mechanism of the hospital budget, to reduce costs.

Section 3 explores in more detail the labour relations structures and processes used to deliver the health care reforms. Again, the politics of the situation has been a central part of the story. Unlike several other states of Australia – and several other English-speaking countries around the world – NSW governments have been relatively moderate in the labour relations reforms they have pursued and they have maintained the traditional collectivist regulatory regime. Consequently, there has been no mass redundancies, no wholesale assault on the wages and working conditions of employees, no attempt to attack unions that represent those employees or to exclude them from decision-making processes and no major changes in bargaining structures. This apparently stable labour relations situation, however, masks the growing pressures caused by management-inspired changes in work practices and staff shortages that have produced increasing work intensification. The final section – Section 4 – draws the threads of the argument together.

The politics and management of health care reform

Health care policy in Australia is complicated by constitutional and political factors, but a common theme can be identified in the events of recent years – namely, the increasing influence of neo-liberal ideologies and the pressures that this produces on health care funding. The responses of health care managers to these pressures have broadly been to "do more with less".

The Constitutional context

As in many other areas of Australian economic and social life, government has long played a central part in the funding, provision and regulation of health care services. Both of the two main levels of government in the Australian federal system (namely, Commonwealth and state) are centrally involved, with their respective roles being determined by the Constitution. The most significant section of that Constitution is s51(xxiiiA), which was added by way of an amendment in 1946. This confers broad powers on the Commonwealth government to make laws with respect to:

> ...the provision of maternity allowances, widows' pensions, child endowment, unemployment, <u>pharmaceutical, sickness and hospital benefits, medical and dental services</u> (but not so as to authorise any form of civil conscription), benefits to students and family allowances... (emphasis added)

Prior to this amendment the Commonwealth had limited powers on health-related matters. The new section enabled the Commonwealth government to legislate for cash benefit programs to:

> ...pay for doctors' services, prescribed drugs and nursing homes, which are overwhelmingly provided by the private sector, and has enabled the Commonwealth to implement a national health insurance program and to dictate the structure and regulation of private health insurance... [1]

Accordingly, the Commonwealth government is directly responsible for financing medical services, pharmaceutical benefits and aged and residential care services. Since 1984, the Commonwealth government has implemented these responsibilities through a universal insurance scheme called Medicare. However, this scheme is only administered by the Commonwealth, while the States have the responsibility of operating public hospital services, mental health programs, community and support programs and women's and children's services [1]. This responsibility required state governments to find additional funding to supplement that received from the federal government.

This partial overlapping of constitutional responsibilities for health care has, predictably, produced considerable tension between Commonwealth and State governments of all political persuasions.

State governments have limited revenue-raising capacity, forcing them to rely heavily on the Commonwealth funding, which State governments frequently argue is inadequate. In response, Commonwealth governments routinely reject such arguments and accuse State governments of failing to allocate sufficient of their own funds to health and of reallocating Commonwealth funds to projects or purposes that were not sanctioned by the Commonwealth. In addition, Commonwealth governments seek to influence state health policy by imposing conditions on the funding grants [1]. Faced with such funding restrictions imposed by the Commonwealth, State governments have used costing shifting to alleviate the tension. For example, with the overlap and duplication of services in the health matrix, state governments have an incentive to move from providing services with capped budgets to those services in uncapped areas. These debates are well illustrated by the following account from a major daily newspaper [2]:

... The NSW President of the Australian Medical Association, Dr Kerryn Phelps, said: 'The hospitals have put in place all the efficiencies that they possibly can... now they need some funding'. The "unsustainable stress" the system was under was the result of 20 years of chronic underfunding, she said.

The NSW Minister for Health, Mr Knowles, also attacked the Federal Government over funding, and called on the Federal Minister for Health, Dr Michael Wooldridge, to accept an arbitrated decision over a dispute between the States and the Commonwealth over indexation in the latest Health Care agreement – the document which determines how much the Federal Government provides the States for hospitals.

If the Commonwealth accepted the decision, it would mean an extra $49.2 million for NSW hospitals, he said. 'At a time when our public hospital system is clearly under stress and their attempts to get more people into private health insurance through a $1.7 billion rebate scheme has been a dismal failure.'

But a spokeswoman for Dr Wooldridge said the Commonwealth had given NSW an extra $95 million towards hospitals this year and $230 million the year before.

Dr Wooldridge said on radio: 'Not only did NSW not put in an extra cent themselves, they took away $42 million of that $95 million I gave. So there's $42 million that I gave them for hospitals that they're spending on the Olympics or something else.'

Mr Knowles denies the allegation, saying that State Government was obliged to put all such funding directly into hospitals and that the State's health budget overall had increased by $300 million this year...'

Trends in health care policy

In addition to the contradictions of the Australian constitution that generate tensions between Commonwealth and State governments, party politics are also a rich source of conflict over health policy. The (broadly Westminster) parliamentary systems that operate at both Commonwealth and State levels have produced two main political groupings, which represent the only real alternative governments: the broadly social democrat Labor Party and the more conservative Coalition between the Liberal and National Parties. Conflict between these two groupings over health was most intense at Commonwealth level during the 1970s and 1980s, when they advocated significantly different policies and when health issues featured prominently in Commonwealth election campaigns [3, 4]. The Medicare scheme introduced by the Hawke Labor government in 1984, however, reduced some of this conflict. Medicare rapidly gained public support during the 1980s and it became increasingly difficult for the Liberal-National Party Coalition to challenge the principles embodied in it.

Under the Medicare scheme, public funding for health care comes from general taxation plus a levy of 1.5 percent on the taxable income of all tax payers. Benefits under the Medicare scheme include access to public hospital care at no charge and cash benefits related to the cost of private medical services. With respect to the latter, patients are entitled to a rebate on the cost of medical services provided outside hospitals, by private practitioners, on a fee-for-service basis. The rebate is calculated at 85 percent of a fee set by the Medical Benefits Schedule (MBS); the remaining 15 percent plus any additional sums resulting from doctors charging fees beyond those set in the MBS are paid by the patient [1]. The Commonwealth and State governments also operate other cash benefit programs that include subsidies for nursing home care and prescription medicines supplied by private pharmacists (PBS). The Health Insurance Commission administers both Medicare and the Pharmaceutical Benefits Scheme (PBS) on behalf of the Commonwealth government.

Supplementing the public provision of services under the Medicare arrangements, the private health insurance sector provides insurance coverage for a range of services that are not publicly funded, the most common of which is services in private hospitals. However, the proportion of all Australians who took out private health insurance was declining throughout the 1980s and by the late 1990s only around one-third of the Australian population was covered by voluntary private health insurance arrangements [1]. In 1999 and 2000, the Liberal Coalition government commenced the introduction of a suite of initiatives to improve the proportion of voluntary private health insurance coverage in Australia.

Within the context of broad consensus over the principles of Medicare, there remained some health policy differences between the major political parties, at both State and Commonwealth levels. The most conspicuous concerned the relative importance placed on the private and public sectors – the more conservative Liberal-National Party Coalition saw a greater role for the private sector in health than did the Labor Party. At Commonwealth level, after the election of the Howard Liberal-National Coalition government in 1996, this manifested in policy towards private health insurance. In response to the continuing decline in private insurance coverage, the Howard government introduced major incentives to encourage taxpayers to join private health insurance schemes and thereby shift from the public to the private sector [5]. This had the effect of increasing the proportion of Australians with private health insurance from a low of 30 percent in 1998 to approximately 45 percent in 2000. At the end of 2004, the proportion continued to hover around 45 percent [6], but the cost of the policy and its benefits in easing the burdens on the public hospital system remain matters of some controversy. At State level, the Liberal-National Coalition placed greater emphasis on private hospitals than did its Labor Party counterparts [7]. For example, in 1991 the NSW Liberal-National Coalition government departed from traditional policy by announcing a joint public-private sector proposal to develop a new hospital in the country town of Port Macquarie. The privately owned hospital, which opened in 1995, contracts with the State government to deliver health care services provided elsewhere in the state by public hospitals [8].

However, despite these differences, the most important feature of Australian health policy during the later 1980s and 1990s was the remarkable similarity between the two major political groupings. The basis of this apparent unity was the increasing influence on both of neo-liberal philosophies [9, 10]. Generally, this meant that market relations were privileged over state intervention, the public sector was considered too large and ripe for reduction through downsizing and privatization, while greater efficiency and more private sector-type management regimes were expected in the sections of the public sector that remained.

In the health care sector, the pressures for smaller government and a more efficient public sector embodied in neo-liberalism collided with a number of sector-specific cost pressures. As elsewhere, the population in Australia was rapidly aging as the "baby-boomers" reached retirement and there was an associated increase in medical needs [1]. At the same time, the population was shifting geographically as new regions grew and older regions, where existing health care facilities were concentrated, declined. Finally, new (and increasingly expensive) medical technologies were emerging that consumed greater proportions of the available expenditure [1, 11].

There were several health policy responses to these pressures in New South Wales that were essentially common across the political parties. First, considerable rhetoric emerged about needing to move away from the provision of diagnosis and treatment to prevention methods; that is, from "curative" medicine to "wellness" medicine. Particularly important here was a growth in health improvement education and promotion programs [12]. Given that approximately 12 percent of the NSW population were admitted to hospital each year, consuming 57 percent of the total state health budget [13], both major political parties argued that health prevention or "wellness" policies made good microeconomic sense because they were more efficient than the treatment or curative approach to health service provision. Significant or sustained action and resources, however, rarely matched this rhetoric.

Second, there was a conscious and substantial trend towards de-institutionalization. There were significant reforms in aged-care policy, with the emphasis moving to community-based programs from costly institutionalized residential care [1]. Strategies in individual hospitals were to decentralize and to de-institutionalize the care of patients with a focus on continuity of care from the point of access to the hospital up to and including the patient's return to the community. Beyond reducing costs, it was argued that the added benefit of this approach was the improvement of access and equity of services within the institutions themselves. This combined with the new focus on "prevention through education" programs and greater communication with the patient's carers, community nurses and general practitioners to produce improved discharge planning processes that facilitated continuity of care and the earlier release of patients from hospitals. Some hospitals even instituted "Hospital in the Home" Projects where patients who were discharged from hospitals were visited by hospital staff in their homes.

Third, along with de-institutionalization, there was an attempt to move resources to geographical areas of population growth and to decentralize the provision of health care. In 2000, the NSW government, for example, spent a considerable amount of time and funding on developing strategies to ensure that rural and non-capital city metropolitan areas were provided with a more equitable range of services [14]. In addition, assistance was provided to ease access to metropolitan information services by establishing toll-free telephone advisory services for rural GPs and supporting the establishment of Professional Chairs in Rural and Remote Nursing at several universities. Other strategies were in the areas of aboriginal and mental health, where attempts were made to improve the health status of the population of the former group and to reduce the morbidity of patients in the latter group, by improvizing access to and integration of services [11, 5].

Finally, there were significant changes in the management of public hospitals that reflected the desire to spread private sector methods of management into the public sector generally and the public health sector specifically [15]. Devolution meant that previously monolithic organizations were broken into smaller units or cost centres. The new managers of these units were given budgets and explicit quantitative targets and then assessed according to their achievement of these targets. Within limits that will be discussed below, managers were given greater autonomy in the methods by which targets were achieved.

Funding pressures and public hospital budgets

Unlike the private hospital sector, where individual profit-seeking companies manage autonomously despite the occasional coordination from employers' associations (see, for example, [16]), New South Wales public hospitals are administered through a fairly traditional public sector system, which channels responsibility and accountability up from individual hospitals through a government department (NSW Health) to the minister and, thereby, to the parliament. In this case, NSW Health is the agency responsible for the provision of public health care services. NSW Health is managed by a Director-General, who reports to the NSW Minister for Health. In this way, the government of the day, through its health policy, broadly dictates the objectives and strategies by which health care services are delivered.

In line with the broader trend towards the "new public management" [17], NSW Health has regularly reviewed and changed its structures and modes of operation. An important aspect of these changes was the decentralization of management structures and decision making to regional Area Health Services, a trend that began in the late 1970s but accelerated during the 1980s and 1990s. Under the provisions of the *Area Health Services Act (NSW)* 1986, for example, Area Health Service Boards were established in major regional areas across the state. NSW Health argued that by replacing a large number of individual hospital boards, these Area Health Services created economies of scale while at the same time decentralizing administration to the regional level, thereby providing a greater degree of autonomy and authority at the local level. In a sense this gave local communities more control over how their health resources would be allocated, given that most Area Health Service Boards had some general community representation. A number of subsequent restructures resulting in 17 Area Health Services across New South Wales and the clarification of the system of Area Health Services, including their funding and administration, culminated in the *Health Services Act (NSW)* 1997. By 2000 funding and accountability pressures had increased. In 2004, based on recommendations of an Independent Pricing and Regulatory Tribunal (IPART), the 17 Area Health Services were re-shaped into eight larger Area Health Services to minimize administrative duplication, improve accountability and increase community and clinician involvement in health service decision making. The proposed outcome of this review would be redirection of funds to clinical or front-line services [18].

The allocation of the health budget in NSW up until the 1989/90 financial year was on an historical basis. Historical funding was based on a snapshot of past utilization in that each year Area Health Services were allocated a budget matching the budget from the previous year with additional funding for new or enhanced services [19]. This funding method came under criticism on both equity and efficiency grounds. With respect to the former, it did not consider the changing trends in population. As a result, the majority of health infrastructure had become concentrated in the inner Sydney metropolitan areas, while population growth was concentrated on the North and Central Coast and in the Western suburbs of Sydney. With respect to the latter, the historically-based system reinforced the status quo, often rewarding inefficiencies by automatically maintaining the level of funding each year.

After 1989/90, NSW introduced a new funding method based on a complex formula that combined activity-based and population-based systems. This was to be implemented over a 10-year period in order to minimize fluctuations in funding levels and to enable the development of physical infrastructure. The key innovation of this new funding method was the separation of funding for tertiary health care services, using activity data, and funding for primary and secondary health services on the basis of population. This hybrid funding method, named the "Resource Allocation Formula" by NSW Health, had two main strengths [19]. On the one hand, the activity base for tertiary services, which utilized Diagnostic Related Groups (DRGs), allowed for efficiency comparisons between organizations and for incentives to reduce costs per bed-day or to discharge patients from hospital as quickly as possible. On the other hand, the population base for funding primary and secondary health care services was seen as fairer and more equitable because it allocated resources according to the size and demographic composition of the population.

The main impact of this method was to allocate Area Health Services a fixed income according to population and to give them responsibility for the planning of health services to ensure that expenditure did not exceed this income. This clearly complemented the trends towards the regionalization of health care services, by allowing local services to prioritize service developments within the community and to maximize activity efficiencies. This new accountability was reinforced by new performance appraisal systems for senior managers of the Area Health Services. The NSW government created a Senior Executive Service in the public sector in 1989 and during the 1990s NSW Health started to negotiate salary packages and performance management systems that ensured that Chief Executive Officers of the Area Health Services had strong incentives to enforce budget limits [20].

If Area Health Services became increasingly accountable for setting and meeting budgets during the 1990s, how did they spend their money? Some indication of the cost pressures during the period can be gained from an analysis of the overall health budget in New South Wales. Over the five years between 1994 and 1999, the total budget allocated to NSW Health from the NSW State Treasury increased by an average 7–8 percent per annum [21]. In isolation, this suggests a rosy picture for health services. This picture is reinforced when it is recognized that within this total expenditure capital spending actually fell steadily throughout the period, which meant that the recurrent component of the budget actually increased at a variable rate within the 7–10 percent range each year [21].

Despite the solid increases in total recurrent expenditure, however, Area Health Services were actually under considerable cost pressures during the 1990s. This arose from two sources. First, labour costs rose by more than the average increase in recurrent expenditure. Depending on which items are included in the definition of "employee-related expenses" (i.e. labour costs) – for example, whether Visiting Medical Officer (specialist medical consultants) costs are included – approximately 30–40 percent of NSW Health budget relates to labour costs. Within this category of labour costs, salaries and wages experienced an approximate 30 percent growth over the five years from 1994 to 1999. And yet area health service budgets did not increase accordingly.

This squeezing of the labour component of health sector budgets was actually part of a larger plan by which NSW governments sought to force efficiencies on the public sector generally. In 1996, the Carr Labor government established the Public Service Management Office within the Premier's Department to coordinate all public sector activities and introduced "whole-of-government" agreements over wage increases with the NSW Labor Council. However, the government consciously chose not to fund the total wage increase for the period because it expected that departments would make efficiency gains and implement cost-cutting measures to fund the remainder of the agreed wage increases [22].

The second source of cost pressures was disproportionate increases in the cost of other non-labour expenditure items in the budgets of Area Health Services. As noted above, the growth in the complexity of treating the health of the population resulted in increasing costs in the complex areas of pharmaceuticals, pathology, and technology and equipment. Expenditure on pharmaceuticals, for example, increased by an average annual rate of 8 percent over the 1989–1996 period compared to 4 percent for health expenditure generally [1], while new diagnostic procedures meant that pathology and other relatively expensive diagnostic tests ballooned as a proportion of health care expenditure [11]. In a similar vein, the cost of drugs increased by 48 percent and medical and surgical supplies by 46 percent over the 1994–1999 period [21]. Leeder [23] suggests that these increases were the direct result of the improved technologies, which in the health sector, unlike other industries, resulted in expenditure increases rather than savings.

It can thus be seen that during the 1990s changes in funding arrangements put the managers of Area Health Services in New South Wales – and by extension the managers of individual hospitals – under considerable and continued budgetary pressure. They assumed new responsibilities to set budgets and to ensure expenditure fell within budgeted limits. At the same time, labour costs and significant non-labour cost items rose at rates higher than increases in recurrent outlays.

Managerial responses – more patients, less resources

Health managers responded to the funding and budgetary pressures in three main ways [19]. Firstly, they sought to vary the admission rates of patients. This represents a particularly swift method of reducing expenditure, especially if it involves reductions in elective surgery or the closure of beds or wards. In areas with unplanned admissions, such as emergency medicine, this strategy was generally only adopted for short periods during which only life-threatening cases were accepted. Less urgent cases were diverted to other hospitals. Secondly, the average length of stay of patients was reduced. Thirdly, the cost per bed-day was reduced.

The success of health managers in these strategies can be seen in Table 7.1, which presents aggregated data for New South Wales Health that are compiled from key activity measures for each financial year from 1991/92 to 1998/99 [24]. These years were selected because they provide consistent reporting over most of the decade of the 1990s, while no more recent data are officially and publicly available. By any benchmark, these data indicate a remarkable increase in productivity within the NSW public hospital system during the 1990s. More specifically, they suggest three trends. First, Table 7.1 shows that hospital "Admissions" over the eight-year period rose (albeit unevenly) from just over one million to around one and a quarter million – an increase of approximately 23 percent. At the same time, the number of "Non-Admitted Inpatient Occasions of Service" increased by approximately 50 percent from just over 14 million to well over 21 million. These numbers clearly indicate that significantly more people were being treated in NSW public hospitals by the end of the period than at the beginning, while the increase in outpatients was almost double that in inpatients.

Second, the increased numbers of inpatients were treated with fewer physical resources. For example, the Average Number of Available Beds each year actually decreased by 11 percent, from over 23,000 to just over 20,500. This corresponded with an increase of around 39 percent in the "Caseflow Rate" (i.e. annual throughput per bed), from 44.5 to 62.0. An additional measure of this more intense usage of beds in the hospitals was the "Bed Occupancy Rate" that increased from 77.7 percent to 84.8 percent across the entire service. Finally, a clear component of these trends was the tendency for patients to move more quickly through the system from admission to discharge – there was an 18 percent decrease in the "Average Length of Stay of Acute Episodes".

Table 7.1 Activity, Performance and Workforce Data

Indicator	1991/2	1992/3	1993/4	1994/5	1995/6	1996/7	1997/8	1998/9	% inc/dec
Admissions	1,032,558	1,114,827	1,232,434	1,202,676	1,253,755	1,242,232	1,265,318	1,267,957	23% inc
Total Non Inpatient Occasions of Service *	14,188,483	14,556,094	13,649,975	15,469,013	15,976,520	17,459,872	17,715,618	21,335,300	50% inc
Average Available Beds	23,224	21,157	24,088	23,699	23,369	22,304	21,284	20,536	11% dec
Caseflow rate (annual throughput per bed)	44.5	52.7	51.2	50.7	53.7	55.7	59.4	62.0	39% inc
Bed occupancy rate (%)	77.7	89.5	83.1	83.6	83.0	82.8	83.8	84.8	9% inc
Average Length of Stay of Acute Episodes	7.0	6.7	6.0	5.9	5.7	5.7	5.6	5.9	18% dec
Full-time Equivalent (EFT) Staff	63,780	65,476	67,305	67,139	73,002	70,627	69,729	69,091	8% inc
Admissions/EFT	16.2	17.0	18.3	17.9	17.2	17.6	18.1	18.4	13% inc
NAPOOS/EFT	222.5	222.3	202.8	230.4	218.9	247.2	254.1	308.8	38% inc

Note: where necessary figures rounded to one decimal point

* Includes non inpatient primary and community-based services, outpatient and emergency services including diagnostics, mental health services and rehabilitation and extended care services

Key:

Admission – the number of patients who undergo admission, that is the administrative process by which a hospital records the commencement of an episode of accommodation, whether it is same day or overnight

EFT – equivalent full-time

NAPOOS – non admitted patient occasions of service

Source: NSW Health Department (1991/2 – 1998/9), NSW Public Hospital/Health Comparison Data Books, Sydney [24].

Third, not only was the increased number of patients treated with fewer physical resources, but there were also comparatively fewer human resources. The total number of staff employed by NSW Health – measured by "Full-Time Equivalent Staff" – increased by about 8 percent, from less than 64,000 to just over 69,000. This percentage increase, however, clearly fell short of the rate of increase in both outpatients and inpatients. The former is measured by the ratio of "Non-Admitted Inpatient Occasions of Service" to Full-Time Equivalent Staff, which increased by approximately 38 percent. The latter is measured by Admissions per Full-Time Equivalent Staff member, which increased by around 13 percent.

The labour relations of health care reform

The health care reforms described above were introduced through an incremental rather than a revolutionary process. This generally moderate approach to labour relations reflects the larger labour relations policies of NSW governments over the period. The labour relations "Archilles heel" of the health care reforms, however, lies in an issue that has so far not found its way onto the bargaining table – work intensification.

The industrial relations framework and the politics of labour relations reform in NSW

As with health care policy, labour relations policy in Australia is complicated by the federal system of government, which gives powers to make laws in this area to both the Commonwealth and State governments. In line with the neo-liberal philosophies which gained increasing support amongst all Australian governments from the late 1980s, the substantive nature of the regulatory regimes at both levels generally moved away from the previously centralized, collectivized and prescriptive systems of conciliation and arbitration towards more decentralized and facilitative systems based on collective bargaining and even on individual bargaining. This trend was especially conspicuous at the Commonwealth level, where the later years of the Labor government (i.e. 1991–1996) saw enterprise bargaining become the dominant mode of regulation and non-union forms of enterprise bargaining being permitted for the first time since the turn of the century. The Liberal-National Coalition government elected in 1996 went even further by severely restricting the activities of unions and promoting individual contracts [25]. The State systems varied considerably, with some (like Victoria in 1992 and Western Australia in 1993) going even further than their Commonwealth counterpart towards individualization, while others were far more cautious [26, 27].

Initially it appeared that New South Wales would lead the trend towards radical labour relations reform because of moves by the Liberal government in 1991 to adopt a more "market-oriented" approach. However, that conservative government encountered political difficulties that frustrated their more radical ambitions [28] and then, in 1995, a Labor government was elected that eschewed individualization and retained elements of the former collectivist system of conciliation and arbitration [27]. Under the main regulatory instrument, the *Industrial Relations Act* 1996 (NSW), the NSW system establishes an Industrial Relations Commission that oversees a range of bargaining options for the parties involved: *awards* – which are generally, but not necessarily, industry-wide in coverage – can be handed down by members of the Commission to impose legally-binding minimum employment standards; *industrial agreements* – which are generally, but not necessarily, enterprise-specific – are negotiated between unions and employers and can be given legal effect by the Commission; while *non-union industrial agreements* – collective agreements negotiated directly between employer and employee without union involvement – can also be ratified by the Commission under certain circumstances. Disputes between the parties are conciliated and, if necessary, arbitrated by the Commission [29].

The modest differences between New South Wales governments of different political persuasions over general industrial relations policies were replicated in their management of the public sector. The Liberal-National Coalition government that held office between 1988 and 1995 embarked on many neo-liberal reforms that were evident elsewhere, such as privatization, private sector management techniques and the decentralization of wage bargaining [30]. Its Labor Party successor also pursued efficiencies and cost-cutting in the public sector through downsizing, contracting out and corporatization of public enterprises. However, the new government's closer relationship with the union movement imposed far-reaching limits. For instance, several public enterprises – such as electricity and water – remained in public ownership, unlike other states where such enterprises have been privatized. Plans for competitive tendering for public sector tasks – such as rail maintenance – were withdrawn. And most importantly in respect of labour relations, wage bargaining was actually centralized to "whole-of-government" arrangements between the government and the state-level union confederation, the NSW Labour Council [22], shifting wage negotiations away from the agency-specific pattern maintained by the previous government.

The management of human resources

Consistent with the "new public management" model, the thrust of the regionalization of public health operations was supposed to include decentralization of decision making to the Area Health Services, which acquired their own one-line budgets and greater autonomy in the way they allocated budgeted resources within their region. The reality, however, was rather more complex because NSW Health retained considerable centralized control. Human resource policy is one area where this central control is most conspicuous.

The main source of managerial control was section 115 of the *Health Services Act*, which states that NSW Health is deemed to be the employer of all public health sector employees in New South Wales. In formal terms, then, Area Health Services acquired the autonomy to make decisions about the terms and conditions of employment in their regions only when those responsibilities were delegated to them by NSW Health under section 115(4). NSW Health rarely made such delegations.

One area in which NSW Health retained complete central control was specific human resource issues that were determined unilaterally by the Director-General of NSW Health and imposed upon the Area Health Services. In late 1998, for example, NSW Health issued a 46-page Code of Conduct policy, which prescribed acceptable behaviours and actions in relation to employment. Area Health Services were advised that these represented absolute minimum standards that could be exceeded but not reduced. A revised policy on Displaced Employees was circulated with similar instructions in 2000. Other central controls over the so-called autonomy of Area Health Services may be evidenced through the NSW Labor Government's Corporate Services Reforms over the period 1995–1999. As a result of this larger policy, the number of payroll and HRM information systems in the health sector across the state were reduced to just two, to ensure uniformity and reduce duplication. Intranet and internet services were established, allowing the centralization, rationalization or cost minimization of some human resource management services. According to the Labor Government, the result of these corporate service reforms has been an important contribution to the $100 million dollar increase in the 1996 health budget [31].

Another area in which NSW Health retained considerable central control was over industrial matters negotiated with unions. For example, with the exception of a brief period of "enterprise bargaining" during the period of the Liberal-National Coalition government in the mid-1990s, all bargaining with unions over new awards or collective agreements during the 1990s was conducted on a state-wide level [32]. The committee acting on behalf of "employers" in these negotiations has been dominated by NSW Health, albeit with some Area Health Service representation.

NSW Health delegated greater authority to the Area Health Services in the more traditional staff management areas such as recruitment, selection and termination of employment, training and development, occupational health and safety and employee assistance programs. However, even here, NSW Health insisted that all of these functions be practised within centralized policy guidelines.

The substance of NSW Health policies also changed during the late 1990s, broadening in scope and becoming more sophisticated. For example, a detailed human resource management plan for the period 1998–2003, entitled *HR2003 Framework* [33] and subtitled "a framework for human resource management and workforce relations strategic directions", contained the following six "result areas": (1) workforce planning, (2) recruitment and retention, (3) staff performance management, (4) the working environment, (5) capability, learning and development, and (6) human resource information. Each "framework result area" had detailed corresponding objectives and key actions. Several features of this *HR2003 Framework* [33] are relevant.

First, as the sub-title indicates, *HR2003 Framework* [33] was a strategic document aimed at developing the organization and clearly sought to link the goals of the workforce with the goals of the organization. This stands in stark contrast to the previous NSW Health plan developed in 1996, which was a far more narrow and reactive statement of management objectives.

Second, the language of the framework document was clearly prescriptive "Human Resource Management", with the emphasis on the development of staff that indicates a rhetorical preference for the "soft" form of HRM rather than its "hard" counterpart [34]. This represented a marked departure from previous management plans that had a much narrower focus on "industrial relations" issues. The entire focus of the previous 1996 statement, for example, was on awards, agreements, award restructuring and simplification, competencies, rewards, and elimination of restrictive work practices.

Third, unions are recognized in the *HR2003 Framework* [33] under the "working environment" result area, but only insofar as they will work collaboratively with management and staff to "...improve the efficiency, effectiveness and quality of human resources management". There was, however, no indication that the framework itself had been the subject of any consultation or negotiation with unions – it was a document developed solely by management.

Finally, the Director General indicated in his message that the framework was not prescriptive but was rather a set of targets towards which each Area Health Service should strive in order to ensure high quality human resource management and workforce relations. The reality, however, from an Area Health Service and employee perspective, was that it was highly unilateralist and implementation rested mostly upon managerial prerogative. Many of the initiatives it contained were also contradictory. While regionalization was championed as the modern way to manage health care, the economic reality of the management of the public health dollar has resulted in increased centralization. So, despite the "strategic" and "soft HRM" rhetoric of NSW Health, the regionalized structure of health management in New South Wales was more centralized than it appeared, especially with respect to human resources and labour relations, and the apparently new and sophisticated human resource policies rarely corresponded to actual practices.

The continued presence of unions

Despite the apparent support amongst public health managers for a new approach to human resource management, there was no conscious attempt to undermine union membership or to challenge the role of unions as bargaining agents. As Table 7.2 shows, union membership in the public hospital sector declined significantly during the 1990s, but this decline was actually less than that experienced across

Table 7.2   Union Membership as a Proportion of Total Employment

Category	1990 %	2000 %
All Industries (Australia)	41	25
Health & Community Services (Australia)	49	32
Public Sector Hospitals & Nursing Homes (NSW)	63*	50

Note: * 1994 figure
Source: Australian Bureau of Statistics, *Trade Union Membership* (Catalogue No. 6325.0) and unpublished data from the same survey [78].

all industries. Aggregate union membership in Australia fell from 41 percent to 25 percent between 1990 and 2000, while membership in the broad industrial classification of "Health and Community Services" fell from 49 to 32 percent over the same period. These industry data, however, included the private and public sectors as well as both hospitals and the lowly-unionized community services sector. Unpublished disaggregated data for NSW reveals that union membership declined from 63 percent in 1994 to approximately 50 percent in 2000 for "public sector hospitals and nursing homes", clearly indicating that union membership in public hospitals remained high compared to most other industries.

The structure of union representation in public health care also remained stable in its strongly occupational basis. As Appendix 7.1 shows, almost every distinct occupational and professional group in public hospitals continued to have its own union and this traditional occupational union structure largely survived the period of union amalgamations during the 1990s that affected unions in other Australian industries [35, 36]. There were some changes. A small union representing non-clinical health managers, the Health Officers' Association, for example, merged with the larger Health and Research Employees' Association during the early 1990s. There was also a transfer of coverage rights between the Public Service Association (PSA) and the Health and Research Employees Association (H&REA) in 1998, which meant that H&REA became responsible for representing the clinical support service employees and the non-specialist medical officers. The PSA retained coverage (to the exclusion of the H&REA) of administrative staff working in the head office of NSW Health. These changes, however, were minor and unimportant in the overall scheme.

Finally, all of the health care unions continued to be recognized by NSW Health for bargaining purposes and, as will be shown below, they continued to negotiate awards and collective agreements that regulated wages and many working conditions. This recognition was, however, far from open-ended and health care managers remained keen to restrict the scope of union influence. The NSW Nurses' Association, for example, found it far easier to be actively involved with NSW Health and the NSW Minister for Health in attempting to develop strategies to overcome the shortage of qualified and skilled nurses, particularly critical care nurses, than getting its voice heard on related issues such as workforce casualization and work intensification.

The stability of bargaining structures

Throughout the period of reform, the wages and working conditions of virtually all employees in NSW public hospitals continued to be regulated by awards and collective industrial agreements (see above) determined within the New South Wales – as opposed to the Commonwealth – labour relations system. *Awards* are written documents that prescribe legally-binding minimum terms and conditions of employment. Formally, awards are determined by the NSW Industrial Relations Commission, but the reality in this sector is that they are mostly "consent awards" which are the result of bargaining between employers and unions, with the Commission only rarely being called upon to resolve disputes by compulsory arbitration. Awards in the sector are mostly based on occupation (see Appendix 7.1), but they cover all hospitals within the jurisdiction of NSW Health; that is, they are state-wide. This means that the parties involved in negotiating awards are NSW Health, aided by Area Health Service personnel who may sit on the employers' negotiating committee, and state-level officials of individual occupational unions.

Collective agreements are most often supplements to rather than substitutes for awards. The bargaining agents involved vary – according to the level of management involved in individual Area Health Services and/or hospitals and their counterpart union representatives, who may be full-time officials or workplace delegates. The outcomes of collective bargaining can be written agreements, which can be formalized by the Industrial Relations Commission, but more often they are unwritten working arrangements that are part of the organizational memory. The incidence of this form of bargaining depends mostly on the power of local unions, which varies considerably across regions, hospitals and even wards. Another important factor is the issue at stake; local work practices, especially those associated with workplace safety or idiosyncratic health care arrangements, are commonly regulated in this way where unions are strong enough to demand consultation and joint decision making.

The pattern of bargaining in public hospitals changed little during the 1990s and early 2000s. This stability can be seen in two ways. First, the persistently strong role of state-wide awards in this sector was unusual in Australia given the widespread growth of "enterprise bargaining" during the 1990s [25, 32]. Apart from the preferences of both NSW Health and most health sector unions for this form of regulation, the key factor explaining the arrangement was the NSW government. The more conservative Greiner government that held power during the first half of the 1990s embraced enterprise bargaining, but efforts to decentralize bargaining in this way in the NSW public sector (including public hospitals) in the 1993–1996 period were not successful, and the Carr Labor government that took its place reversed the trend back towards sectoral awards [37, 32]. Indeed, negotiations – especially over wage issues – became even more centralized after 1996 in that the Carr government has negotiated framework agreements with the NSW Labour Council to regulate wage increases across the entire NSW public sector [22].

Second, the scope of bargaining did not expand. By far the dominant industrial issue in public hospitals throughout the period was wages. Awards in this sector regulated a wide range of non-wage issues (including hours of work, allowances and wage loadings, the provision of meals and accommodation, appointment and promotions procedures, union rights and grievance procedures; for more detail, see [32]). In particular, there continued to be few award provisions or clauses in collective agreements that directly regulated what rapidly became a key workplace issue – namely, the workloads of employees. The absence of regulation meant that such workplace changes (and the resulting productivity increases) in the sector were often introduced either through informal collective bargaining or by managerial unilaterialism and were generally driven by budgets and cost-cutting.

Allen's [38] case study of work intensification at a Queensland public hospital provides an example of what appears to be the common managerialist process of change that occurs in New South Wales. That is, the number of patients being treated in the hospital was simply increased, with resulting increases in bed utilization and shorter patient stays, but without corresponding increases in staff numbers. In the absence of clear and enforceable workload limits in awards or collective agreements, there was no mechanism by which unions could easily intervene, while clinical managers and employees who were well aware of budgetary restrictions were forced to reluctantly accept the higher workloads.

O'Donnell's [39] case study of changes in work organization for non-clinical support staff at two Sydney hospitals illustrates the collective bargaining process. Here, the workplace changes involved employees who had previously performed different tasks (i.e. cleaning, meal preparation, patient portering etc) and paid under different wage classifications were brought together under a single classification and "multi-skilled" so that they could be used to perform any of the tasks. No award changes were required, because the broad wage classification already existed, but unions and their members opposed the changes, partly because they resulted in considerable work intensification. Union resistance ultimately failed, however, not least because of the pressure to cut costs through an explicit threat that the work would be contracted out if reduced costs were not achieved.

This regulatory gap with respect to workloads in New South Wales public hospitals not only left an important industrial issue for many employees to managerial prerogative, but it also contrasted with developments in other states. One regulatory mechanism – in the form of staffing levels being linked to formulas embodied in computer software programs – was included in collective agreements in South Australia in the early 1990s and led to some redress for nurses in that state [40]. An alternative method was the insertion of a maximum workload formula into some nurses' awards in Victoria mid 2000 after a sustained union campaign [41].

Staffing practices

Unlike other Australian states, such as Victoria, where downsizing [17] and outsourcing [42] had a significant effect on employment, reform in NSW has been more gradual and its impact on employees more benign [17, 43]. In the latter case, reforms were driven by changes in funding and focused on organizational restructuring and improved productivity through bed management practices [43–47]. These initiatives changed many employment profiles and job tasks, but reduced labour requirements were generally managed through staffing freezes (see various Premier's Department Circulars and [48]). Where redundancies were considered necessary, employees were given the opportunity for redeployment in other areas of the public sector and some salary maintenance according to NSW Health's extensive policy and procedure for managing displaced employees [49]. While the policy was not a collective agreement, one of its general principles was that where restructuring resulted, or threatened to result, in redeployment or redundancy, management must at the earliest opportunity consult with relevant unions [49].

The NSW Health redeployment and redundancy policy assisted in preventing widespread industrial action by providing some job security. However, the policy only applies to permanent employees. By 2000, unions were becoming increasingly concerned that health managers were using temporary and short-term contracts to circumvent the policy, particularly for non-clinical staff, and the Health and Research Association was able to negotiate "permanency clauses" into awards effective from 1 January 2000. The general principle of these provisions was that employees engaged in meaningful work on a continuing basis are entitled to an expectation of permanency of employment [50].

Despite the slight increase in aggregate employment in public hospitals during the 1990s, there were – and there continues to be – significant staff shortages in some occupations. The two most conspicuous examples are nurses [51] and rural doctors [52]. In response to the former, NSW Health and the NSW Nurses Association cooperated on a nursing staff shortage campaign after 2000, when there were approximately 1,100 full-time equivalent nursing vacancies in NSW and approximately 5,000 around Australia [53]. The campaign, called "Nursing 4 Life," focuses on recruitment and retention strategies such as building partnerships; undertaking needs analysis, marketing and promotional activities; and reviewing job structures and career paths within nursing classifications. In the short term, these did not alleviate the problem, but the NSW Health Department Progress Report (September 2001) [54] noted that:

> ...a significant number of strategies have been implemented over recent years [and] had these strategies not been progressed, the nursing workforce situation would be even more challenging. [54]

Nonetheless on the same page the Progress Report indicated that:

> ...The Department of Health Reporting System (DOHRS) nursing figures for July 2001 highlight that in the public sector, AHSs [Area Health Services] were "actively recruiting" approximately 1,800 FTE positions. At the same time they were using approximately 2,800 FTE casual staff, including 690 agency nursing staff... [54].

The use of casual employees reflects an obvious strategy to manage the fluctuations in activity [54–56] and may also reflect the choice of nurses themselves to work casually. The NSW Nurses Association, however, argued that the shortage of nurses and the growing dependence on casuals were indicative of the low wages earned by nurses and that increased wages would lead to a large proportion of trained and qualified nurses returning to the public hospital system. Their claim may be partially correct, but research commissioned by the Association suggests that many other factors may be preventing nurses from working in the public hospital sector, including the changes in hospital management systems, shift work, the heavy nature of the work, limited opportunities for career progression, increasing community expectations, harassment and violence within the workplace, and the increasing intensification of work in the public hospital system [57].

Strikes

The health care reforms in New South Wales were introduced without significant industrial disputation. Unions were by no means pleased with many of the changes taking place in the public sector generally and in health specifically, and health sector unions took part in several large-scale protests. However, strikes in public hospitals were rare during the 1990s and when they did occur, they were almost always small and localized in nature. The relative industrial peace in New South Wales contrasted with earlier periods, especially the 1980s [58], and with the experiences of other states [59].

There were, however, signs in New South Wales in the early 2000s that industrial peace was under threat. In response to a comparative decline in wages, staff shortages and work intensification, the NSW Nurses Association commenced its "What's a Nurse Worth?" campaign in 2001. As part of this campaign, the union called a strike on 18 October 2001 – the first state-wide stoppage in more than a decade [60]. While the stoppage only lasted two hours, it highlighted the growing frustrations of nurses. NSW Health (and thereby the government) agreed to fund wage increases of 16 percent over four and a half years in five instalments, but refused the union's additional claim of 15 percent to compensate for past declines and the matter went to arbitration. The result was a major inquiry into the wages of nurses before the Full Bench of the Industrial Relations Commission through what was called a "Nurses Special Wage Case". Hearings in this inquiry began in June 2002 and on 19 December 2002 an interim decision of the NSW Industrial Relations Commission was handed down increasing the weekly rates of pay by 6 percent. Almost one year later, on 11 December 2003, the Full Bench of the NSW Industrial Relations Commission handed down its final decision, which addressed a number of outstanding matters including further wage increases and qualification allowances. The award was varied to incorporate an agreed clause on reasonable workloads for nurses, effective from 16 December 2003. However the impact of this clause may be limited as it is not a prescriptive patient-to-staff ratio clause as it found in other state nursing awards such as Victoria. The NSW clause is procedural in nature, detailing reasonable workload principles, the role and structure of reasonable workload committees, and the treatment of grievances in relation to workloads, which leaves open the negotiation of reasonable workloads, their interpretation and application at local workplaces [61, 62].

Wages

Wage increases for five major awards in the NSW public hospital sector for the period from January 1994 to December 2000 are presented in Figure 7.1. During this period, there were essentially two wage rounds, each producing agreements that operated for three years. The first wage round ran from 1994 to 1996/7, depending on the start and finish dates of each award, while the second ran from 1996/7 to 1999/2000. Data for subsequent rounds was not available for collection as part of the larger research study.

Before analyzing the substantive outcomes of the wage rounds, two features of the data reported in Figure 7.1 need to be emphasized. First, they relate to increases in base wages and salaries only. In other words, they do not include overtime, time-in lieu, shift penalty, extra leave or allowance rates. The wage increases for Senior Medical Practitioners

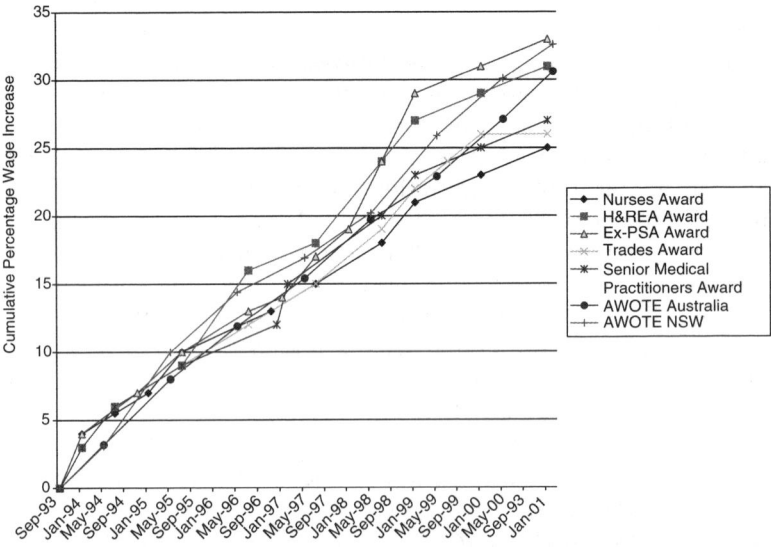

Figure 7.1   Cumulative Percentage Wage Increase

Note: The AWOTE data details the percentage increases for average weekly ordinary time earnings for full-time adult employees (that part of the total earnings attributable to award, standard or agreed hours of work). The data was sourced from the Australian Bureau of Statistics, Average Weekly Earnings, States and Australia catalogue 6302.0. [79]

Source: The wage data were sourced from NSW Health Department Policy Circulars from the period. These circulars are prepared by NSW Health Department staff for relevant Area Health Services/Hospitals staff and outline the award changes/variations and the relevant implementation dates. Awards and Determinations for the occupational groups were also used as source documentation (for a sample of such documents, see Appendix 1).

only relate to base salary and do not include private practice drawing rights or allowances, fringe benefits or salary packaging benefits. Second, they report only cumulative percentage wage increases, not absolute wages or salaries.

Recognizing the limitations of the data, it can be seen from Figure 7.1 that the five awards delivered roughly similar cumulative wage increases of around 15 percent to their respective occupational groups in the first round that ended towards the end of 1996. The non-clinical staff represented by the H&REA gained slightly higher increases, while the nurses received the lowest increase.

The second round of bargaining from late 1996 to 2000 produced a wider range of wage outcomes. The clinical support groups, formerly represented by the PSA but latterly by the H&REA, received the most significant increases, totaling around 33 percent over the three years, followed by the non-clinical support groups. Again, the lowest increases were gained by the nurses and the trades groups.

The respective wage positions of the five occupational groups over the full 6–7 year period show that cumulative wage increases ranged from around 33 percent for clinical support groups to 25 percent for nurses.

As well as reporting absolute wage increases from the respective awards, Figure 7.1 also provides a comparison between public health sector wage increases and those across all industries in both Australia and New South Wales, as measured by the Average Weekly Ordinary Time Earnings (AWOTE) series from the Australian Bureau of Statistics. These comparisons show that only the clinical and non-clinical support groups received wage increases above the all-industries average during the period in question.

Work intensification

Section 2 above demonstrated significant productivity increases in NSW public hospitals during the 1990s. Some of this increased productivity was attributable to more efficient management practices. The Report by the NSW Health Council in 2000 correctly identified a number of innovative measures being undertaken by various wards, departments and hospitals to accommodate the pressure of increasing demands. For example, initiatives as part of the National Demonstration Hospitals Program improved the planning and scheduling of surgical procedures and consequently achieved a reduction by 26 percent in unplanned re-admissions within a month of surgery and a 50 percent decrease in the cancellation of surgery on the day of admission [13].

However, much of the increased productivity appears to be attributable to simply doing more with less – the health workforce was working harder to accommodate the increasing patients numbers, with a corresponding trend towards work intensification. Allen's unpublished thesis of 1996 describes a similar trend in Queensland hospitals as a "quicker and sicker" discharge plan; that is, patients are treated quicker and discharged sicker [63]. He also correctly identifies the effects of this type of plan on staff. On the one hand, when the duration of the hospital stay reduces, there is less time for staff to complete the treatment/care regime within the hospital. In other words, inpatients received the most intensive components of their treatment whilst they were in hospital. Furthermore, once the initial patient is discharged, another patient fills the bed, requiring new treatments. On the other hand, when patients are discharged earlier the treatment regime simply continues as an outpatient service, increasing the load on staff in this area. In this way, the workload intensifies for the staff involved in both inpatient and outpatient areas. Even the very positive analysis of the NSW system provided by the Report of the NSW Health Council, which generally concluded that the current system appeared to provide excellent, accessible and affordable health care, recognized that "the system is feeling the pressure of increased patient demand and rising costs" [13].

The process of work intensification described by the aggregate statistics was generally achieved through incremental change, but it produced urgent short-term crises in particular locations and at particular times. Winter is a time of the year when acute shortages of beds almost inevitably lead to media reports that focus on the impact on patients. For example, on 9 November 1999, the *Sydney Morning Herald* reported [64]:

Emergency wards at five Sydney public hospitals were closed yesterday to all patients except those with life-threatening conditions. A chronic bed shortage meant people with severe cancer pain or pneumonia, who would normally have been admitted, were turned away.... In September, Westmead Hospital was closed to all but life-threatening cases 52 percent of the time. Last month it was closed about a third of the time...All the State's hospitals have recently closed their so-called "winter beds" – whole wards designed to be opened for colder months, when the higher incidence of respiratory illnesses put pressure on emergency departments.

The impact of these crises on staff workloads rarely received the same media attention. One senior health bureaucrat, however, was recently quoted as acknowledging the pressures that high rates of bed occupancy rates create for staff:

Occupancies in the late 80s percentile are difficult to manage and above 90 percent cause stress for hospital and management staff [65].

The same newspaper article went on to assert that these crisis situations were common occurrences:

...NSW Audit Office data shows (sic) Central Coast Area Health Service (AHS) hospital bed occupancies jumped 2 percent to 96.6 percent last year [i.e. 1999], Hunter AHS occupancies increased to 88.3 percent, while Illawarra AHS bed occupancy was 91.8 percent. Metropolitan Sydney fared no better, with at least 88 percent of hospital beds occupied last year in northern Sydney, southern Sydney and western Sydney AHSs, as well as Wentworth AHS [65].

By the end of the 1990s, staff shortages and excessive workloads were becoming the focus of public comment and staff protests. For example:

A coalition of senior doctors from Sydney's top teaching hospitals has called for a major review of Australia's health care system, including Medicare, to resolve what they describe as a crisis in hospitals... [66]
...You're pushed so much and have got so many people to look after that you don't get any time to sit down and spend any quality time with the individual patients...Consider the responsibility: you've got 165 acute neuropatients to look after and you're getting paid as much as someone packing shelves. It doesn't seem right (Neurosurgical Nurse, John Hunter Hospital). [67]

In Victoria, such protests have been coordinated into an industrial campaign by the nurses' union to introduce workload limits by specifying in the appropriate awards a maximum patient-nurse ratio [68–71]. However, no such campaign had emerged in New South Wales until recently. Indeed, the emphasis of union strategy seemed to be merely on wages and salaries rather than workloads, which is consistent with centralized "whole of government" wage agreements. The most common response, for example, of the nurses' union to the widely acknowledged shortage of nurses was to push the government for higher wage increases in order to attract nurses back to the wards [67, 72–75]. One possible reason for pursuing wages over workload issues may be that the relevant public hospital nurses awards have not traditionally regulated the work practices or workloads of nurses in a prescriptive manner, which makes demonstrating intensified workload levels or their implementation somewhat more difficult to demonstrate [76, 77]. However, the special wages case [61, 62] discussed above did initiate important changes in relation to regulating nursing workloads, the effects of which are yet to be evaluated.

Conclusions

There are many pressures on the NSW public hospital system, stemming from governments that expect lower costs and greater efficiency, from the broader population that is demanding greater access to health care services and from new technologies, drugs and procedures that are increasingly expensive, despite the better clinical outcomes they offer. This scenario is not unusual.

However, unlike many other jurisdictions, these pressures in New South Wales have not been addressed through radical changes in labour laws or industrial relations institutions. The public hospital sector continues to be highly unionized, managers – at the levels of NSW Health, Area Health Services and individual hospitals – have rarely tried or succeeded in excluding unions and the regulatory system has not deregulated or decentralized to the significant detriment of employees.

Nonetheless, employees in New South Wales public hospitals are feeling the pressure. Their wages have increased, but not significantly more (or less) than those of other workers. Work intensification is very different issue, though. Managers and employees are expected to do more with less, the number of patients is increasing, the services they are receiving must be provided more intensively and staff numbers are not keeping pace. The formal institutions of industrial relations rarely provide an adequate mechanism to address such issues. Changes in work practices, whether they are innovative ways of doing things or just more of the same, are mostly introduced unilaterally by management in an attempt to meet the budgetary objectives they receive from higher authorities. Unions have found opposition difficult, while the professionalism of employees often leads them to accept the changes, albeit reluctantly. The pressure, however, is building and it remains to be seen how much longer it can continue.

Bibliography

[1]   Donato R., Scotton R. The Australian Health Care System. In: Mooney G., Scotton R., editors. Economics and Australian Health Policy. St Leonards: Allen & Unwin, 1999.

[2]   Whelan J. Pressure mounts for more hospital funding. *Sydney Morning Herald*, 10 November 1999.

[3]   Palmer G. Health Insurance and Financing. In: Head B., Patience A., editors. From Fraser to Hawke: Australian Public Policy in the 1980s. Melbourne: Longman Cheshire, 1989.

[4]   Gray G. Health Policy. In: Jennett C., Stewart R., editors, Hawke and Australian Public Policy. Melbourne: Macmillan, 1990.

[5]   Commonwealth Department of Health & Aged Care. Reforming the Australian Health Care System: The Role of Government, Occasional Papers: New Series No. 1. AGPS: Canberra, 1999.

[6]   Private Health Insurance Administration Council, 2004 http://www.phiac.gov.au/statistics/membershipcoverage

[7]   Degeling G., Thomas D. Health Policy. In: Laffin M., Painter, M., editors. Reform and Reversal: Lessons from the Coalition Government in NSW 1988–1995. Melbourne: Macmillan, 1995.

[8]   Collyer F. Privatisation and the Public Purse: The Port Macquarie Base Hospital. *Just Policy* 1997; 10: 27–39.

[9]   Pusey M. Economic Rationalism in Canberra. Sydney: Cambridge University Press, 1991.

[10] Bell S. Ungoverning the Economy. Melbourne: Melbourne University Press, 1997.

[11] George J., Davis A. States of Health: Health and Illness in Australia, 3rd edition. South Melbourne: Longman, 1998.

[12] Galbally R. Placing Prevention at the Centre of Health Sector Reform. In: Bloom A., editor. Health Reform in Australia and New Zealand. South Melbourne: Oxford University Press, 2000.

[13] New South Wales Health Council. A Better Health System for NSW, Sydney: NSW Government, 2000.

[14] NSW Ministerial Advisory Committee on Health Services in Smaller Towns. Report to the Minister for Health: A Framework for Change (Sinclair Report). Sydney: NSW Health Department, 2000.

[15] Davis A. Managerialised Health Care. In: Rees S., Rodley G., editors. The Human Costs of Managerialism, Sydney: Pluto Press, 1995.

[16] Allen C., Barry M. The Private Hospitals' Association of Queensland. In: Sheldon P., Thornthwaite L., editors. Employer Associations and Industrial Relations Change. Sydney: Allen & Unwin, 1999.

[17] Stoelwinder J., Viney R. A Tale of Two States: New South Wales and Victoria. In: Bloom A., editor. Health Reform in Australia and New Zealand. South Melbourne: Oxford University Press, 2000.

[18] New South Wales Health. Planning Better Health: Background Information. July 2004.

[19] Gilbert R., Gibberd B., Stewart J. The New South Wales Resource Allocation Formula: a method for equitable health funding. *Australian Health Review* 1992; 15 (1): 6–21.

[20] NSW Health Department SES Guidelines (http://www.health.nsw.gov.au).

[21]   NSW Health Department. Annual Reports. Sydney: NSW Health Department, 1991/2–1998/99.

[22]   O'Donnell M. Continuity and Change: The New South Wales Public Sector Under Labor. *Australian Journal of Public Administration* 2000, 59 (4): 93–9.

[23]   Leeder S. Healthy Medicine: Challenges facing Australia's health services. St Leonards: Allen & Unwin, 1999.

[24]   NSW Health. NSW Public Hospital/Health Comparison Data Books. Sydney: NSW Health Department, 1991/92–1998/99.

[25]   Bray M. Ostenfeld S. Recent Developments in Australian Industrial Relations: A Unique Experience?. *New Zealand Journal of Industrial Relations* 1999, 24 (3): 219–29.

[26]   McCallum R., Ronfeldt P. Our Changing Labour Law. In: Ronfeldt P., McCallum R., editors. Enterprise Bargaining, Trade Unions and the Law. Sydney: Federation Press, 1995.

[27]   Shaw J. In Defence of the Collective: New South Wales Industrial Relations in the 21st Century. *Journal of Industrial Relations* 1997; 39 (3): 388–404.

[28]   Jamieson S. Industrial Relations. In: Laffin M., Painter M., editors. Reform and Reversal: Lessons from the Coalition Government in NSW 1988–1995, Melbourne: Macmillan, 1995.

[29]   Shaw J. A Balanced Industrial Relations Reform Package for New South Wales. *Journal of Industrial Relations* 1996; 38 (1): 57–69.

[30]   Painter M. Microeconomic Reform and the Public Sector. In Laffin M., Painter M., editors. Reform and Reversal: Lessons from the Coalition Government in NSW 1988–1995, Melbourne: Macmillan, 1995.

[31]   NSW Premier's Department. Reform and Redirection: Using Corporate Services Reform to Enhance Government Services in NSW. Sydney: NSW Government Printer, 1999.

[32]   White N., Bray M. An Exceptional Case? (The Lack of) Enterprise Bargaining in NSW Public Hospitals. In Burgess J., Macdonald D., editors. Developments in Australian Enterprise Bargaining. Melbourne: Tertiary Press, 2003.

[33]   NSW Health Department, HR2003 Framework.

[34]   Legge K. Human Resource Management: Rhetorics & Realities. London: Macmillan, 1995.

[35]   Lambert R. State of the Union: An Assessment of Union Strategies. *The Economic and Labour Relations Review* 1991; 2 (2): 1–24.

[36]   Tomkins M. Trade Union Amalgamations: Explaining the Recent Spate of Mergers in Australia. Labour & Industry 1999; 9 (3): 61–78.

[37]   McCallum R. Two Approaches to Industrial Relations Reform in New South Wales: The Making of the Industrial Relations Act of 1991 and 1996. In: Nolan D., editor. The Australiasian Labour Law Reforms: Australia and New Zealand at the End of the Twentieth Century. Sydney: Federation Press, 1998.

[38]   Allan C. The Elasticity of Endurance: Work Intensification and Workplace Flexibility in the Queensland Public Hospital System. *New Zealand Journal of Industrial Relations* 1997, 23 (3): 133–151.

[39]   O'Donnell M. Empowerment or Enslavement? Lean Production, Immigrant Women and Service Work in Public Hospitals. Labour & Industry 1995; 6 (3): 73–94.

[40] Willis E. Enterprise Bargaining and Work Intensification: an Atypical Case Study from the South Australia Public Hospital Sector, *New Zealand Journal of Industrial Relations* 2002; 27 (2): 221–232.

[41] Commissioner Blair. Decision in Victorian Hospitals' Industrial Association and the Australian Nursing Federation. Australian Industrial Relations Commission Print K6359. 31 August 2000.

[42] Young S. Public Health in Victoria: The Reform Process. In: Burgess J., Strachan G., editors. Research on Work, Employment and Industrial Relations: Proceedings of the 14th AIRAANZ Conference – Volume 2: Newcastle, 2000.

[43] Braithwaite J. Competition, Productivity and the Cult of "More is Good" in the Australian Health Care Sector. *Australian Journal of Public Administration* 1997; 56 (1): 37–44.

[44] Braithwaite J. Identifying the Elements in the Australian Health Service Management Revolution. *Australian Journal of Public Administration* 1993; 52 (4): 417–430.

[45] Braithwaite, J. Strategic Management and Organisational Structure: Transformational processes at work in hospitals. *Australian Health Review* 1993; 16 (4): 383–404.

[46] Boyce R. A. Organisational governance structures in allied health services: A decade of change. *Australian Health Review* 2001; 24 (1): 22–36.

[47] Boyce R. A. Hospital Restructuring – the implication for allied health professionals. *Australian Health Review* 1991; 14 (2): 147–154.

[48] NSW Premiers Department, Ministerial Memorandum 99–10 – Suspension of Advertising and Filling of Vacancies, 1999.

[49] NSW Health Department. Managing Displaced Employees Policy – Circular No. 2000/78, 2000.

[50] Health Industry Status of Employment Interim (State) Award.

[51] NSW Health Department. NSW Nursing Workforce Research Project Report 2000, 2000.

[52] Wolff A. M. Recruitment of medical practitioners to rural areas: A practical approach from the coalface. *Australian Health Review* 1997; 20 (2): 4–12.

[53] Knowles C. Minister Launches Campaign to Fill 1,100 Nursing Jobs. Minister for Health Media Release, 9 June 2000.

[54] NSW Health Department, Recruitment and Retention of Nurses Progress Report, 2001.

[55] Allan C. Stabilising the Non-Standard Workforce: Managing Labour Utilisation in Private Hospitals. Labour & Industry 1998; 8 (3): 61–76.

[56] Allan C. Patterns of Labour Use in a Private Hospital Case Study in Queensland. In Sonder L., editor. Current Research in Industrial Relations: Proceedings of the 9th AIRAANZ Conference, Melbourne, February 1995.

[57] ACIRRT. Stop Telling Us to Cope Report. Sydney: University of Sydney, 2002.

[58] Strachan G. Not Just a Labour of Love: Industrial Action by Nurses in Australia. *Nursing Ethics* 1997; 4 (4): 294–302.

[59] Stanton P. The Impact of Enterprise Bargaining on Union Membership and Organisation in the Victorian Health Sector. Paper Presented to "Ten Year of Enterprise Bargaining" Conference, Newcastle, May 2001.

[60] NSW Nurses Association, http://www.nswnurses.asn.au.

[61] Public Hospital Nurses (State) Award (No. 3), Re [2002] NSWIRComm 325.

[62] Public Hospital Nurses (State) Award (No. 4) Re [2003] NSWIRComm 442.

[63] Allan C. Labour Utilisation in Queensland Hospitals. Unpublished PhD Thesis. Brisbane: Griffith University, 1996.

[64] Ragg M., Whelan, J. Hospitals bar all but the dying. *Sydney Morning Herald*, 9 November 1999.

[65] Allen L. NSW hospital bed occupancy up. *Australian Financial Review*, 22 March 2001.

[66] Whelan J. Doctors despair over sick system. *Sydney Morning Herald*, 13 August 1999.

[67] Davison N. Running out of care. *Newcastle Herald*, 21 July 2001.

[68] Cave M., Skulley M. Nurses lead Victoria into workplace chaos. *The Australian Financial Review*, 13 August 2001.

[69] Workplace Express. IRC to arbitrate Victorian nursing dispute, 20 July 2001.

[70] Leyden F. Angry nurses converge on city. *The Age*, 17 July 2001.

[71] Shaw M., Toy M-A. Surgery at risk as nurses take action. *The Age*, 10 August 2001.

[72] *Newcastle Herald*, We are worth more: nurses. 20 July 2001.

[73] Allison L. Nurses' work bans start today. *Newcastle Herald*, 9 August 2001.

[74] Allison L. Nurses close to mass walkout. *Newcastle Herald*, 11 August 2001.

[75] Robinson M. Hospital Beds hit by dispute. *Sydney Morning Herald*, 8 August 2001.

[76] White N., Bray M. The Changing Role of Nurse Unit Managers: A Case of Work Intensification?. Labour & Industry 2003: 14 (2): pp. 1–19.

[77] White N., Bray M., Awards, Managerial Prerogative and Workplace Change: Case Study Evidence from the Health Sector. Paper Presented to 18th AIRAANZ Conference, February 2004, Noosa.

[78] Australian Bureau of Statistics – Catalogue 6310.0, Employee Earnings, Benefits and Trade Union Membership.

[79] Australian Bureau of Statistics – Catalogue 6302.0, Average Weekly Earnings of Employees.

Appendix 7.1 Public Health Sector Unions and Awards as at 1999

Occupation	Union	Employee Coverage	Award
Nursing	NSW Nurses Association *	All Nurses including managers and unskilled aides	Public Hospital Nurses' (State) Award
Medical	Australian Salaried Medical Officers Federation	Specialist Medical Officers (Staff Specialists, Post Graduate Fellows etc)	Salaried Senior Medical Practitioners (State) Award
			Salaried Senior Medical Practitioners (State) Determination – Specialist Medical Officers only
		Medical Superindentents (election available between awards and associations)	Salaried Senior Medical Practitioners (State) Award
	Health & Research Employees Association # +		Public Hospitals (Medical Superintendents) Award
	Australian Medical Association	Visiting Medical Officers	Public Hospitals (Visiting Medical Officers Sessional Contracts) Determination 1994
	Health & Research Employees Association # +	Interns, Residents, Registrars	Public Hospital (Medical Officers) Award
		Career Medical Officers	Public Hospital (Career Medical Officers) Award
Allied Health/ Clinical Support Staff	Health & Research Employees Association # +	Physiotherapists, Occupational Therapists, Speech Pathologists	Public Hospital Physiotherapists, Occupational Therapists and Speech Pathologists (State) Award
			Public Hospital (Professional & Associated Staff) Conditions of Employment (State) Award
		Dieticians	Scientific Officers (Public Hospital Dieticians) State Award

Appendix 7.1   Public Health Sector Unions and Awards as at 1999 – continued

Occupation	Union	Employee Coverage	Award
		Social Workers	Public Hospital Social Workers (State) Award Health Employees Conditions of Employment (State) Award
		Hospital Scientists	Hospital Scientists (State) Interim Award
		Biomedical Engineers	Public Hospital Engineers' (Biomedical Engineers) (State) Award
		Medical Record Librarians	Public Hospital Medical Record Librarians Award
		Pharmacists	Health Employees Pharmacists (State) Award
		Radiographers	Health Employees Medical Radiation Scientists (State) Award
Non-Clinical Support Staff	Health & Research Employees Association +	Non-Clinical Managers, eg, Finance, HR, Business Managers ^	Health Managers (State) Award
		General Administrative Staff, eg Supply or Catering Managers	Health Employees General Administrative Staff (State) Award
		Administrative & Clerical Staff	Health Employees Administrative Staff (State) Award
		Information Technology Staff	Health Employees Computer Staff (State) Award
		Catering, Cleaning, Security & Gardening Staff	Health Employees (State) Award

Appendix 7.1 Public Health Sector Unions and Awards as at 1999 – *continued*

Occupation	Union	Employee Coverage	Award
Trades	Construction, Forestry, Mining & Energy Union	Carpenters, Painters, Tilers, Plasterers, etc	Public Hospital Employees' Skilled Trades (State) Award
	Electrical Trades Union	Electrical Tradespersons	
	Plumbers and Gasfitters Employees Union	Plumbers, Gasfitters and Drainers	

* State Branch of the national Australian Nurses Federation
# Covered by the Public Service Association prior to 31 May 1998
+ State Branch of the national Health Services Union
^ Previously covered by the Health Officers Association which amalgamated with the Health & Research Association in 1995

8
Comparative Analysis and Conclusions
Kurt Wetzel

The foregoing chapters examine the particulars of health reform industrial relations in five jurisdictions. This section considers the evidence
drawn from those restructuring experiences, looking at common principles or themes, similar features and instructive points of comparison.
It argues that specific approaches to restructuring can be linked to
identifiable industrial relations outcomes and that there are lessons to
be learned from the five case studies.

Government

The political inclinations of governments involved in reforming health
care systems are generally reflected in one of three policy paradigms.
The assumptions underlying each paradigm are typically carried into
the operating modes that guide the processes of implementing industrial relations restructuring schemes and the sector's on-going labour
relations. While there is no reason to expect perfect alignment of a
government's political beliefs, policy paradigms, choice of operating
modes and the sector's industrial relations climate, it is reasonable to
search for discernible patterns linking political beliefs and industrial
relations themes.

Health reform is conducted within three political climates. First,
social democratic agendas focus primarily upon reforming public
health delivery systems. Social democrats' objective is to improve
public systems' capacity to deliver quality health services effectively.
The "incrementalist reform" paradigm is most consistent with a social
democratic approach to health reform. It involves an effort to preserve
a publicly funded and provided health care delivery system by restructuring it. Of the jurisdictions examined, this paradigm is most evident

in Saskatchewan and in New Zealand starting in the late 1990s under the Labour Party.

By contrast, neoconservative governments treat health reform as only one component of a much larger political agenda. That agenda focuses on marketizing the provision of public services. The "market revolutionary" reform paradigm is intended to import competing providers, profit sector-like efficiency and business methods into the public sector, including public health services. In doing so, it focuses on fundamentally transforming the way the public sector operates. Market revolutionary policies are rooted in ideology. The Thatcher government, New Zealand during the 1980s and early 1990s, and Alberta fit this characterization.

The third political regime within which health reform occurs, "policy eclecticism," is less a product of guiding principles or ideology. Instead, government policy and programs reflect temporal and contextual pressures, for example, political, fiscal and administrative. Hence, policy and programs are an eclectic or opportunistic mix. The New South Wales and Blair governments most closely reflect this approach.

Governments' policy paradigms embody their industrial relations perspectives, which are manifested in operating or implementation modes. The choice of operating modes reflects the degree to which industrial relations issues are strategic considerations on the part of those who plan and implement health reform or whether they are treated as afterthoughts that can be addressed on an *ad hoc* basis. As identified and explored in this book, three modes predominate: unilateralism, third partyism and the negotiating model. Although one mode may be favoured, in reality governments employ a mix of practices.

Incrementalist reform/negotiating model

The social democratic policy and program paradigm, incremental reformism, focuses on improving the effectiveness and efficiency of publicly provided health services by restructuring, not revolutionizing, the public sector. It is part of a New Deal-like tradition which assumes that the public sector can equitably and effectively address public needs by delivering services. Indeed, governments should manifest civil society's will by means of an active public sector. This set of political values treats universally accessible, publicly funded health care as both emblematic of a just society and an efficient means of delivering services.

For social democratic governments, health reform represents an opportunity to reconceive, reorganize and reinvigorate public health systems and improve their capacity to address health needs. This belief is informed more by practical experience and a product of values than theory or ideology. Where it proclaims a vision, that vision is grounded in thinking about improving health. Incremental reformist policies might embrace "wellness" as a guiding principle and goal. The challenge facing incrementalist reformers in the health sector is to find organizational structures and ways of operating that enable them to accomplish more with available resources. Incremental reform health policies can occasion extensive and disruptive organizational change.

The prevalent industrial relations operating mode for implementing policy change and operating under incremental reformism is typically the "negotiating model." This mode reflects the pluralistic assumption that those who are likely to be affected by change, including workers and their representatives, should have input into decisions affecting them. Their involvement has the potential to improve decision making and to foster commitment in the workplace and to the change process. Under ideal circumstances, unions, management and government might develop collaborative relationships committed to preserving the public health care delivery system.[1] Social democratic parties might also hope to win labour's electoral support.

The search for mutually satisfactory accommodations involves a willingness by those in power to negotiate and consult with unions on structural and transitional matters including representational issues, labour force adjustment programs, job evaluation systems and the structure of bargaining. Union recognition and respect for collective agreements and unwritten understandings are *sine qua non*s. By involving unions in making decisions as to how, if not whether, change should occur, the negotiating model is used to avoid the polarization and ill will that unilateral action courts. It treats compromise and delay required to reach accords as the price for collaborative change and sustainable arrangements.

The model's allure is longer-term effectiveness. It does not promise short-term efficiency or prompt results. It can be used to build understanding and relationships based on trust and respect, which may extend the boundaries of shared decision making. The negotiating model anticipates routine communication and extensive information sharing. Ideally, the actors could develop relationships that allow them to address complex, intractable health restructuring and ongoing industrial relations issues collaboratively and in ways that improve the health care delivery system's effectiveness and make it a good place to work.

As Saskatchewan's experience with free collective bargaining in the health sector attests, when resources are limited, the challenge of maintaining or expanding the ambit of the negotiating model beyond traditional adversarialism is enormous. For the model to work, government must apply it consistently, even under difficult circumstances. Its unseemly and untimely (from the nurses' perspective) intervention to preclude an impending strike generated a political and industrial relations backlash. The government is now reticent to intervene in disputes.

Saskatchewan's labour-friendly government is wary of contemplating or unable to comprehend the task of transforming relationships.[2] The actors' mindsets and experience may not equip them to move beyond adversarialism. Broader adoption of the negotiating model leads to the creation of reciprocal rights and obligations and can raise workers' and unions' expectations and management's apprehensions. Management may be reluctant to see any erosion of managerial prerogative. Unions' inherent conservatism and internal political dynamics may make them both leery of innovative departures wherein they assume greater responsibility and unreliable partners in trust-based endeavours. Opposition parties may use attempts to innovate as evidence of "selling out" to labour. Indeed, this government's strategy seems to have involved forcing change by trimming budgets but not specifying the desired outcomes or change processes.

In Saskatchewan, such experimentation as has occurred has been undertaken away from government. It is, after all, labour and management who must live and deal with the complex organizational and operational issues. Despite the promising results of these efforts to address complex non-wage issues, monetary issues have remained the source of conflict. The negotiating model recognizes both the actors' distinctness and their interdependence, the potential for conflict as well as cooperation.[3] It allows that conflict, including job action, is normal. Although laws designating certain employees as essential and barred from striking[4] as well as third-party arbitration may be used, in its purest form, the negotiating model allows an unfettered right to strike.

In New Zealand, the latest Labour government has implemented a policy calling for expanded participation. Its recent labour legislation, which is intended to expand the ambit of joint decision making, and the Public Service Alliance's embrace of collaborative decision making may combine to provide an incipient model for different relationships using the negotiating model.

Market revolutionary reform/unilateralism

Influenced by thinking pioneered by Frederich Hayek[5] and developed by Chicago school economists, neoconservatives regard state intervention, including public health care delivery systems, as inefficient and ultimately a threat to individual freedom. Instead of an active public sector, advocates of this ideology would minimize the state's role, lower taxes, eliminate deficits, reduce debt and, wherever possible, rely on markets to meet society's needs. Neoconservatives may seek to alter the premises upon which the public sector operates by introducing systemic, indeed radical, change aimed at marketizing it.

Short of a wholesale privatization of public services, which could prove politically untenable, neoconservative governments can embrace a "market revolutionary" policy and program paradigm. This paradigm is rooted in microeconomics, i.e. public choice and agency theories.[6] The thinking holds that where government is a monopoly provider of public services, it has no incentive to maximize efficiency. Market revolutionary programs are designed to transform the way in which services are delivered by introducing market competition or market-like mechanisms to the public sector.[7] The driving force behind market revolutionary health reform programs is economic theory and a drive for efficiency, not new visions of health.

At a minimum, market revolutionary reform entails having health organizations operate according to the private sector example. It focuses on creating an ambiance for "business-like" efficiency, often overseen by managers with non-health sector backgrounds. This approach is evident in the market revolutionary reform programs of Britain, Alberta and New Zealand in the 1980s and early 1990s. Health organizations may be called upon to prepare business plans for which they are accountable. The approach is similar to the "corporatization" process used in New Zealand when government departments providing printing, postal, telephone, electrical, banking and rail services were transformed into profit maximizing "state-owned enterprises." Most were ultimately privatized.[8]

Market revolutionary policies and programs typically expand the private sector's role as a health service provider. Private sector providers offer a range of health services in Britain, New Zealand and Australia. Market revolutionary policies may encourage public health organizations to contract out non-core services (e.g. dietary, cleaning, laboratory), as is the case in New Zealand, or in Britain, where the Conservatives instituted compulsory tendering. In New Zealand there is tendering for specific medical procedures such as cataract and bypass surgery. Policies may include de-insuring certain health services.

Market revolutionary programs may also involve creating "public markets." In its purest form, this entails the "funder" (i.e. government) establishing "purchasers" (e.g. regional health authorities) to buy health services from competing public, private not-for-profit and for-profit "providers." Tender winners become accountable to the purchasers for delivering the specified services.[9] This is a direction being followed in New Zealand and Britain and contemplated by Alberta.

Market revolutionary ideology does not treat employees as stake-holders or unions as partners. Rather, workers are apt to be regarded as labour market commodities and unions as rent-seeking interest groups, indeed retrogressive artifacts of a bygone industrial era. Collective agreements can be impediments to achieving the efficiency and flexibility that markets promise. Unions can block, slow or distort efforts to reform health services delivery. Therefore, market revolutionary policies seek to weaken unions, if not to administer a *coup de grace* to unionism. This may include legislation designed to limit unions' power by ending their right to take collective action, as in Alberta, and restricting their capacity to represent their members, for example, New Zealand's elimination of management's duty to recognize and bargain with unions. Policies may also involve the creation of institutional environments designed to limit unions' capacity to withstand the impact of market forces (e.g. decentralized bargaining). Again, the New Zealand example is compelling.

The market revolutionary's preferred mode for implementing health reform and operating the system includes a strong element of "unilateralism". This involves acting expeditiously and vigorously relying on the state's powers and managerial prerogative. Unilateralism is associated with a view of private sector management, in which change occurs top down, is intended to yield prompt results, and ignores industrial relations niceties. It envisions those in positions of power addressing complicated issues decisively, without becoming mired in protracted, rancorous processes for sharing information, examining implications and details, and reaching messy compromises. Longstanding protocols, collective agreements and legislation upon which unions might have relied may be ignored or summarily changed. Thus, government is not obliged to consult on policy decisions, and managers of semi-autonomous units are empowered to restructure the workplace, pursue flexibility and take important personnel actions. Marketizers in New Zealand, Britain and Alberta have all used these approaches.

The allure of unilateralism is efficiency. The approach is bold, purposeful, even blitz-like. Industrial relations issues are treated as ancillary considerations that can be attended to on an *ad hoc* or *post hoc* basis to bring them into conformity with the change program. Labour is expected to adapt and, optimally, to help adjust the health system to reform. The unilateralist approach to negotiations may be perfunctory. Bargaining agendas are limited and perhaps focused on extracting concessions from unions.[10] Management and government are especially empowered during economic downturns.

Unilateralists have two approaches to conflict. First, government may proscribe strikes. Unresolved differences may be resolved by fiat or arbitrated by third parties, perhaps by a "neutral" whose discretion is limited. These policies rely on union members quiescently obeying laws banning job action, even when they feel unfairly treated. This is the approach adopted by Alberta. Second, government may adopt institutional and structural changes that make it more difficult for unions to organize and bargain effectively, without disallowing strikes. New Zealand's market revolutionaries accomplished this by decentralizing bargaining to the health unit level.

Market revolutionaries are not deterred by the prospect that their programs and methods may generate resentment among the health workforce. Unilateralism is typically used to capitalize on opportunities to implement change without dwelling on industrial relations or political consequences. Neoconservatives do not court the labour vote. Their constituency is found among those who favour using the market or marketlike mechanisms to improve efficiency and, ideally, to reduce the size of the public sector, thereby allowing taxes to be lowered.

As long as the fiscal, political and labour market circumstances marginalize unions and heighten workers' insecurities, unilateralist practices can carry the momentum of a market revolutionary agenda. Unilateralism yields short-term results. However, changes wrought by market revolutionary reform and unilateralism can have the unintended consequence of strengthening unions and setting the stage for a test of wills. If workers' insecurities ease, their respect for or fear of government diminishes, and feelings of organizational loyalty erode, workers may sanction job actions, leave the industry and/or work to defeat the government.

Policy eclecticism

Whereas incremental and market revolutionary reform paradigms flow from political values or ideological conviction, the third paradigm, "policy eclecticism," reflects a pragmatic search for programs of whatever derivation. Policy eclecticism could involve opportunistic regression to a mean for governments that lack political conviction. It may also be a default option for those without the political means for converting their beliefs into coherent programs. Governments with social democratic predispositions caught in political environments that have shifted to the right may hesitate to embrace incremental reformist policies. One might expect to find elements of both market revolutionary and incrementalist reform paradigms in health restructuring initiatives typified by policy eclecticism.

The Economist characterizes the policy direction of Britain's New Labour Party government, elected in 1997, in such terms. Its purported lack of an ideological "compass" is symptomatic of a government with "no single big idea" that has adopted the shibboleth "whatever works" as a guiding principle.[11] Along similar lines, Bach notes that trade unions have criticized the Blair government for retaining its neoconservative predecessor's policies while employers fault its perceived willingness to re-regulate labour markets in favour of unions.[12]

While New Labour favours an active public sector, it has embraced the Conservatives' performance management systems to monitor and direct health units and tendering programs. Although not espousing market mechanisms, it advocates strong private sector involvement and is leery of provider capture. However, New Labour uses inclusive language and seeks to involve labour in implementing its health program. Not surprisingly, unions are apprehensive about what may be the advent of a stealthy privatization initiative. They are concerned that the government may be seeking local flexibility to set terms and conditions of employment within a national framework. New Labour's "modernization" mantra is conducive to various interpretations that fit the policy eclecticism paradigm.

Labor governments in New South Wales are well known for their political pragmatism and ideological ambiguity, which have led to an eclectic approach to health policy. This has been reinforced by the need to deal with Commonwealth governments (Labor until 1996 and then neoconservative) that have been influenced by economic rationalism. State governments have not sought to destroy unions or to dismantle longstanding institutions of conciliation and arbitration, but their health agendas have emphasized stronger and better public sector management in the name of delivering more cost-effective health outcomes. Substantial privatization was only briefly part of this agenda during the earlier conservative coalition government.

It is difficult to characterize precisely an operating mode consistent with policy eclecticism. Indeed, it may include a mix of unilateralism, the negotiating model and "third partyism," a practical technique for avoiding or diffusing conflict by resolving disputes impartially and rationally. Third partyism is associated with a sense of fairness and trust in neutrals whose expertise, independence and freedom to exercise discretion are acknowledged. It can be used to address intractable, complicated, high-stakes issues that are beyond the capacity of the actors to resolve without delay or conflict. This operating mode places a priority on maintaining industrial peace. Third partyism can be prescribed in policy as a default option or used as an *ad hoc* device.

Management

Much of what management experiences in the health reform process is common across jurisdictions. It is both a target of and a tool for restructuring. Compared to its private sector counterparts, health management typically has less opportunity to provide preliminary input into the process of determining the shape, direction and timetable of industry reform. Government's ideology, its fiscal and statutory or administrative industrial relations policies, and its health reform programs serve as contextual factors for health management. Moreover, government determines the type and amount of consideration that industrial relations issues receive and the strategies to be adopted to address them. Health sector management is a "policy taker". Government significantly influences the what, how and who of reform for management. Its policies affect the sector's attitudinal structures and the way the parties relate to each other.

Management's task is to implement the operational and organizational specifics of government policy, as directed by health boards. This may involve restructuring to create large, complex multi-site and -service organizations or small, nimble and competitive units, while simultaneously delivering ongoing health services. Government provides the resources to be used in transitions to new health regimes, i.e. it controls the funding. It also specifies the pace at which restructuring is to proceed.

Management addresses the downstream industrial relations consequences of reform's impact on organizations and workplaces. If resources are limited and budgets are tight, management may find itself facing a frustrated, insecure, suspicious and resentful workforce with low morale, tendencies toward militancy and high turnover rates. Since reform is an on-going rather than discrete process, organizational restructuring can occur repeatedly, thereby disturbing, exhausting and demoralizing workers. Where reform is less urgently pursued, more collaboratively implemented and better funded, there may be more good will, optimism and commitment throughout the workforce. Government influences the choice of the type of managers retained to implement reform. The sector can draw from the ranks of career professional health managers, recruit private sector managers with no health experience, or rely upon clinicians, who may be less well prepared to assume complex managerial roles but perhaps more aware of the impact of change on the public.

Restructuring is a managerially intensive undertaking. However, the rationalization of service delivery and the drive for efficiency may lead to reductions in the number of managers. Health organizations are loath to be perceived as cutting front-line workers' jobs without first trimming management ranks. This results in broadening the remaining managers' scopes of responsibility. While some managers may see themselves as being handed a rare opportunity to implement much-needed and leading edge change, others may experience reform as work intensification that leaves them feeling undervalued and overwhelmed. Resentment may build if they are not remunerated for added responsibilities or if they are blamed for not meeting unachievable objectives.

Management's industrial relations roles differ widely among jurisdictions. A major determinant of that role is government's oft-proclaimed predilection for decentralizing decision making. The government and management balance is unpredictable, dynamic and protean. Whatever the nature of the understandings, government may engage in politically inspired intervention. The size and organizational structure of health units and bargaining structures also help set the ambit of management's role. Government may be actively and directly involved in bargaining at a central level, or it may have its interests represented by an industry association. If bargaining occurs at the unit level, management is likely to conduct negotiations. Management's approach to dealing with its employee representatives is prescribed by government.

Market revolutionary New Zealand's funder/purchaser/provider split was designed to preclude government meddling with an empowered, efficiency-driven management. This model conferred unilateralist powers and operational autonomy upon health units, which were to become competitive organizations. An industry association composed of competitors would have been anathema. Decentralized bargaining allowed health units to set divergent, uncoordinated industrial relations courses. Under this fractured structure, management was able to roll back weak unions' employment conditions. Local practices and contract terms (e.g. pay structures, rates and benefits) became widely divergent. The New Zealand experience demonstrates management's need for a capacity to accommodate policy shifts. Subsequent governments have changed industrial relations policy and management's role. Health units are being called upon to work more collegially with each other as well as more collaboratively with unions. A nascent push is under way to recentralize bargaining.[13] Much as in the UK, government has shifted the prescribed operating mode from unilateralism to a negotiating model that includes soft human resource management and attempts at building social partnerships with unions.

By contrast, the Alberta government, which shares the New Zealand revolutionaries' ideology, has remained in power and retained market revolutionary policies. The industry's bargaining structures, unilateralist operating mode and governance structures have not changed. Health regions operate as fiefdoms overseen by trustees (all of whom are appointed) and administrators whose personal or political contacts enable them to manage health unit-government relationships. This government believes in strong, accountable management to act as the conduit for its will. There is no funder/purchaser/provider split; nor is the government-regional health unit relationship brokered by an industry association. Indeed, health reform brought the demise of Alberta's broad-purpose industry association, supplanting it with a weak, limited-purpose organization.

Alberta's strengthening labour markets and the fallout from reform have combined to generate an industrial relations backlash. Emboldened, even rebellious, workers whose unions have been strengthened by restructuring have begun to insist they be recompensed for their sacrifices. Government, not management, is the leading protagonist in Alberta's politicized bargaining.

Starting with the Conservatives, management of the UK's health system underwent transformations along the lines experienced in New Zealand. The unified national health system was fragmented into as many as 536 health care trusts run by managers instructed to adopt a private sector perspective. A purchaser/provider split was introduced to encourage competition among providers. Senior managers' authority, status and compensation rose. As in Alberta, government devolved operational managerial authority while maintaining political control and capacity to specify the objectives that management is accountable for achieving.

Management was empowered with operational discretion to enact flexible work practices and mandated to adopt market-like practices such as competitive tendering. Management was urged but not empowered to conduct wage bargaining locally. Due to the political sensitivity of health sector decision making, centralized pay determination structures were not transformed. Resistance by organized health professionals, political intervention and endemic resource constraints have combined to limit the effectiveness of management initiatives.

In 1997, Britain's political pendulum swung from the Conservatives to a policy eclectic New Labour government set on "modernizing" public service delivery. This government has changed the emphasis and tone of health policy while maintaining much of its essence, including central control. Instead of pursuing ideology-inspired market-like mechanisms, New Labour has taken an approach reminiscent of Alberta's. It sets and monitors management performance targets. Its primary care trusts serve in both provider and purchaser capacities. Like its predecessor, New Labour is wary of provider capture. It has retained a competitive tendering policy and private financing but uses the language of social partnership. Instead of focusing on ownership, it prefers to regulate private, voluntary and public service providers. The government willingly consults with the increasingly apprehensive unions about its program's implications. It has pledged to increase health spending for five years.

Although New Labour has discontinued performance-based pay, policy remains aggressively managerial. Government has devolved a variety of employee relations functions to the trusts. The role of health trust personnel specialists has gone from being perfunctory to one of integrating personnel considerations into the trusts' business plans. Middle managers are expected to assume greater decision-making responsibility in personnel matters. Management is focusing more on communicating with employees and increasing the flexibility of the workforce. It is also trying without notable success to decentralize wage bargaining. Other issues, however, remain the focus of local bargaining. Labour market conditions and staff shortages are forcing management to address work-life issues as it reconfigures the workforce and reallocates responsibilities among different classes of workers. The combined effect of New Labour's changes has occasioned management transformation, calling for greater use of human resource management practices.

Health managers in New South Wales have not had to adapt to far-reaching statutory, political or institutional change under either the earlier Liberal-National Coalition government or the Labor government elected in 1995. There has, however, been persistent pressure in the direction of a neoconservative agenda. Even the Commonwealth Labor government of the early 1990s was a source of these trends, but the pressure intensified after the election of its more conservative successor. The state Labor government might have eschewed privatization, but private-sector-like management techniques and cost control were important elements of its health sector policies, which included wellness programs, deinstitutionalizing service delivery, reallocating resources to areas of population growth, and creating regional administrative units.

Industrial relations in New South Wales were centrally led. They were characterized by a longstanding system of sector-wide awards negotiated between unions and the centralized Department of Health. The Department also remained the formal employer of health sector employees and retained control over most aspects of manpower planning, recruitment and retention, performance management and industrial relations. Within this context, however, strict budget controls and new performance management systems forced local managers to initiate workplace changes in the pursuit of improved productivity and reduced costs. There was no attack on unions or their members' wages, conditions or security. Unions' participation was actually welcomed provided they agreed to work collaboratively towards improving the effectiveness of health organizations.

In contrast to the New South Wales government's inclination to intervene in personnel matters, Saskatchewan's incrementalist reform NDP government has left management to its own devices. Its health reform vision included devolution, participation, and cost reduction. Communities, not bureaucrats, determined the initial health districts' boundaries, and boards were partially elected. The Department of Health's role was curtailed.

While the Saskatchewan government proffered no industrial relations vision, it did embrace the negotiating model. It moved collaboratively to address restructuring's disruptive consequences for health workers being laid off, transferred or moved to reduced status, and their unions, whose representational rights were affected. It also acceded to the unions' wishes to retain centralized bargaining and maintain the right to take collective action.

Management, in the form of a multi-purpose industry association, was assigned the role of representing government's monetary and health units' operational interests in provincial bargaining. Recognizing the complexity of the bargaining issues generated by restructuring, the industry association and two unions undertook successful interest-based bargaining initiatives. The association has assumed myriad roles, including coordinating a province-wide joint job evaluation system, shared systems and training programs, administering employee benefits, and carrying out an array of member services. It has become an industry focal point, providing a collective industry voice with which to address government and external bodies.

Management's situation at the unit level has been less auspicious. Management was assigned the formidable task of merging and integrating the disparate, pre-existing freestanding units into health service delivery organizations to accord with local needs. Restructuring was to be carried out using resources found within existing budgets, which had been trimmed. By comparison with other jurisdictions, Saskatchewan did not emphasize management's role; rather, it assumed that management would be up to the task. But restructuring overwhelmed, exhausted and demoralized the ill-equipped and under-resourced managers. Government made matters worse by intervening in the industry's affairs. The nadir was reached in 1999, when government injected itself into provincial bargaining with the nurses, aggravating a bitter two-week strike. Government has since backed off.

The experiences of these five jurisdictions reveal a range of distinctions and commonalities in managements' approaches to the industrial relations of health reform. It is evident that even after neoconservative governments have lost power, there is no fundamental retreat from the essence of market revolutionary policies. The UK, New South Wales and New Zealand cases indicate that new governments may soften robust market revolutionary polices and strident unilateralism, but the direction does not change. There is no going back. Governments use fiscal pressures and the need for efficiency to keep management operationally empowered. The softening is likely to be evinced in tone and the emergence of human resource management practices to cope with the strengthening demand for health professionals. Hence, health management must be ready to adapt.

It is also apparent that governments have an abiding wish to hold onto or reclaim power rather than decentralize. While regional service delivery is common, power devolution can be illusory or evanescent. Management is as likely to be the sector's handmaid as its leader. The Saskatchewan experience suggests that an active, membership-driven industry association can become both a vehicle for building a health sector identity and collegiality and a voice for the industry.

Health workers and unions

The impact of health restructuring on labour can be categorized by type of bargaining relationships associated with various institutional arrangements and industrial relations policy contexts. Restructuring can also be characterized in terms of how union members and different types of unions experience it.

Government policy and institutional change

The institutional and policy contexts within which restructuring occurs include a broad mix of statutory, budgetary, structural and administrative arrangements. They incorporate governments' ideologies, industrial relations perspectives and operating modes. These combine to have an enormous impact on unions' capacity to operate effectively, or even survive. The policy environment determines unions' rights to represent workers, their opportunity to participate in those aspects of the health restructuring process that affect them and their members, and relative power. Thus, organizational restructuring leading to the creation of larger or smaller independent health units, the structure of bargaining, labour relations laws and the jurisdiction's industrial relations history contribute to the industrial relations context.

After generations of centralized mandatory unionism, New Zealand's market revolutionary industrial relations and health restructuring policies were not union-friendly. In addition to imbuing management with unilateralist ardour, trimming health budgets and creating regional health units, which were to bargain local instead of national agreements, the government enacted the *Employment Contracts Act*. The Act made union membership voluntary and removed management's obligation to recognize or bargain with unions. Most unions went into survival mode as management sought concessions. Some merged; others were simply ignored or marginalized. A new government with incremental reformist policies consistent with the negotiating model has increased unions' opportunities for input and improved their prospects without markedly expanding their statutory rights. This is a boat that unions are loath to rock.

The Alberta government has pointedly excluded unions from health reform planning and decision-making processes. It extended a statutory strike ban and restrictive arbitration system to the entire health sector. However, unions' representation rights within this Wagner-like labour policy framework were addressed smoothly through voluntary local arrangements.[14] The resulting union amalgamations consolidated the larger unions' power. After examining the local bargaining option, employers largely opted to retain provincial bargaining. The government imposed wage cuts and freezes. Its funding policies led to workforce reductions. Unlike New Zealand, where dietary and housekeeping work was tendered, Alberta used tendering primarily as a threat to extract concessions rather than as a policy. At the outset of restructuring, managerial unilateralism and calls for sacrifice intimidated workers into quiescence. Militancy emerged only after the labour markets improved, the "fiscal crisis" ended, and workers realized that their sacrifices would not be recompensed. Even compliant unions recognized that militant action was a *sine qua non* for improving their situations and used threats and job actions that are illegal to achieve their objectives. In Alberta, neither side has given any quarter when it had the power advantage.

The social democratic Saskatchewan government's industrial relations policy has been to encourage free collective bargaining. Saskatchewan provides for the right to strike. It has incremental reformist policies and, with notable exceptions, adheres to the negotiating model. Restructuring initially resulted in layoffs and reductions in work status. Government negotiated a labour force adjustment program. The most significant institutional challenge accompanying health restructuring involved reorganizing unions' representational structures to make them compatible with a regionalized health system. Distrust borne of longstanding union rivalries and reluctance to cede members to rivals precluded a negotiated settlement. A third party was called upon to devise a system for reassigning representation rights. As in Alberta, the results of restructuring solidified the larger unions' power, and centralized bargaining remained the norm. Bargaining involved no rollbacks in the terms and conditions of employment. The first bargaining round under the new regime provided the parties with a fruitful learning experience. It included innovative collaboration, a misguided government intervention and strikes that revealed the limits of union power.

As in New Zealand, restructuring in Britain has spanned two political regimes. The market revolutionaries fragmented the centralized health system into more than 500 health care trusts, which assumed responsibility for key non-wage determination human resource management functions. Management was expected to take on private-sector-like ways, including compulsory competitive tendering of union jobs, and a purchaser/provider split was adopted. Despite the Conservatives' wish to move from centralized pay bargaining, which had taken place voluntarily between government and unions without management involvement, to decentralized pay bargaining, the process has mostly remained unchanged. New Labour has attempted to move toward a two-tier arrangement of national bargaining for doctors, nurses and support staff, which involves trusts dealing with local conditions that have pay implications. Local bargaining structures have involved multi-union tables, with small unions becoming marginalized. Their professional power, however, ensures their continuing importance. Management has increasingly been able to bypass unions and deal directly with the membership as well as create generic classifications of health workers. The change of government has shifted the tone rather than the substance of the changes to the health system. Privatization of service delivery remains a union concern.

New South Wales experienced comparatively little institutional restructuring. Traditional union bargaining rights were retained and, with the exception of some minor swaps in union coverage between unions, union representation continued largely as before. Similarly, despite the regionalization of management and some attempts in the 1993–96 period by the conservative Liberal government to introduce enterprise bargaining, the centralized bargaining structures supported by both the unions and the Department of Health remained intact. Membership in health unions declined, but less than in other industries.

Membership issues

Union members can be profoundly affected by health reform. They take their concerns to their unions, anticipating that the matters will be addressed. Health reform generates two categories of membership issues, transitional and emergent. *Transitional membership issues* are typically products of organizational and workplace restructuring. If sites or services are closed or merged, workers may be transferred to new workplaces, shifted to other unions and assigned different duties. They may be reassigned to different employers, including contractors. Restructuring can affect workers' job security and job status. Full-time employment may be replaced by part-time, temporary or casual status, or even unemployment. Restructuring can also raise issues regarding the status of collective agreements, seniority rights and redundancy arrangements.

The way transitional issues are dealt with reflects the operating mode the government endorses. In Saskatchewan, government, employers and unions concluded agreements to address workplace mergers, transfers and workforce adjustment. In New South Wales as well, these issues were mostly addressed through negotiations with unions. The Alberta government unilaterally imposed a labour adjustment program while leaving the merger/transfer matters to the local parties. Market revolutionary New Zealand left these matters to the discretion of local management. A major transitional issue for union members in the UK and New Zealand has been tendering of work to the private sector. Whereas this was accomplished in New Zealand, unions in Britain under New Labour have successfully fought to maintain affected workers' terms and conditions by treating transfers to the private sector as secondments.

Emergent membership issues are the operational consequences of reform. In contrast to transitional issues, which can be addressed summarily, emergent issues are more enduring. One such issue is work intensification. As health organizations strive to improve their efficiency, work processes are intensified. Workers may find themselves dealing with sicker patients but with insufficient resources. Thus, many find their jobs increasingly demanding and stressful. Reform implemented on short budgets can leave health care workers feeling overworked, ill paid, badly treated and resentful. They may miss the old order and see little cause for optimism about the future. Morale, recruitment and retention problems can develop. Workers may experience reform in ways that reduce their organizational commitment.

Workers' response to the deterioration of working conditions in Britain has prompted the government to begin espousing family-friendly policies designed to make health organizations and careers in health more attractive. Attempts to create trust-level flexibility have generated pay inequity issues within health trusts. These issues are increasing as personnel functions are decentralized. Like the UK, New South Wales has attempted to introduce new human resource policies to make the sector more attractive to nurses and other health professionals, but implementation of these policies has been limited. As well, many issues associated with work intensification remain unresolved, leading to morale problems that spill over into recruitment difficulties.

In Alberta and Saskatchewan, health unions and workers are aware that restructuring and/or labour markets have increased labour's bargaining power. Health workers have become more amenable to militant action aimed at addressing their concerns.

Another emergent issue stems from management's desire to deploy labour more flexibly, in ways that blur occupational distinctions and erode professional demarcations. Inter-occupational jurisdictional issues involving the transfer of tasks to workers with less training – a response to shortages of skilled labour and budgetary limitations – threaten some workers' job security and work patterns and provoke inter-union discord.

Unions as organizations

There are four major hierarchically arrayed groupings of health workers: medical staff (a group largely beyond the scope of these papers); registered nurses; non-medical health professionals; and support staff. Education and skill levels distinguish the groups.

Health unions are on the receiving end of health restructuring initiatives and the environment within which it occurs. They must adapt and adjust in order to survive. Due to the differences in the nature of their memberships, these unions are affected by restructuring in distinct and different ways. Each experiences its own a mix of common ambient factors, for example, government policies and operating modes, public attitudes, membership support, and bargaining and organizational structures. Those that emerge dominant are those that are powerfully positioned in the labour market and, to a lesser extent, politically well connected. The losers are likely to include smaller unions, those whose members' skills are not in short supply, and those lacking strong leadership. They are vulnerable to being ignored or intimidated by management and government and raided by rival unions.

Support workers' unions

The case of the New Zealand's Service and Food Workers' Union (SFWU), which represents dietary and housekeeping health workers, demonstrates what low-wage workers have to fear from health restructuring. The removal of unions' right to recognition and mandatory union membership, decentralized bargaining, contracting out and management unilateralism, for example, imposing contracts, decimated SFWU. Its members' low skill levels and the competitiveness of the labour market left the union with little bargaining power. Wages and benefits declined to "hospitality sector" levels and membership declined.

Falling dues revenues and the decentralization of bargaining forced SFWU to restructure internally. It cut and decentralized staff. To address its locals' burgeoning needs, it moved from the "servicing" model of unionism to the "organizing" model. The union has sought to generate a core of grassroots leaders and activists to build a local presence. Locals must address individual members' needs, bargain and organize. Like support unions in other jurisdictions, especially the UK, it has sought a merger partner. SFWU has become a more political union, seeking to build alliances with community, environmental and church groups and maintaining its links with the Labour Party. Its survival rests with a sympathetic government.

In the UK, Unison had some broadly similar experiences stemming from the move toward decentralization. The British government is proposing a social partnership to win workers' acceptance of its modernization agenda as well as moving to improve their work lives. Overall, these support unions have been weakened rather than renewed by health restructuring. They realize that to get along, it is prudent to go along.

Support unions' effectiveness, in part, reflects the scope of their memberships. Inclusive or quasi-industrial support workers' unions, which represent administrative and skilled maintenance personnel, non-degreed technical workers, auxiliary nurses, as well as housekeeping and dietary staff, fare better than narrower support unions. Where bargaining is centralized and the law makes union membership mandatory and obliges employers to recognize and bargain with unions, support unions can emerge from restructuring more powerful, even if their political connections are not compelling. Their job actions can cripple the industry. This has been the experience in Alberta and Saskatchewan.

Internal political dynamics in support unions can shift, especially where traditional leadership is replaced by aggrieved, militant and, increasingly, female leaders. Quasi-industrial support unions are better able to resist government and management's insistence that they follow public service or hospitality sector settlement patterns. Indeed, they may demand their version of a "health industry pattern" which includes settlements reached with health professionals, including those in other jurisdictions. Militant quasi-industrial health unions can "punch above" their labour market weight. Dominant support workers' unions in Saskatchewan and Alberta fit this mold.

Technical, professional and nursing unions

Health restructuring has coincided with shortages of nurses and (sub)professionals, improving their market and bargaining positions. In some cases, restructuring has aggravated the situation by deliberately or inadvertently driving workers from the sector. Tales of workers experiencing reduced employment status, layoffs, unattractive remuneration and work intensification have made health careers appear unattractive. The combined impact of market forces, a sense of grievance and, in some cases, memberships enlarged by union mergers has strengthened professional unions.

Registered nurses are distinguished by a homogeneity, solidarity and potential for militant professionalism. For many, restructuring is associated with understaffing, overwork and growing disaffection; they view service quality as being compromised. This overwhelmingly female group shares a common identity, training, and perspective. Nurses' unions are large and strategically positioned. Their members enjoy a positive public image and favourable labour markets. Where reform has been accompanied by union mergers, membership growth and strong central control, they have grown powerful. Their concerns increasingly include patient care issues that encroach upon areas of traditional management prerogative as well as improved wages and working conditions. Where the work of registered nurses is threatened by auxiliary nurses, nurses' unions have become willing to begin organizing these less qualified competitors.

Nursing unions' response to the three operating modes is clear. Where bargaining is centralized, unilateralism can generate backlashes that governments hesitate to confront. These unions have shown a willingness to engage in legal and illegal job actions. Their approaches to negotiations have been traditional, not characterized by interest-based bargaining. They often have the necessary power to achieve their objectives. Third partyism can be successful if it is carried out in ways that recognize rather than deny or negate the validity of nurses' market arguments.

Unions representing multi-occupational groups of (sub)professionals face the challenge of satisfying the professional status and market aspirations of fractured and uncohesive memberships. This problem is compounded when bargaining is decentralized, as per the British experience. Unions can more proficiently defend and promote their members' professional and workplace group interests when they address them centrally. Those interests are more vulnerable and easily undermined locally. Generating a sufficiently sophisticated, committed coterie of local activists to address issues such as job territory encroachment by "helper" grades and the growth of a private sector presence, which threatens to shift jobs to private sector providers, is an enormous challenge for unions. This is particularly true under conditions of work intensification. At the central level, unions are more apt to be staff run or influenced.

Blessed with robust labour markets and adjoining professional standard-setting bodies, health professionals' unions are potentially powerful. Their members' mobility and importance to modern health services systems have prompted employers to monitor turnover rates and recruitment problems as well as look for ways to satisfy these workers' work life aspirations. This has led to human resource management initiatives aimed at individual or smaller groups of workers. Such initiatives can be carried out directly with an employee, without involving her union.

The union representing medical specialists in New Zealand demonstrates these well-positioned unions' capacity to adapt to restructuring. The Association of Salaried Medical Specialists (ASMS) easily accommodated the end of both mandatory union membership and centralized bargaining. Management unilateralism had the effect of aggravating and unifying the doctors, who voluntarily joined ASMS. Members' high skill levels, a strong labour market, professional solidarity, astute leadership and willingness to take meaningful reprisals against management make the union strong. Decentralized bargaining allowed ASMS to whipsaw the fragmented employers in the tradition of a craft union dealing with employers individually rather than as a group. Given that the market for health professionals is (inter)national, it seems reasonable to conduct bargaining nationally to prevent inter-unit and cross-jurisdiction whipsawing.

Health professionals' unions range from those that are loath to strike to ones that are coming to regard nursing unions' militancy as worthy of emulation. Strike-averse unions may be particularly well suited to third partyism. The problem lies in keeping the rest satisfied.

It should concern governments that these unions have issues that prompt strike action.

Unions representing health professionals have actively explored creative approaches to bargaining. In New Zealand, the Public Service Association advocates labour-management collaboration. The Health Sciences Association of Saskatchewan has experimented with interest-based bargaining, although it changed course in 2002 by undertaking a four-week strike. There is reason to believe that unions representing health professionals are increasingly inclined toward behaving like trade unions capable of building strategic partnerships with government and management.

Non-degreed technicians, who strive to be treated like or included with the professionals, may find themselves in support unions. While technicians may feel that their concerns are not being addressed, support unions are reluctant to give up a group of members that increases their bargaining power. Technical workers may emerge as fractional bargaining units that can plague unions and employers.

Conclusion

Health restructuring has far reaching implications for the sector's industrial relations; it can irreversibly alter the old order. As one considers the industrial relations of health restructuring across the five jurisdictions examined here, it becomes evident that three broad factors shape a government's strategic health reform decisions and the course of its reform undertaking: the government's ideological or policy perspectives; the government's desire to devolve decision-making power or to exercise it at a central political or bureaucratic level; and the urgency of the government's fiscal situation. These factors combine to help shape the health reform vision, the actors' roles, and the pace and means by which restructuring is implemented. Awareness of the interplay among these factors is essential to understanding cause and effect in the health sector's industrial relations.

The question of the degree of centralization is largely a separate issue from a government's political values. Since all governments are ultimately politically accountable for the performance of their health services system, they face the choice having a system that has its operational and industrial relations matters controlled at the centre or one that endeavours to devolve greater responsibility to health units or shares it with an industry association. Governments, however, are reluctant to relinquish control. They are keen to establish accountability arrangements and set performance objectives. They make or approve budgets, determine operating units' goals and monitor them. All of this has structural and operational implications at the health unit level. Moreover, governments exercise ultimate authority, including the prerogative to behave erratically and intrusively.

The matter of who does what and at which level has enormous implications for management. The extent to which management should control and conduct organizations' industrial relations is an issue on which governments are ambivalent. It varies across jurisdictions. Governments can be differentiated by the degree to which they devolve authority, the specificity of their prescriptions and their proclivity for intervening. Management's role is to adjust their organization in response to government's plans and changing expectations while implementing restructuring and continuing to provide health services.

A related issue is whether and how management or health units are able to participate in sector-level industrial relations. This role contemplates either personal politics or professional health sector management having a voice at the strategic level. Management's periodic frustration with health sector industrial relations can be driven as much or more by political considerations as by operational or organizational concerns. Governments are not obliged to solicit or accommodate managements' concerns in their decisions.

Health reform is always about money, the third factor. Since labour is a major operating expense, one way of controlling costs is to increase output. This involves some combination of fewer, cheaper, harder working and/or more effectively deployed employees, who happen to be unionized. Actions designed to contain costs – work intensification, organizational restructuring and consolidations, work force reductions, introduction of market-like mechanisms, pay restraint – can combine to generate union and union membership issues. Attempts to improve efficiency can generate problems in organizations where workers are dedicated to providing compassionate care but also concerned about employment security and balancing their work and non-work lives. Unions have the dual role of reflecting their members' concerns about changes flowing from restructuring as well as perennial workplace issues and their own institutional concerns to both government and management. They prefer to negotiate accommodations, but they may have solutions imposed on them by government, management or perhaps a third party. Unions recognize that the choice of including or excluding them is political. Hence, to be effective, they must be involved both politically and organizationally.

Notes

1. William Lazonick, *Competitive Advantage on the Shop Floor* (Cambridge: Harvard University Press), 1990, pp. 299–332. This work identifies characteristics of an ideal private sector relationship.
2. Dan Cameron, "The Crisis in Public Sector Bargaining in Saskatchewan," *Policy Options*, (September 2001): 1–7.
3. Richard E. Walton, Joel E. Cutcher-Gershenfeld and Robert. B. McKerskie, *Strategic Negotiations: A Theory of Change in Labor-Management Relations* (Boston: Harvard Business School Press), 1994, pp. 28–9.
4. Bernard Adell, Michel Grant and Allen Ponak, *Strikes in Essential Services* (Kingston: IRC Press), 2002, pp. 1–15.
5. Friedrich A. Hayek, *The Road to Serfdom* (Chicago: University of Chicago Press), 1944.
6. M. Olson, *The Logic of Collective Action* (Cambridge: Harvard University Press), 1965; P. Gorringe, "A Review Article: The Economic Institutions of Capitalism:

Firms, Markets and Relational Contracting" (Oliver E. Williamson, author), *Australian Journal of Management* 12 (1987): 125–43.

7. Janice Gross Stein, *The Cult of Efficiency* (Toronto: Anansi), 2001.

8. Pat Walsh and Kurt Wetzel, "State Restructuring, Corporate Strategy and Industrial Relations: State-owned Enterprise Management in New Zealand," *British Journal of Industrial Relations* 31, 1 (1993): 57–74.

9. Stein, *The Cult of Efficiency*.

10. Walton, Cutcher-Gershenfeld and McKerskie, pp. 24–7.

11. "Whatever works," *The Economist*, May 4, 2002, p. 56.

12. Stephen Bach, "Public Sector Employment Relations Reforms under Labour: Muddling through on Modernisation," *British Journal of Industrial Relations* 40, 2 (2002): 319–339.

13. "National Negotiations – Here We Come!" *The Specialist*, 53 (December 2002): 1–2.

14. Wagner-type labour policy provides for "winner take all" "exclusive bargaining rights," whereby the union supported by the majority is certified to represent the bargaining unit. "Union shop" provisions make union membership compulsory for all members of certified bargaining units. Wagnerism imposes a duty for management to recognize and bargain in good faith with certified unions. Thus, if workplaces represented by different unions are consolidated, larger unions stand to gain members. They also get new members when previously non-union workplaces are merged with unionized ones.

Index

adversarialism   88, 97, 105, 117, 120,
    156, 201
AFL *see* Alberta Federation of Labour
aged-care policy (New South Wales)
    168–9
agency theory   49, 202
AHA *see* Alberta Health Care
    Association
AHS *see* Area Health Services
Alberta (Canada)   90, 127
    bargaining structure   145–6, 155
    bargaining unit restructuring
        141–2
    contracting out   145
    employers' associations   135–8,
        154
    government industrial relations
        policy   132–3
    Klein government   129–30, 148
    labour force adjustment   143–4
    labour relations restructuring
        processes   141, 154
    petroleum markets   128
    RHAs and health reform agenda
        133–5, 154
    transfer/merger settlements   142–3
    unions   132–3, 138–41, 154–6,
        212–13
Alberta Cancer Board   133, 153
Alberta Federation of Labour   (AFL)
    140, 148, 151
Alberta Healthcare Association (AHA)
    135–6, 141, 145
Alberta Labour Relations Board
    (ALRB)   132, 138
role in bargaining unit restructuring
    141–2, 155, 159 n.36
role in collective bargaining   150,
    151, 152, 156
Alberta Mental Health Board   133,
    153
Alberta Progressive Conservatives
    (PCs)   130

Alberta Roundtables on Health   130
Alberta Union of Public Employees
    (AUPE)   140, 141, 143, 145, 149,
    150, 151–2, 156, 157
ALRB *see* Alberta Labour Relations
    Board
Area Health Boards Act 1983
    (New Zealand)   51
Area Health Services (AHS)
    (New South Wales)   170–2, 177,
    178, 179, 181, 184, 189, 190
Area Health Services Act 1986
    (New South Wales)   170
ASMS *see* Association of Salaried
    Medical Specialists
Association of Salaried Medical
    Specialists (ASMS) (New Zealand)
    52, 60–2, 64, 73–4, 75, 77,
    84 n.80, 85 n.82, 219
Auckland Healthcare   61, 83 n.54
Audit Commission (NHS)
    2001   27
    2002   22
Audit Society   13
AUPE *see* Alberta Union of Public
    Employees
Australia   162
    see also New South Wales
    Commonwealth government
        164–5
    Liberal-National Coalition
        government   167, 176
awards   176, 178, 181, 182, 196–7

bank working   27
bargaining   8, 9, 10, 207, 208, 210–11
    see also collective bargaining
    enterprise   175, 178, 181–2, 214
    fees   77
    political   120, 123
    provincial   111, 141, 146, 210,
        211, 213
    wage   25, 31, 176–7, 209, 214

223